D1044733

ANIMAL STORIES

Young Reader's Library

ANIMAL STORIES

Edited by Ernest Thompson Seton

Originally published as *The Animal Story Book*

DERRYDALE BOOKS
NEW YORK

Foreword copyright © 1991 by Outlet Book Company, Inc.
All rights reserved.

This 1991 edition is published by Derrydale Books, distributed by
Outlet Book Company, Inc., a Random House Company, 225 Park Avenue
South, New York, New York 10003.

Printed and bound in the United States of America

Library of Congress Cataloging-in-Publication Data

Animal story book.
    Animal stories / edited by Ernest Thompson Seton.
        p.   cm. — (Young reader's library)
    Reprint. Originally published: The animal story book. Boston :
Hall and Locke Co., c1902.
    Summary: A collection of fifty-eight classic animal tales by
writers including Aesop and La Fontaine.
    ISBN 0-517-03761-0
    1. Fables. [1. Fables.]   I. Seton, Ernest Thompson, 1860–1946.
II. Title. III. Series.
PZ8.2.A535An   1991
398.2—dc20   90-14015
                                                        CIP
                                                         AC

8   7   6   5   4   3   2   1

CONTENTS

PAGE

FOREWORD ix

OUR FOUR–FOOTED FRIENDS xi
BY ERNEST THOMPSON SETON

THE FOX AND THE CROW 1
FROM THE FABLES OF ÆSOP.

THE WOLF AND THE LAMB 3
FROM THE FABLES OF ÆSOP.

THE LION AND THE MOUSE 5
FROM THE FABLES OF ÆSOP.

THE FOX AND THE GOAT 6
FROM THE FABLES OF ÆSOP.

THE LION, THE TIGER, AND THE FOX 8
FROM THE FABLES OF ÆSOP.

THE LARK AND HER YOUNG ONES 9
FROM THE FABLES OF ÆSOP.

THE LION, THE FOX, AND THE WOLF 11
FROM THE FABLES OF ÆSOP.

THE COCK AND THE FOX 13
FROM THE FABLES OF ÆSOP.

THE HEN AND THE FOX 15
FROM THE FABLES OF ÆSOP.

THE FOX, THE WOLF, AND THE HORSE 16
FROM THE FABLES OF ÆSOP.

THE CAT AND THE FOX . . . . . . : 18
FROM THE FABLES OF ÆSOP.

PAGE

THE DOG THAT DROPPED THE SUBSTANCE FOR THE
    SHADOW   19
    FROM THE FABLES OF LA FONTAINE.

THE FOX WITH HIS TAIL CUT OFF   20
    FROM THE FABLES OF LA FONTAINE.

THE CITY RAT AND THE COUNTRY RAT   22
    FROM THE FABLES OF LA FONTAINE.

THE ASS LOADED WITH SPONGES AND THE ASS LOADED
    WITH SALT   24
    FROM THE FABLES OF LA FONTAINE.

BELLING THE CAT   26
    FROM LANGLAND'S VISION OF PIERS PLOWMAN.

THE OLD HARE AND THE ELEPHANTS   29
    FROM THE HITOPADEÇA. TRANSLATED BY SIR EDWIN ARNOLD.

THE TIMID HARE AND THE FLIGHT OF THE BEASTS . .   31
    FROM THE JĀTAKA. TRANSLATED BY H. N. FRANCIS.

SAINT GERASIMUS AND THE LION   36
    BY ABBIE FARWELL BROWN.

REYNARD THE FOX   50

ANDROCLES AND THE LION   72

MY LION FRIEND   77
    BY MONSIEUR GERARD.

A LION STORY   87
    BY SIR SAMUEL BAKER.

A NARROW ESCAPE FROM A TIGER   99
    BY ROBERT COCHRANE.

TRAPPING A LEOPARD 111
    BY ROBERT COCHRANE.

THE GRIZZLY BEAR 118
    BY WASHINGTON IRVING.

THE GIRLS, THE BEAR, AND THE ALLIGATORS 123
    BY ROBERT COCHRANE.

A FIGHT BETWEEN A LION AND A CROCODILE 129
    BY H. RIDER HAGGARD.

SAGACITY OF THE ELEPHANT 133
    BY ROBERT COCHRANE.

PAGE

WORKING ELEPHANTS AT RANGOON 141
    BY ROBERT COCHRANE.

MOTI GUJ — MUTINEER 145
    BY RUDYARD KIPLING.

EXPLOITS OF SAMSON 156
    BY ROBERT COCHRANE.

A MAD ELEPHANT 161
    BY MR. JAMES INGLIS.

MONKEY STORIES 165
    BY ROBERT COCHRANE.
        MONKEYS IN CONFINEMENT 177
        MY PET APE 178

THE EARLY DAYS OF BLACK BEAUTY 186
    BY ANNA SEWELL.

A PARROT WHICH ANSWERED QUESTIONS 197
    BY SIR WILLIAM TEMPLE.

SOME PARROTS I HAVE KNOWN 199
    BY ROBERT COCHRANE.

A PHOTOGRAPHER'S PARROT 210
    BY ROBERT COCHRANE.

MY PET STARLING 219
    BY ROBERT COCHRANE.

TALES OF INSTINCT AND REASON 230
    BY LADY JULIA LOCKWOOD.
        RESCUED BY A DOG 230
        A SAGACIOUS DOG 232
        A DOG THAT PUNISHED ITS PUPS 235
        SOME MONKEY TRICKS 237
        SAGACIOUS RATS 243
        A DOG WITH TWO HOMES 246
        ABOUT BEES 248

RAB AND HIS FRIENDS 254
    BY JOHN BROWN, M.D.

OUR NEW NEIGHBORS AT PONKAPOG 275
    BY THOMAS BAILEY ALDRICH.

Contents

	PAGE
MOUFFLOU	283
BY OUIDA .	
A STORY OF A CHIPMUNK	315
BY JOHN BURROUGHS.	
THE HOMESICKNESS OF KEHONKA	319
BY CHARLES G. D. ROBERTS.	
THE STORY OF A HOMER	334
BY FRANK M. GILBERT.	
HOW RED WULL HELD THE BRIDGE	345
BY ALFRED OLLIVANT.	
MALDONADA AND THE PUMA	351
BY W. H. HUDSON.	
THE CAPTAIN'S DOG	354
BY LOUIS A. ENAULT	
ROYAL'S FATE	364
BY FLORA L. SHAW.	
THE CIVILIZED FOX	380
BY CHARLES DUDLEY WARNER.	

FOREWORD

The Young Reader's Library offers reprint editions of selected volumes from a classic series of children's books originally published at the turn of the century.

Animal Stories, or *The Book of Animal Stories*, as it was first called, presents fifty-eight classic and timeless tales of the animal kingdom, suitable for reading out loud or alone. From the moment man first made the acquaintance of animals he began to tell stories about them. Drawing on the wealth of wonderful stories available, naturalist Ernest Thompson Seton has selected tales by Aesop, La Fontaine, Washington Irving, Rudyard Kipling, Anna Sewell, and W. H. Hudson, among many others.

You'll meet Reynard the Fox, Moti Guj the Elephant, Black Beauty, the Timid Hare, lions, crocodiles, an unusual parrot, and a grizzly bear, as well as dogs, cats, monkeys, and mice—and even the occasional human being. For most animal stories are, at heart, actually tales of the world of men, although they are disguised in the characters of animals. The tales in *Animal Stories* are no exception to this great tradition of storytelling. The delightful fables, daring deeds, and fascinating lives of the animals presented in this lovingly illustrated volume offer hours of reading and entertainment for all generations.

LOIS HILL

New York
1991

OUR FOUR–FOOTED FRIENDS

BY

ERNEST THOMPSON SETON.

AUTHOR OF "WILD ANIMALS I HAVE KNOWN," "THE SANDHILL STAG," "THE BIOGRAPHY OF A GRIZZLY," "LIVES OF THE HUNTED."

THE animal story is seen to-day in its greatest development and importance. It is not a modern invention; from the days when first man made the acquaintance of animals, he must have told stories about them. We can trace the gradual development of Beast Lore from the mere hunting tale, in which the animal was a thing to be hated and destroyed, and the man a hero for doing so, — a class of story not entirely out of vogue, — through the fables of the Æsop kind, and the prolonged allegory, of which Reynard the Fox is a fair example, to the modern animal story in which man is the hated enemy, and the animal the noble-minded hero.

Whatever criticisms may be made on this last with its reversal of the situation, it yet marks a new and better epoch, — the epoch of sympathy for the animal.

There was a stage in human growth when sympathy for any one of another tribe was scoffed at, or even considered criminal. But this sympathy came; men learned that justice is wider than the tribal limit, though it was still considered absurd to waste pity on slaves. In time, even that became first a possible, then an accepted thing. The broadening sympathy which is, after all, the law of love, thus took in all of mankind, and is following further along the lines drawn by the Great Hindu, who taught that in this broadest sympathy should be included the whole living world.

We have not yet got as far as that, but we are moving that way — led by the children. It is a noble cause; it is a great and good thing, and should by all means be helped. Not chiefly because it saves the animals from much suffering, but because of the effect on ourselves. It is an old saying that hate hurts the hater: giving blesses the giver. A recent writer has pointed out that murder, in European countries, is prevalent in exactly the same ratio as cruelty to animals. This statement has not yet been contradicted so far as I know, and indeed as a broad principle it is unassailable and has long been recognized in our jurisprudence; witness the exclusion of butchers from juries that are to try a man for his life. We are safe then in drawing this inference,— In promoting kindness to the animals we are begetting kindness for mankind. Experience has shown that the best way to aid in the good work is not by preaching or by philosophies, but by putting within reach of the rising generation the animal stories best calculated to lead them into sympathy with these, their Little Brethren.

The Hunting Story in which the sympathy of the hearer is with man, is represented in this Volume by various Adventures with Lions, Tigers, Bears, Leopards, etc.

The Fables by Æsop and Lafontaine are the best examples in the newer field, wherein each animal was used as an impersonation, or as the embodiment of a quality.

In the various Fox Fables, not invented, but collected by Æsop, we recognize the originals that grew together into the story of " Reynard the Fox."

The mere allegory led to an attempt to portray the actual life of the animal, or rather to endow it with human mind and speech, while it retained its own limitations. Many volumes of these have been written, most of them unworthy of preservation. However, they did good work as a class. They were the bridge between the utterly fanciful and the true animal worlds. A few of them have established a place that appears to be permanent. Black Beauty is one of the most famous, and Kipling's Tales will probably stand always as the unique classics of this literature.

Next we find a style of animal story that shows the man and the animal associated, which like the hunting story aims to record actual events, but in which the man and the beast do not appear as enemies. In these the dog naturally is prominent. Rab and Moufflou are classical canine examples. The celebrated story of Androcles and the Lion is of doubtful authenticity, but the much more wonderful adventure of Maldonada with the Puma seems to withstand the attacks of all critics. In all of these, however, the chief interest and sympathy is human.

The latest kind of animal story and probably the best, because the truest, is that which aims to tell the history of the animal just as it is, without humanizing in the least, but in sympathy with the animal. This is the most scientific and satisfactory of all. This is the class to which I aim to make my own belong. The writings of Mr. Charles G. D. Roberts are among the most eminent examples in this field, and demonstrate how much better and more wonderful is the truth about the animal world, than any fairy tale that can be concocted about it.

THE FOX AND THE CROW

(FROM THE FABLES OF ÆSOP.)

A FOX once saw a Crow fly with a piece of cheese in its beak and settle on a branch of a tree. "That's for me, as I am a Fox," said Master Renard, and he walked up to the foot of the tree. "Good-day, Mistress Crow," he cried. "How well you are looking to-day; how glossy your feathers; how bright your eye. I feel sure your voice must surpass that of other birds, just as your figure does; let me hear but one song from you that I may greet you as the Queen of Birds." The Crow lifted up her head and began to caw her best, but the moment she opened her mouth the piece of cheese fell to the ground, only to be snapped up by Master Fox. "That will do," said he. "That was all I wanted. In exchange for your cheese I will give you a piece of advice for the future — Do not trust flatterers."

> The flatterer doth rob by stealth,
> His victim, both of wit and wealth.

THE WOLF AND THE LAMB

(FROM THE FABLES OF ÆSOP.)

A HUNGRY Wolf one day saw a Lamb drinking at a stream, and wished to frame some plausible excuse for making him his prey. " What do you mean by muddling the water I am going to drink ? " fiercely said he to the Lamb. " Pray, forgive me," meekly answered the Lamb; " I should be sorry in any way to displease you, but as the stream runs from you towards me, you will see that such cannot be the case." " That's all very well," said the Wolf; " but you know you spoke ill of me behind my back a year ago." " Nay, believe me," replied the Lamb, " I was not then born." " It must have been your brother, then," growled the Wolf. " It cannot have been, for I never had any," answered the Lamb. " I know it was one of

3

your lot," rejoined the Wolf, " so make no more such idle excuses."   He then seized the poor Lamb, carried him off to the woods, and ate him.   But before he died he gasped out,

"Any excuse will serve a tyrant."

THE LION AND THE MOUSE

(From the Fables of Æsop.)

A LION, tired with the chase, lay sleeping at full length under a shady tree. Some Mice, scrambling over him while he slept, awoke him. Laying his paw upon one of them, he was about to crush him, but the Mouse implored his mercy in such moving terms that he let him go. Some time after the Lion was caught in a net laid by some hunters, and, unable to free himself, made the forest resound with his roars. The Mouse whose life had been spared came, and with his little sharp teeth gnawed the ropes asunder and set the Lion free.

THE FOX AND THE GOAT

(FROM THE FABLES OF ÆSOP.)

A FOX and a Goat once journeyed together. The Goat was a simple creature, seldom seeing beyond his own nose; while the Fox, like most of his kind, was a master of knavery. They were led by thirst to descend a deep well, and when they had both drunk freely, the Fox said, "Now, Master Goat, what shall we do? Drinking is all very well, but it won't get us out from here. You had better rear up against the wall; then, by the aid of your horns, I can get out, and, once out, of course I can help you." "By my beard," said the Goat, "that's a good plan. I should never have thought of that. How I wish I had your brains, to be sure!" The Fox,

6

having got out in the way described, began to rail at his companion. "Make the most of your patience, old fellow," said he, "for you'll need it all. If you had half as much brains as beard, you would never have gone down there. I am sorry that I can't stay longer with you, but I have some business that must be seen to. So, good-by."

THE LION, THE TIGER, AND THE FOX

(FROM THE FABLES OF ÆSOP.)

A LION and a Tiger happened to come together over the dead body of a Fawn that had been recently shot. A fierce battle ensued, and as each animal was in the prime of his age and strength, the combat was long and furious. At last they lay stretched on the ground, panting, bleeding, and exhausted, each unable to lift a paw against the other. An impudent Fox, coming by at this time, stepped in and carried off before their eyes the prey for which they had both suffered so much.

THE LARK AND HER YOUNG ONES

(From the Fables of Æsop.)

A LARK, who had Young Ones in a field of corn which was almost ripe, was afraid lest the reapers should come before her young brood were fledged. Every day, therefore, when she flew away to look for food, she charged them to take notice of what they heard in her absence, and to tell her of it when she returned. One day when she was gone they heard the master of the field say to his son that the corn seemed ripe enough to be cut, and tell him to go early to-morrow and desire their friends and neighbors to come and help to reap it. When the old Lark came home, the Little Ones fell quivering and chirping around her, and told her what had happened, begging

her to remove them as fast as she could. The mother
bade them to be easy, " for," said she, " if he depends
upon his friends and his neighbors, I am sure the corn
will not be reaped to-morrow." Next day she went out
again, and left the same orders as before. The owner
came, and waited. The sun grew hot, but nothing was
done, for not a soul came. " You see," said he to his
son, " these friends of ours are not to be depended upon,
so run off at once to your uncles and cousins, and say
I wish them to come betimes to-morrow morning and
help us to reap." This the Young Ones, in a great
fright, reported also to their mother. " Do not be
frightened, children," said she; " kindred and relations
are not always very forward in helping one another;
but keep your ears open, and let me know what you
hear to-morrow." The owner came the next day, and,
finding his relations as backward as his neighbors, said
to his son, " Now, George, listen to me. Get a couple
of good sickles ready against to-morrow morning, for it
seems we must reap the corn by ourselves." The
Young Ones told this to their mother. " Then, my
dears," said she, " it is time for us to go indeed, for
when a man undertakes to do his business himself, it is
not so likely that he will be disappointed." She removed her young ones immediately, and the corn was
reaped the next day by the old man and his son.

THE LION, THE FOX, AND THE WOLF

(From the Fables of Æsop.)

THE King of the Forest was once long and seriously ill, and his Majesty's temper not being at all improved by the trial, the Fox, with his usual discretion, kept away from Court as much as he could. He slunk about, however, as near as he could without being seen, and one day overheard the Wolf talking to the Lion about him. The Wolf and the Fox were never good friends, and the Wolf was now calling the Lion's attention to the fact that the Fox had not shown his face for a long time at Court, and added that he had strong reasons for suspecting that he was busily engaged in hatching some treason or other. The Lion thereupon commanded that the Fox should be brought at once to his presence, and the Jackal was accordingly sent to look for him. The Fox, being asked what he had to say for himself, replied that his absence, so far from arising from any want of respect for his sovereign,

11

was the result of his extreme concern for his welfare. He had gone far and wide, he said, and consulted the most skilful physicians as to what was the best thing to be done to cure the King's most grievous malady. "They say," stated he (and here he gave a malicious leer at the Wolf), "that the only thing to save your Majesty's life is to wrap yourself in the warm skin torn from a newly-killed Wolf." The Lion, eager to try the experiment, at once dragged the Wolf toward him and killed him on the spot.

THE COCK AND THE FOX

(FROM THE FABLES OF ÆSOP.)

A COCK, perched among the branches of a lofty tree, crowed aloud. The shrillness of his voice echoed through the wood, and the well-known note brought a Fox, who was prowling in quest of prey, to the spot. Renard, seeing the Cock was at a great height, set his wits to work to find some way of bringing him down. He saluted the bird in his mildest voice, and said, " Have you not heard, cousin, of the proclamation of universal peace and harmony among all kinds of beasts and birds? We are no longer to prey upon and devour one another, but love and friendship are to be the order of the day.

13

Do come down, and we will talk over this great news at our leisure." The Cock, who knew that the Fox was only at his old tricks, pretended to be watching something in the distance, and the Fox asked him what it was he looked at so earnestly. "Why," said the Cock, "I think I see a pack of Hounds yonder." "Oh, then," said the Fox, "your humble servant; I must be gone." "Nay, cousin," said the Cock, "pray do not go: I am just coming down. You are surely not afraid of Dogs in these peaceable times!" "No, no," said the Fox; "but ten to one whether they have heard of the proclamation yet."

THE HEN AND THE FOX

(FROM THE FABLES OF ÆSOP.)

A FOX, having crept into an outhouse, looked up and down for something to eat, and at last spied a Hen sitting upon a perch so high that he could by no means come at her. He therefore had recourse to an old stratagem. "Dear cousin," said he to her, "how do you do? I heard that you were ill and kept at home; I could not rest, therefore, till I had come to see you. Pray let me feel your pulse. Indeed, you do not look well at all." He was running on in this impudent manner, when the Hen answered him from the roost, "Truly, dear Renard, you are in the right. I was seldom in more danger than I am now. Pray excuse my coming down; I am sure I should catch my death." The Fox, finding himself foiled, made off and tried his luck elsewhere.

THE FOX, THE WOLF, AND THE HORSE

(FROM THE FABLES OF ÆSOP.)

A FOX, seeing a Horse for the first time, grazing in a field, at once ran to a Wolf of his acquaintance, and described the animal that he had found. "It is, perhaps," said the Fox, "some delicious prey that fortune has put in our path. Come with me, and judge for yourself." Off they ran, and soon came to the Horse, who, scarcely lifting his head, seemed little anxious to be on speaking terms with such suspicious-looking characters. "Sir," said the Fox, "your humble servants here would with pleasure learn the name by which you are known to your illustrious friends." The Horse, who was not without a ready wit, said his name was there curiously written upon his hoofs for the information of those who cared to read it. "Gladly would

I," replied the sly Fox, suspecting in an instant something wrong, " but my parents were poor and could not pay for my education; hence, I never learned to read. The friends of my companion here, on the contrary, are great folk, and he can both read and write, and has a thousand other accomplishments." The Wolf, pleased with the flattery, at once went up, with a knowing air, to examine one of the hoofs which the horse raised for his convenience; and when he had come near enough, the Horse gave a sudden and vigorous kick, and back to earth fell the Wolf, his jaw broken and bleeding. " Well, cousin," cried the Fox, with a grin, " you need never ask for the name a second time, now that you have it written so plainly just below your eyes."

THE CAT AND THE FOX

(FROM THE FABLES OF ÆSOP.)

THE Cat and the Fox were once talking together in the middle of a forest. "Let things be ever so bad," said Renard, "I don't care; I have a hundred shifts if one should fail." "I," said the Cat, "have but one; if that fails me I am undone." Just then a pack of Hounds burst into view. The Cat flew up a tree, and sat securely among the branches, and thence saw the Fox, after trying his hundred shifts in vain, overtaken by the Dogs and torn in pieces. Miss Puss, who had been looking on, said: "Better one safe way than a hundred on which you cannot reckon."

THE DOG THAT DROPPED THE SUB-
STANCE FOR THE SHADOW

(FROM THE FABLES OF LA FONTAINE.)

THIS world is full of shadow-chasers,
    Most easily deceived.
    Should I enumerate these racers,
      I should not be believed.
    I send them all to Æsop's dog,
    Which, crossing water on a log,
    Espied the meat he bore, below;
    To seize its image, let it go;
    Plunged in; to reach the shore was glad,
With neither what he hoped, nor what he'd had.

THE FOX WITH HIS TAIL CUT OFF

(FROM THE FABLES OF LA FONTAINE.)

A CUNNING old fox, of plundering habits,
 Great crauncher of fowls, great catcher of
  rabbits,
Whom none of his sort had caught in a nap,
Was finally caught in somebody's trap.
By luck he escaped, not wholly and hale,
For the price of his luck was the loss of his tail.
Escaped in this way, to save his disgrace,
He thought to get others in similar case.
One day that the foxes in council were met,
"Why wear we," said he, "this cumbering weight,
Which sweeps in the dirt wherever it goes?
Pray tell me its use, if any one knows.
 If the council will take my advice,
 We shall dock off our tails in a trice."

" Your advice may be good," said one on the ground;
" But, ere I reply, pray turn yourself round."
Whereat such a shout from the council was heard,
Poor bob-tail, confounded, could say not a word.
To urge the reform would have wasted his breath.
Long tails were the mode till the day of his death.

THE CITY RAT AND THE COUNTRY RAT

(FROM THE FABLES OF LA FONTAINE.)

A CITY rat, one night,
    Did, with a civil stoop,
A country rat invite
    To end a turtle soup.

Upon a Turkey carpet
    They found the table spread,
And sure I need not harp it
    How well the fellows fed.

The entertainment was
    A truly noble one ;
But some unlucky cause
    Disturbed it when begun.

It was a slight rat-tat
  That put their joys to rout:
Out ran the city rat;
  His guest, too, scampered out.

Our rats but fairly quit,
  The fearful knocking ceased.
"Return we," cried the cit,
  "To finish there our feast."

"No," said the rustic rat;
  "To-morrow dine with me.
I'm not offended at
  Your feast so grand and free, —

"For I've no fare resembling;
  But then I eat at leisure,
  And would not swap for pleasure
So mixed with fear and trembling."

THE ASS LOADED WITH SPONGES, AND
THE ASS LOADED WITH SALT

(FROM THE FABLES OF LA FONTAINE.)

A MAN, whom I shall call an ass-eteer,
    His sceptre like some Roman emperor bearing,
    Drove on two coursers of protracted ear,
The one, with sponges laden, briskly faring ;
        The other lifting legs
        As if he trod on eggs,
        With constant need of goading,
        And bags of salt for loading.
O'er hill and dale our merry pilgrims passed,
Till, coming to a river's ford at last,
They stopped quite puzzled on the shore.
Our asseteer had crossed the stream before ;
    So, on the lighter beast astride,
        He drives the other, spite of dread,
        Which, loath indeed to go ahead,
    Into a deep hole turns aside,

24

And, facing right about,
　Where he went in, comes out;
For duckings two or three
　Had power the salt to melt,
　So that the creature felt
His burdened shoulders free.
The sponger, like a sequent sheep,
Pursuing through the water deep,
　Into the same hole plunges
Himself, his rider, and the sponges.
All three drank deeply; asseteer and ass
For boon companions of their load might pass;
　Which last became so sore a weight,
　　The ass fell down,
　　Belike to drown,
　His rider risking equal fate.
A helper came, no matter who.
The moral needs no more ado:
　That all can't act alike, —
　The point I wished to strike.

BELLING THE CAT

(FROM LANGLAND'S VISION OF PIERS PLOWMAN.)

WITH that there ran, all at once, a rout of rats, and small mice, more than a thousand, with them, and came to council for their common profit. For a Cat of a Court came when he liked and caught them easily, and seized them whenever he would, and played with them perilously, and pushed them about. "For fear of divers dangers we dare not look about us; and, if we grumble at this game, he will vex us all, scratch us, or claw us, or hold us in his clutches so that our life becometh hateful before he letteth go of us. If we could by any device withstand him, we might lord it up above, out of his reach, and live at our ease."

A rat of renown, very ready of tongue, said that, to his mind this was the sovereign remedy: "I have

seen men," he said, "in the city of London, bearing
bright rings about their necks, and some with collars
of cunning workmanship; they run loose both in
warren and waste wherever they please, and, at other
times, they go elsewhere, as I hear tell. Were there
a bell on their collar, methinketh men might know
where they were going, and run away. And right
so," said that rat, "reason telleth me to buy a bell
of brass, or of bright silver, and fasten it on to a
collar for our common good, and hang it upon the
Cat's neck, and then we can hear whether he moveth
or resteth or runneth to play; and if he like to play
then we can know it, and appear in his presence as
long as it pleaseth him to sport; and, if he grow
wrathful, beware, and shun his path."

All the rout of rats agreed to this plan; but, when
the bell was bought and hanged upon the collar, there
was no rat in all the company who durst, for the realm
of France, have bound the bell about the Cat's neck,
nor durst hang it about the Cat's throat to win all
England. And they thought themselves not bold
enough and their counsel weak, and they held their
labor lost, and all their long devising.

A mouse, who had good parts, methought, brushed
forth sternly to the front, and stood before them all,
and, to the rout of rats, spake these words: "Though
we killed the Cat, yet would there come another to
scratch us and all our kind, though we should creep
under benches. Therefore I counsel all the commons
to let the Cat be, and never be so foolhardy as to show
him the bell. For I heard my sire say, seven years
ago, that where the Cat is a Kitten the court is very

miserable. Holy Writ witnesseth to that, whoso will read it: 'Woe to thee, O land, whose king is a boy.' For no man may have rest there by night for the rats; while the cat catcheth rabbits, our carrion he coveteth not, but feedeth himself with naught but venison — may we never defame him! For better is a little loss than a long sorrow — the sorrow of confusion amongst us all, if the Cat died, though we got rid of a tyrant. For we mice would destroy many men's malt, and also ye rout of rats would rend men's clothes were there not that Cat of the Court who can catch you; and had ye rats your will, ye would not rule yourselves. As for me," said the mouse, "I see so much that would come afterwards that never shall the Cat or the Kitten be vexed by my counsel. And talk no more of this collar, that never cost me aught, and though it had cost my goods I would not confess it, but suffer him to do as he pleaseth, fastened and unfastened, to catch what he may. Therefore every wise man I warn: let him look well to his own."

What this dream meaneth, ye merry men, divine ye; for I dare not.

THE OLD HARE AND THE ELEPHANTS

(FROM THE HITOPADEÇA, TRANSLATED BY EDWIN ARNOLD.)

ONCE on a time very little rain had fallen in the due season; and the elephants, being oppressed with thirst, thus accosted their leader: "Master, how are we to live? The small creatures find something to wash in, but we cannot, and we are half dead in consequence; whither shall we go then, and what shall we do?" Upon that the king of the elephants led them away a little space; and showed them a beautiful pool of crystal water, where they took their ease. Now it chanced that a company of hares resided on the banks of the pool, and the going and coming of the elephants trampled many of them to death, till one of their number, named Hardhead, grumbled out, "This troop will be coming here to water every day, and every one of our family will be crushed." "Do not disquiet yourself," said an old buck named Good-speed; "I will contrive to avert it," and so saying, he set off, bethinking himself

29

on his way how he should approach and accost a herd of elephants; for,

Elephants destroy by touching, snakes with point of tooth beguile;
Kings by favor kill, and traitors murder with a fatal smile.

"I will get on the top of a hill," he thought, "and address the elephants thence."

This being done, and the lord of the herd perceiving him, it was asked of the hare, "Who art thou? and whence comest thou?"

"I am an ambassador from His Godship the Moon," replied Good-speed.

"State your business," said the elephant-king.

"Sire," began the hare, "an ambassador speaks the truth safely by charter of his name. Thus saith the Moon then: 'These hares were the guardians of my pool, and thine elephants in coming thither have scared them away. This is not well. Am I not "S'ās'anka," whose banner bears a hare, and are not these hares my votaries?'"

"Please your worship," said the elephant-king with much trepidation, "we knew nothing of this; we will go there no more."

"It were well," said the sham ambassador, "that you first made your apologies to the divinity, who is quaking with rage in his pool, and then went about your business."

"We will do so," replied the elephant with meekness; and being led by night to the pool, in the ripples of which the image of the Moon was quivering, the herd made their prostrations; the hare explaining to the Moon that their fault was done in ignorance, and therefore they got their dismissal.

THE TIMID HARE AND THE FLIGHT OF THE BEASTS

(FROM THE JĀTAKA, TRANSLATED BY H. N. FRANCIS.)

ONCE upon a time when Brahmadatta reigned in Benares, the Bodhisatta came to life as a young lion. And when fully grown he lived in a wood. At this time there was near the Western Ocean a grove of palms mixed with vilva trees. A certain hare lived here beneath a palm sapling, at the foot of a vilva tree. One day this hare after feeding came and lay down beneath a young palm tree. And the thought struck him : "If this earth should be destroyed, what would become of me?" And at this very moment a ripe vilva fruit fell on a palm leaf. At the sound of it, the hare thought, "This solid earth is collapsing," and starting up he fled without so much as looking behind him. Another saw him scampering off as if frightened to death, and asked the cause of his panic flight. "Pray, don't ask me," he said. The other hare cried, "Pray, sir, what is it?" and kept running after him. Then the hare stopped a moment and without looking back he said, "The earth

31

here is breaking up." And at this the second hare ran
after the other. And so first one and then another
hare caught sight of him running, and joined in the
chase till one hundred thousand hares all took flight
together. They were seen by a deer, a boar, an elk, a
buffalo, a wild ox, a rhinoceros, a tiger, a lion, and an
elephant. And when they asked what it meant and
were told that the earth was breaking up, they too took
flight. So by degrees this host of animals extended to
the length of a full league.

When the Bodhisatta saw this headlong flight of the
animals, and heard the cause of it was that the earth
was coming to an end, he thought: "The earth is nowhere coming to an end. Surely it must be some sound
which was misunderstood by them. And if I don't
make a great effort, they will all perish. I will save
their lives." So with the speed of a lion he got before
them to the foot of a mountain, and lion-like roared
three times. They were terribly frightened at the lion,
and stopping in their flight stood all huddled together.
The lion went in amongst them and asked why they
were running away.

"The earth is collapsing," they answered.

"Who saw it collapsing?" he said.

"The elephants know all about it," they replied.

He asked the elephants. "We don't know," they
said; "the lions know." But the lions said, "We
don't know; the tigers know." The tigers said, "The
rhinoceroses know." The rhinoceroses said, "The wild
oxen know." The wild oxen, "The buffaloes." The
buffaloes, "The elks." The elks, "The boars."
The boars, "The deer." The deer said, "We don't

know; the hares know." When the hares were questioned, they pointed to one particular hare and said, " This one told us."

So the Bodhisatta asked, " Is it true, sir, that the earth is breaking up ? "

" Yes, sir, I saw it," said the hare.

" Where," he asked, " were you living when you saw it ? "

" Near the ocean, sir, in a grove of palms mixed with vilva trees. For as I was lying beneath the shade of a palm sapling at the foot of a vilva tree, methought, ' If this earth should break up, where shall I go ? ' And at that very moment I heard the sound of breaking up of the earth and I fled."

Thought the lion: " A ripe vilva fruit evidently must have fallen on a palm leaf and made a ' thud,' and this

hare jumped to the conclusion that the earth was coming to an end, and ran away. I will find out the exact truth about it." So he reassured the herd of animals, and said : " I will take the hare and go and find out exactly whether the earth is coming to an end or not, in the place pointed out by him. Until I return do you stay here." Then, placing the hare on his back, he sprang forward with the speed of a lion, and putting the hare down in a palm grove, he said, " Come, show us the place you meant."

" I dare not, my lord," said the hare.

" Come, don't be afraid," said the lion.

The hare, not venturing to go near the vilva tree, stood afar off and cried, " Yonder, sir, is the place of dreadful sounds," and so saying, he repeated the first stanza :

> " From the spot where I did dwell
> Issued forth a fearful 'thud';
> What it was I could not tell,
> Nor what caused it understood."

After hearing what the hare said, the lion went to the foot of the vilva tree, and saw the spot where the hare had been lying beneath the shade of the palm tree, and the ripe vilva fruit that fell on the palm leaf, and having carefully ascertained that the earth had not broken up, he placed the hare on his back and with the speed of a lion soon came again to the herd of beasts.

Then he told them the whole story, and said, " Don't be afraid." And having thus reassured the herd of beasts, he let them go. Verily, if it had not been for the Bodhisatta at that time, all the beasts would have rushed into the sea and perished. It was all owing to the Bodhisatta that they escaped death.

> Alarmed at sound of fallen fruit,
> A hare once ran away ;
> The other beasts all followed suit,
> Moved by that hare's dismay.

They hastened not to view the scene,
  But lent a willing ear
To idle gossip, and were clean
  Distraught with foolish fear.

They who to Wisdom's calm delight
  And Virtue's heights attain,
Though ill example should invite,
  Such panic fear disdain.

These three stanzas were inspired by Perfect Wisdom.

SAINT GERASIMUS AND THE LION

(FROM THE BOOK OF SAINTS AND FRIENDLY BEASTS.)

BY ABBIE FARWELL BROWN.

ONE fine morning Saint Gerasimus was walking briskly along the bank of the River Jordan. By his side plodded a little donkey bearing on his back an earthen jar; for they had been down to the river together to get water, and were taking it back to the monastery on the hill for the monks to drink at their noonday meal.

Gerasimus was singing merrily, touching the stupid little donkey now and then with a twig of olive leaves to keep him from going to sleep. This was in the far East, in the Holy Land, so the sky was very blue and the ground smelled hot. Birds were singing around them in the trees and overhead, all kinds of strange and beautiful birds. But suddenly Gerasimus heard a sound unlike any bird he had ever known; a sound which was not a bird's song at all, unless some newly invented kind had a bass voice which ended in a howl. The little donkey stopped suddenly, and bracing his fore legs and cocking forward his long, flappy ears, looked afraid and foolish. Gerasimus stopped too. But he was so wise a man that he could not look foolish. And he was too good a man to be afraid of anything. Still, he was a little surprised.

"Dear me," he said aloud, "how very strange that sounded. What do you suppose it was?" Now there was no one else anywhere near, so he must have been talking to himself. For he could never have expected that donkey to know anything about it. But the donkey thought he was being spoken to, so he wagged his head, and said, "He-haw!" which was a very silly answer indeed, and did not help Gerasimus at all.

He seized the donkey by the halter and waited to see what would happen. He peered up and down and around and about, but there was nothing to be seen except the shining river, the yellow sand, a clump of bushes beside the road, and the spire of the monastery peeping over the top of the hill beyond. He was about to start the donkey once more on his climb towards home, when that sound came again; and this time he noticed that it was a sad sound, a sort of whining growl ending in a sob. It sounded nearer than before, and seemed to come from the clump of bushes. Gerasimus and the donkey turned their heads quickly in that direction, and the donkey trembled all over, he was so frightened. But his master only said, "It must be a Lion."

And sure enough: he had hardly spoken the word when out of the bushes came poking the great head and yellow eyes of a lion. He was looking straight at Gerasimus. Then, giving that cry again, he bounded

out and strode towards the good man, who was holding
the donkey tight to keep him from running away. He
was the biggest kind of a lion, much bigger than the
donkey, and his mane was long and thick, and his tail
had a yellow brush on the end as large as a window
mop. But as he came Gerasimus noticed that he
limped as if he were lame. At once the Saint was
filled with pity, for he could not bear to see any
creature suffer. And without any thought of fear, he
went forward to meet the lion. Instead of pouncing
upon him fiercely, or snarling, or making ready to eat
him up, the lion crouched whining at his feet.

"Poor fellow," said Gerasimus, "what hurts you and
makes you lame, brother Lion?"

The lion shook his yellow mane and roared. But
his eyes were not fierce; they were only full of pain as

they looked up into those of Gerasimus asking for help.
And then he held up his right fore paw and shook it to

show that this was where the trouble lay. Gerasimus
looked at him kindly.

"Lie down, sir," he said, just as one would speak to
a big yellow dog. And obediently the lion charged.
Then the good man bent over him, and taking the
great paw in his hand examined it carefully. In the
soft cushion of the paw a long pointed thorn was
piercing so deeply that he could hardly find the end.
No wonder the poor lion had roared with pain! Gerasimus pulled out the thorn as gently as he could, and
though it must have hurt the lion badly he did not
make a sound, but lay still as he had been told. And
when the thorn was taken out the lion licked Gerasimus' hand, and looked up in his face as if he would
say, "Thank you, kind man. I shall not forget."

Now when the Saint had finished this good deed he
went back to his donkey and started on towards the
monastery. But hearing the soft pad of steps behind
him he turned and saw the great yellow lion was following close at his heels. At first he was somewhat em-
barrassed, for he did not know how the other monks
would receive this big stranger. But it did not seem
polite or kind to drive him away, especially as he was
still somewhat lame. So Gerasimus took up his switch
of olive leaves and drove the donkey on without a word,
thinking that perhaps the lion would grow tired and
drop behind. But when he glanced over his shoulder he
still saw the yellow head close at his elbow; and sometimes he felt the hot, rough tongue licking his hand
that hung at his side.

So they climbed the hill to the monastery. Some
one had seen Gerasimus coming with this strange atten-

dant at his heels, and the windows and doors were
crowded with monks, their mouths and eyes wide open
with astonishment, peering over one another's shoulders.
From every corner of the monastery they had run to
see the sight; but they were all on tiptoe to run back
again twice as quickly if the lion should roar or lash
his tail. Now although Gerasimus knew that the house
was full of staring eyes expecting every minute to
see him eaten up, he did not hurry or worry at all.
Leisurely he unloaded the water-jar and put the donkey
in his stable, the lion following him everywhere he
went. When all was finished he turned to bid the beast
good-by. But instead of taking the hint and departing
as he was expected to, the lion crouched at Gerasimus'
feet and licked his sandals; and then he looked up in
the Saint's face and pawed at his coarse gown plead-
ingly, as if he said, "Good man, I love you because you
took the thorn out of my foot. Let me stay with you
always to be your watch-dog." And Gerasimus understood.

"Well, if you wish to stay I am willing, so long
as you are good," he said, and the lion leaped up and
roared with joy so loudly that all the monks who were
watching tumbled over one another and ran away to
their cells in a terrible fright, locking the doors behind
them.

Gerasimus carried the water-jar into the empty kitchen,
and the lion followed. After sniffing about the place
to get acquainted, just as a kitten does in its new home,
the lion lay down in front of the fire and curled his head
up on his paws, like the great big cat he was. And so
after a long sigh he went to sleep. Then Gerasimus

had a chance to tell the other monks all about it. At
first they were timid and would not hear of keeping
such a dangerous pet. But when they had all tiptoed
down to the kitchen behind Gerasimus and had seen the
big kitten asleep there so peacefully they were not
quite so much afraid.

"I'll tell you what we will do," said the Abbot.
"If Brother Gerasimus can make his friend eat porridge and herbs like the rest of us we will let him join
our number. He might be very useful, — as well as
ornamental, — in keeping away burglars and mice. But
we cannot have any flesh-eating creature among us.
Some of us are too fat and tempting, I fear," and he
glanced at several of the roundest monks, who shud-
dered in their tight gowns. But the Abbot himself
was the fattest of them all, and he spoke with feeling.

So it was decided. Gerasimus let the lion sleep a
good long nap, to put him in a fine humor. But when
it came time for supper he mixed a bowl of porridge
and milk and filled a big wooden platter with boiled
greens. Then taking one dish in each hand he went
up to the lion and set them in front of his nose.

"Leo, Leo, Leo!" he called coaxingly, just as a
little girl would call "Kitty, Kitty, Kitty!" to her
pet. The lion lifted up his head and purred, like a
small furnace, for he recognized his friend's voice.
But when he smelled the dishes of food he sniffed and
made a horrid face, wrinkling up his nose and saying
"Ugh!" He did not like the stuff at all. But Gerasimus patted him on the head and said, "You had
better eat it, Leo; it is all I have myself. Share and
share alike, brother."

The lion looked at him earnestly, and then dipped his nose into the porridge with a grunt. He ate it all, and found it not so very bad. So next he tried the greens. They were a poor dessert, he thought; but since he saw that Gerasimus wanted him to eat them he finished the dish, and then lay down on the hearth feeling very tired.

Gerasimus was delighted, for he had grown fond of the lion and wanted to keep him. So he hurried back to the dining hall and showed the empty dishes to the Abbot. That settled the lion's fate. Thenceforth he became a member of the monastery. He ate with the other monks in the great hall, having his own private trencher and bowl beside Gerasimus. And he grew to like the mild fare of the good brothers, — at least he never sought for anything different. He slept outside the door of his master's cell and guarded the monastery like a faithful watch-dog. The monks grew fond of him and petted him so that he lived a happy life on the hill, with never a wish to go back to the desert with its thorns.

Wherever Gerasimus went the lion went also. Best of all, Leo enjoyed their daily duty of drawing water from the river. For that meant a long walk in the open air, and a frolic on the bank of the Jordan. One day they had gone as usual, Gerasimus, the lion, and the stupid donkey who was carrying the filled jar on his back. They were jogging comfortably home, when a poor man came running out of a tiny hut near the river, who begged Gerasimus to come with him and try to cure his sick baby. Of course the good man willingly agreed; this was one of the errands which he loved best to do.

"Stay, brother," he commanded Leo, who wanted to go with him, "stay and watch the foolish donkey." And he went with the man, feeling sure that the lion would be faithful. Now Leo meant to do his duty, but it was a hot and sleepy day, and he was very tired. He lay down beside the donkey and kept one eye upon him, closing the other one just for a minute. But this is a dangerous thing to do. Before he knew it, the other eye began to wink; and the next moment Leo was sound asleep, snoring with his head on his paws. Then it was that the silly donkey began to grow restless. He saw a patch of grass just beyond that looked tempting, and he moved over to it. Then he saw a greener spot beyond that, and then another still farther beyond that, till he had taken his silly self a long way off. And just then there came along on his way from Dan to Beersheba, a thief of a Camel Driver, with a band of horses and asses. He saw the donkey grazing there with no one near, and he said to himself, —

"Aha! A fine little donkey. I will add him to my caravan and no one will be the wiser." And seizing Silly by the halter, he first cut away the water-jar, and then rode off with him as fast as he could gallop.

Now the sound of pattering feet wakened Leo. He jumped up with a roar just in time to see the Camel Driver's face as he glanced back from the top of the next hill. Leo ran wildly about sniffing for the donkey; but when he found that he had really disappeared, he knew the Camel Driver must have stolen him. He was terribly angry. He stood by the water-

jar and roared and lashed his tail, gnashing his jaws as
he remembered the thief's wicked face.

Now in the midst of his rage out came Gerasimus.
He found Leo roaring and foaming at the mouth, his
red-rimmed eyes looking very fierce. And the donkey
was gone — only the water-jar lay spilling on the
ground. Then Gerasimus made a great mistake. He
thought that poor Leo had grown tired of being a vege-
tarian, of living upon porridge and greens, and had
tried fresh donkey-meat for a change.

"Oh, you wicked lion!" he cried, "you have eaten
poor Silly. What shall I do to punish you?" Then
Leo roared louder than ever with shame and sorrow.
But he could not speak to tell how it had happened.
The Saint was very sad. Tears stood in his kind eyes.
"You will have to be donkey now," he said; "you
will have to do his part of the work since he is now a
part of you. Come, stand up and let me fasten the
water-jar upon your back." He spoke sternly and
even switched Leo with his olive stick. Leo had never
been treated like this. He was the King of Beasts,
and it was shame for a King to do donkey's work.
His eyes flashed, and he had half a mind to refuse and
to run away. Then he looked at the good man and
remembered how he had taken out that cruel thorn.
So he hung his head and stood still to be harnessed in
the donkey's place.

Slowly and painfully Leo carried the water-jar up
the hill. But worse than all it was to feel that his
dear master was angry with him. Gerasimus told the
story to the other monks, and they were even more
angry than he had been, for they did not love Leo so

well. They all agreed that poor Leo must be punished;
so they treated him exactly as if he were a mean, silly
donkey. They gave him only oats and water to eat,
and made him do all Silly's work. They would no
longer let him sleep outside his master's door, but they
tied him in a lonesome stall in the stable. And now
he could not go to walk with Gerasimus free and
happy as the King of Beasts should be. For he went
only in harness, with never a kind word from his
master's lips.

It was a sad time for Leo. He was growing thinner
and thinner. His mane was rough and tangled because
he had no heart to keep it smooth. And there were
several white hairs in his beautiful whiskers. He was
fast becoming melancholy; and the most pitiful beast in
all the world is a melancholy lion. He had been hoping
that something would happen to show that it was all a
mistake; but it seemed as though the world was
against him, and truth was dead.

It was a sad time for Gerasimus, too; for he still
loved Leo, though he knew the lion must be punished
for the dreadful deed which he was believed to have
done. One day he had to go some distance to a neighboring town to buy provisions. As usual, he took Leo
with him to bring back the burden, but they did not
speak all the way. Gerasimus had done the errands
which he had come to do, and was fastening the baskets on each side of the lion's back. A group of
children were standing around watching the queer
sight, — a lion burdened like a donkey! And they
laughed and pointed their fingers at him, making fun
of poor Leo.

But suddenly the lion growled and began to lash his tail, quivering like a cat ready to spring on a mouse. The children screamed and ran away, thinking he was angry with them for teasing him. But it was not that. A train of camels was passing at the moment, and Leo had seen at their head a mean, wicked face which he remembered. And as the last of the caravan went by, Leo caught sight of Silly himself, the missing donkey of the monastery. At the

sound of Leo's growl, Silly pricked up his ears and stood on his fore legs, which is not a graceful position for a donkey. Then the Camel Driver came running up to see what was the matter with his stolen donkey. But when he came face to face with Leo, whose yellow eyes were glaring terribly, the thief trembled and turned pale. For he remembered the dreadful roar which had followed him that day as he galloped across the sand holding Silly's halter. The poor donkey was quivering with fear, thinking that this time he was surely going to be eaten piecemeal. But after all this trouble on Silly's account, the very idea of tasting donkey made Leo sick. He only wanted to show Gerasimus what a mistake had been made.

All this time Gerasimus had been wondering what the lion's strange behavior meant. But when he saw Leo seize the donkey's bridle, he began to suspect the truth. He ran up and examined the donkey carefully. Then Leo looked up in his face and growled softly, as if to say : —

" Here is your old donkey, safe and sound. You see I didn't eat him after all. *That* is the real thief," and turning to the Camel Driver, he showed his teeth and looked so fierce that the man hid behind a camel, crying, " Take away the lion! Kill the wicked lion! " But Gerasimus seized Silly by the bridle.

" This is my beast," he said, " and I shall lead him home with me. You stole him, Thief, and my noble lion has found you out," and he laid his hand tenderly on Leo's head.

" He is mine, you shall not have him! " cried the Camel Driver, dodging out from behind the camel, and trying to drag the donkey away from Gerasimus. But with a dreadful roar, Leo sprang upon him, and with his great paw knocked him down and sat upon his stomach.

" Do not hurt him, Leo," said Gerasimus gently. But to the Camel Driver he was very stern. " Look out, Sir

Thief," he said, " how you steal again the donkey of an
honest man. Even the yellow beasts of the desert know
better than that, and will make you ashamed. Be
thankful that you escape so easily."

Then he took the baskets from Leo's back and bound
them upon Silly, who was glad to receive them once
more from his own master's hands. For the Camel
Driver had been cruel to him and had often beaten him.
So he resolved never again to stray away as he had
done that unlucky time. And when they were all
ready to start, Gerasimus called Leo, and he got up
from the chest of the Camel Driver, where he had been
sitting all this time, washing his face with his paws and
smiling.

"My poor old Leo!" said Gerasimus, with tears in
his eyes, "I have made you suffer cruelly for a crime
of which you were not guilty. But I will make it up
to you."

Then happily the three set out for home, and all the
way Gerasimus kept his arm about the neck of his lion,
who was wild with joy because he and his dear master
were friends once more, and the dreadful mistake was
discovered.

They had a joyful reception at the monastery on the
hill. Of course every one was glad to see poor Silly
again ; but best of all it was to know that their dear
old lion was not a wicked murderer. They petted him
and gave him so many good things to eat that he almost burst with fatness. They made him a soft bed,
and all the monks took turns in scratching his chin
for ten minutes at a time, which was what Leo loved
better than anything else in the world.

And so he dwelt happily with the good monks, one of the most honored brothers of the monastery. Always together he and Gerasimus lived and slept and ate and took their walks. And at last after many, many years, they grew old together, and very tired and sleepy. So one night Gerasimus, who had become an Abbot, the head of the monastery, lay gently down to rest, and never woke up in the morning. But the great lion loved him so that when they laid Saint Gerasimus to sleep under a beautiful plane-tree in the garden, Leo lay down upon the mound moaning and grieving, and would not move. So his faithful heart broke that day, and he, too, slept forever by his dear master's side.

But this was not a sad thing that happened. For think how dreadful the days would have been for Leo without Gerasimus. And think how sad a life Gerasimus would have spent if Leo had left him first. Oh, no; it was not sad, but very, very beautiful that the dear Saint and his friendly beast could be happy together all the day, and when the long night came they could sleep together side by side in the garden.

REYNARD THE FOX

HOW THE LION PROCLAIMED A SOLEMN FEAST
AT HIS COURT, AND HOW ISEGRIM THE WOLF
AND HIS WIFE, AND CURTOIS THE HOUND,
MADE THEIR FIRST COMPLAINTS OF REYNARD
THE FOX.

IT was about the Feast of Pentecost
(which is commonly called Whit-
suntide), when the woods are in
their lustyhood and gallantry,
and every tree clothed in the green
and white livery of glorious leaves
and sweet-smelling blossoms, and the
earth is covered in her fairest mantle
of flowers, while the birds with much
joy entertain her with the delight of their harmonious
songs. Even at this time and entrance of the lusty
spring, the Lion, the royal King of beasts, to celebrate
this holy feast time with all triumphant ceremony, in-
tends to keep open court at his great palace of Sanden,
and to that end, by solemn proclamation, makes known
over all his kingdom to all beasts whatsoever, that,
upon pain to be held in contempt, every one should
resort to that great celebration. Within a few days
after, at the time appointed, all beasts both great and

small came in infinite multitudes to the court, only
Reynard the fox excepted, who knew himself guilty in
so many trespasses against many beasts, that his coming thither must needs have put his life in great hazard
and danger.

Now when the
King had assem-
bled all his court
together,
there were
few beasts
found but
made their sev-
eral complaints
against the fox,
but especially
Isegrim the
wolf, who, be-
ing the first
and principal
complainant,
came with all
his lineage and
kindred, and
standing be-
manner: fore the King, spoke in this
ereign Lord "My dread and dearest Sov-
you, that the King, I humbly beseech
of your from the height and strength
great power, and the multi-
tude of your mercies, you will be pleased to take pity
on the great trespasses and unsufferable injuries which
that unworthy creature Reynard the fox hath done to

me, my wife, and our whole family. Now to give your
highness some taste of these, first know (if it please your
Majesty) that this Reynard came into my house by vio-
lence, and against the will of my wife, where, finding
my children laid in their quiet couch, he there assaulted
them in such a manner that they became blind. For
this offence a day was set and appointed wherein Reynard should come to excuse himself, and to take a solemn oath that he was guiltless of that high injury;
but as soon as the book was tendered before him, he
that well knew his own guiltiness refused to swear,
and ran instantly into his hole, both in contempt of
your Majesty and your laws. This, my dread Lord,
many of the noblest beasts know which now are resi-
dent in your court: nor hath this alone bounded his
malice, but in many other things he hath trespassed
against me, which to relate, neither the time nor your
highness's patience would give sufferance thereunto.
Suffice it, mine injuries are so great that none can exceed them, and the shame and villany he hath done
to my wife is such that I can neither bide nor suffer it
unrevenged, but I must expect from him amends, and
from your Majesty mercy."

When the wolf had spoken these words, there stood
by him a little hound whose name was Curtois, who,
stepping forth, made likewise a grievous complaint unto
the King against the fox, saying that in the extreme
cold season of the winter, when the frost was most
violent, he being half starved and detained from all
manner of prey, had no more meat left him to sustain
his life than one poor pudding; which pudding the
said Reynard had most unjustly taken away from him.

But the hound could hardly let these words fly from his lips, when, with a fiery and angry countenance, in sprang Tibert the cat amongst them, and falling down before the King, said, " My Lord the King, I must confess the fox is here grievously complained upon, yet were other beasts' actions searched, each would have enough to do for his own clearing. Touching the complaint of Curtois the hound, it was an offence committed many years ago, and though I myself complain of no injury, yet was the pudding mine and not his;

for I won it by night out of a mill when the miller lay asleep, so that if Curtois could challenge any share thereof, it must be from mine interest."

When Panther heard these words of the cat, he stood

forth and said, " Do you imagine, Tibert, that it were a just or a good course that Reynard should not be complained upon ? Why the whole world knows he is a murderer, a vagabond, and a thief. Indeed he loveth not truly any creature, no not his Majesty himself, but would suffer his highness to lose both honor and renown, so that he might thereby attain to himself but so much as the leg of a fat hen ; I shall tell you what I saw him do yesterday to Kyward the hare, that now standeth in the King's protection. He promised unto

Kyward that he would teach him his *credo*, and make him a good chaplain; he made him come sit between his legs and sing and cry aloud *credo, credo.* My way lay thereby, and I heard the song: then coming nearer,

I found that Mr. Reynard had left his first note and song, and begun to play his old deceit; for he had caught Kyward by the throat, and had I not come at that time, he had taken his life also, as you may see by the fresh wound on Kyward at this present. O my Lord the King, if you suffer this unpunished, and let him go quit, that hath thus broken your peace, and profaned your dignity, and doing no right according to the judgment of your laws, your princely children many years hereafter shall bear the slander of this evil."

"Certainly, Panther," said Isegrim, "you say true, and it is fit they receive the benefit of justice that desire to live in peace."

HOW GRIMBARD THE BROCK SPAKE FOR REYNARD BEFORE THE KING.

Then spake Grimbard the brock, that was Reynard's sister's son, being much moved with anger: "Isegrim, you are malicious, and it is a common saw, *Malice never spake well;* what can you say against my kinsman Reynard? I would you durst adventure, that whichever of you had most injured one another might die the death, and be hanged as a felon. I tell you, were he here in the court, and as much in the King's favor as you are, it would be much too little satisfaction for you to ask him mercy. You have many times bitten and torn my kinsman with your venomous teeth, and oftener much than I can reckon, yet some I will call up to my remembrance.

"Have you forgot how you cheated him with the plaice which he threw down from the cart, when you followed aloof for fear? Yet you devoured the good plaice alone, and gave him no more but the great bones which you could not eat yourself. The like you did with the fat flitch of bacon, whose taste was so good, that yourself alone did eat it up, and when my uncle asked his part, you answered him with scorn, 'Fair young man, thou shalt have thy share.' But he got not anything, albeit he won the bacon with great fear and hazard, for the owner came, and caught my kinsman in a sack, from whence he hardly escaped with life. Many of these injuries hath Isegrim done to Reynard, which I beseech your lordships judge if they be sufferable.

"Now comes Kyward the hare with his complaint, which to me seems but a trifle, for if he will learn to read, and read not his lesson aright, who will blame the schoolmaster Reynard if he give him due correction? for if scholars be not beaten and chastened they will never learn.

"Lastly complaineth Curtois that he with great pain had gotten a pudding in the winter, being a season in which victuals are hard to find; methinks

silence would have become him better, for he had stolen
it; and *Male quæsisti, et male perdidisti* — that is to
say, it is fit that be evil lost which was evil won; who
can blame Reynard to take stolen goods from a thief?
It is reason that he which understands the law and can
discern right, being of great and high birth as my kinsman is, do right unto the law. Nay, had he hanged
up Curtois when he took him with the manner, he had
offended none but the King in doing justice without
leave; wherefore, for respect to his Majesty, he did it
not, though he reaped little thanks for his labor.
Alas, how do these complaints hurt him! mine uncle is
a gentleman and a true man, nor can he endure false-
hood; he doth nothing without the counsel of his
priest. I affirm, since my Lord the King proclaimed
his peace, he never thought to hurt any man. He
eateth but once a day, he liveth as a recluse; he chas-
tiseth his body, and weareth a shirt of haircloth; it is
above a year since he ate any flesh (as I have been
truly informed by them which came but yesterday from
him); he hath forsaken his castle Malepardus, and
abandoned all royal state, a poor hermitage retains
him, hunting he hath forsworn, and his wealth he
hath scattered, living only by alms and good men's
charities; doing infinite penance for his sins, so that
he is become pale and lean with praying and fasting."

Thus, whilst Grimbard his nephew stood preaching,
they perceived coming down the hill unto them, stout
Chanticleer the cock, who brought upon a bier a dead
hen, of whom Reynard had bitten off the head, and
was brought to the King to have knowledge thereof.

HOW CHANTICLEER THE COCK COMPLAINED OF REYNARD THE FOX.

Chanticleer marched foremost, smote piteously his hands and feathers, whilst on the other side the bier went two sorrowful hens — the one was Tantart, the other the good hen Cragant, being two of the fairest hens between Holland and Arden; these hens bore each of them a straight bright burning taper, and these hens were sisters to Copple, which lay dead on the bier, and in the marching they

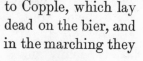

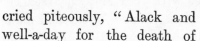

cried piteously, "Alack and well-a-day for the death of Copple, our dear sister." Two young hens bare the bier, which cackled so heavily, and wept so loud for the death of Copple their mother, that the hills gave an echo to their clamor. Thus being come before the King, Chanticleer, kneeling down, spake in this manner:

"Most merciful and my great Lord the King, vouchsafe, I beseech you, to hear our complaint, and redress those injuries which Reynard hath unjustly done to

me, and to my children that here stand weeping.   For
so it is, most mighty sir, that in the beginning of April,
when the weather was fair, I being then in the height
of my pride and glory, because of the great stock and
lineage I came of, and also I had eight valiant sons,
and seven fair daughters, which my wife had hatched,
all which were strong and fat, and walked in a yard
well walled and fenced round about, wherein they had
in several sheds for their guard six stout mastiff dogs,
which had torn the skins of many wild beasts, so that
my children feared not any evil which might happen
unto them.   But Reynard, that false and dissembling
traitor, envying their happy fortune because of their
safety, many times assailed the walls, and gave such
dangerous assaults, that the dogs divers times were let
forth unto him and hunted him away.   Yea, once they
lighted upon him, and bit him, and made him pay the
price for his theft, and his torn skin witnessed; yet
nevertheless he escaped, the more was the pity; albeit,
we were quit of his troubling a great while after.   At
last he came in the likeness of a hermit, and brought
me a letter to read, sealed with your Majesty's seal, in
which I found written, that your highness had made
peace throughout all your realm, and that no manner
of beast or fowl should do injury one to another.   He
affirmed unto me that for his own part he was become
a monk or cloistered recluse, vowing to perform a daily
penance for his sins; and showed unto me his beads,
his books, and the hair shirt next to his skin, saying in
humble wise unto me, 'Sir Chanticleer, never henceforth be afraid of me, for I have vowed nevermore to
eat flesh.   I am now waxed old, and would only re-

member my soul; therefore I take my leave, for I have
yet my noon and my even song to say.' Which spake,
he departed, saying his *credo* as he went, and laid him
down under a hawthorn; at this I was so exceeding
glad, that I took no heed, but went and chuckled my
children together, and walked without the wall, which
I shall ever rue. For false Reynard, lying under a
bush, came creeping betwixt us and the gate, and suddenly surprised one of my children, which he trussed
up in his mail and bore away, to my great sorrow. For
having tasted the sweetness of our flesh, neither hunter
nor hound can protect or keep him from us. Night
and day he waits upon us with that greediness, that of
fifteen of my children he hath left me but four un-
slaughtered, and yesterday Copple my daughter, which
here lieth dead on this bier, was after her murder, by
a kennel of hounds, rescued from him. This is my
plaint, and this I leave to your highness's mercy to
take pity of me, and the loss of my fair children."

THE KING'S ANSWER TO THE COCK'S COMPLAINT, AND HOW THEY SUNG THE DIRGE.

Then spake the King: " Sir Grimbard, hear you
this of your uncle the recluse? he hath fasted and
prayed well; and well, believe me, if I live a year, he
shall dearly abide it. As for you, Chanticleer, your complaint is heard and shall be cured; to your daughter
that is dead, we will give her the right of burial, and
with solemn dirges bring her to the earth, with worship; which finished, we will consult with our lords
how to do you right and justice against the murderer."

Then began the *Placebo Domine*, with all the verses belonging to it, which are too many to recite; and as soon as the dirge was done, the body was interred, and upon it a fair marble stone laid, being polished as bright as glass, in which was engraven in great letters this inscription following:

TOPPLE,
CHANTICLEER'S DAUGHTER,
WHOM REYNARD THE FOX HATH SLAIN,
LIETH HERE BURIED;
MOURN THOU THAT READEST IT,
FOR HER DEATH WAS UNJUST AND LAMENTABLE.

After this the King sent for his lords and wisest counsellors to consult how this foul murder of Reynard's might be punished. In the end it was concluded that Reynard should be sent for, and without all excuse to appear before the King to answer those trespasses should be objected against him, and that this message should be delivered by Bruin the bear. To all this the King gave consent, and calling him before him, said, "Sir Bruin, it is our pleasure that you deliver this message, yet in the delivery thereof have great regard to yourself, for Reynard is full of policy, and knoweth how to dissemble, flatter, and betray. He hath a world of snares to entangle you withal, and without great exercise of judgment, will make a scorn and mock of the best wisdom breathing."

"My Lord," answered Sir Bruin, "let me alone with Reynard, I am not such a truant in discretion, to become a mock to his knavery;" and thus full of jollity the bear departed; if his return be as jovial, there is no fear in his well speeding.

HOW BRUIN THE BEAR SPED WITH REYNARD THE FOX.

The next morning away went Bruin the bear in quest of the fox, armed against all plots of deceit whatsoever. And as he came through a dark forest, in which Reynard had a bypath, which he used when he was hunted, he saw a high mountain, over which he must pass to go to Malepardus. For though Reynard has many houses, yet Malepardus is his chiefest and

most ancient castle, and in it he lay both for defence and ease. Now at last when Bruin was come to Malepardus, he found the gates close shut, at which after he had knocked, sitting on his tail, he called aloud, " Sir Reynard, are you at home ? I am Bruin your kinsman, whom the King hath sent to summon you to the court, to answer many foul accusations exhibited against you, and hath taken a great vow, that if you fail to appear to this summons, that your life shall answer your contempt, and your goods and hon-

ors shall lie confiscate at his highness's mercy. Therefore, fair kinsman, be advised of your friend, and go
with me to the court to shun the danger that else will
fall upon you."

Reynard, lying close by the gate, as his custom was
for the warm sun's sake, hearing those words, departed
into one of his holes, for Malepardus is full of many
intricate and curious rooms, which labyrinth-wise he
could pass through, when either his danger or the
benefit of any prey required the same. There he medi-
tated awhile with himself how he might counterplot
and bring the bear to disgrace (who he knew loved
him not) and himself to honor; at last he came forth,
and said, " Dear uncle Bruin, you are exceeding wel-
come; pardon my slowness in coming, for at your first
speech I was saying my even song, and devotion must
not be neglected. Believe me, he hath done you no
good service, nor do I thank him which hath sent you
this weary and long journey, in which your much sweat
and toil far exceed the worth of the labor. Certainly
had you not come, I had to-morrow been at the court
of my own accord, yet at this time my sorrow is much
lessened, inasmuch as your counsel at this present may
return me double benefit. Alas, cousin, could his
Majesty find no meaner a messenger than your noble
self to employ in these trivial affairs? Truly it appears
strange to me, especially since, next his royal self, you
are of greatest renown both in blood and riches. For
my part, I would we were both at court, for I fear our
journey will be exceeding troublesome. To speak
truth, since I made mine abstinence from flesh, I
have eaten such strange new meats, that my body is

very much distempered, and swelleth as if it would break."

"Alas, dear cousin," said the bear, "what meat is that which maketh you so ill?"

"Uncle," answered he, "what will it profit you to know? the meat was simple and mean. We poor men are no lords, you know, but eat that for necessity which others eat for wantonness, yet not to delay you, that which I ate was honeycombs, great, full, and most pleasant, which, compelled by hunger, I ate too unmeasurably and am thereby infinitely distempered."

"Ha," quoth Bruin, "honeycombs? do you make such slight respect of them, nephew? why it is meat for the greatest emperor in the world. Fair nephew, help me but to some of that honey, and command me whilst I live; for

one little part thereof I will be your servant everlastingly."

"Sure," said the fox, "uncle, you but jest with me."

"But jest with you," replied Bruin; "beshrew my heart then, for I am in that serious earnest, that for one lick thereat you shall make me the faithfullest of all your kindred."

"Nay," said the fox, "if you be in earnest, then know I will bring you where so much is, that ten of you shall not be able to devour it at a meal, only for your love's sake, which above all things I desire, uncle."

"Not ten of us?" said the bear, "it is impossible; for had I all the honey betwixt Hybla and Portugal, yet I could in a short space eat it all myself."

"Then know, uncle," quoth the fox, "that near at hand here dwelleth a husbandman named Lanfert, who is master of so much honey, that you cannot consume it in seven years, which for your love and friendship's sake I will put into your safe possession."

Bruin, mad upon the honey, swore, that to have one good meal thereof he would not only be his faithful friend, but also stop the mouths of all his adversaries.

Reynard, smiling at his easy belief, said, "If you will have seven ton, uncle, you shall have it."

These words pleased the bear so well, and made him so pleasant, that he could not stand for laughing.

Well, thought the fox, this is good fortune, sure I will lead him where he shall laugh more measurably; and then said, "Uncle, we must delay no time, and I will spare no pains for your sake, which for none of my kin I would perform."

The bear gave him many thanks, and so away they went, the fox promising him as much honey as he could bear, but meant as many strokes as he could undergo. In the end they came to Lanfert's house, the sight whereof made the bear rejoice. This Lanfert was a stout and lusty carpenter, who the other day had

brought into his yard a great oak, which, as their manner is, he began to cleave, and had struck into it two
wedges in such wise that the cleft stood a great way
open, at which the fox rejoiced much, for it was
answerable to his wish. So with a laughing countenance he said to the bear, " Behold now, dear uncle,

and be careful of yourself, for within this tree is so
much honey that it is unmeasurable. Try if you can
get into it, yet, good uncle, eat moderately, for albeit
the combs are sweet and good, yet a surfeit is dangerous, and may be troublesome to your body, which I
would not for a world, since no harm can come to you
but must be my dishonor."

" Sorrow not for me, nephew Reynard," said the
bear, " nor think me such a fool that I cannot temper
mine appetite."

" It is true, my best uncle, I was too bold. I pray
you enter in at the end, and you shall find your desire."

The bear with all haste entered the tree, with his
two feet forward, and thrust his head into the cleft,
quite over the ears, which when the fox perceived, he
instantly ran and pulled the wedges out of the tree, so

that he locked the bear fast therein, and then neither flattery nor anger availed the bear. For the nephew had by his deceit brought the uncle into so fast a prison that it was impossible by any art to free himself of the same. Alas, what profited now his great strength and valor? Why they were both causes of more vexation; and finding himself destitute of all relief, he began to howl and bray, and with scratching and tumbling to make such a noise, that Lanfert, amazed, came hastily out of his house, having in his hand a sharp hook, whilst the bear lay wallowing and roaring within the tree.

The fox, from afar off said to the bear in scorn and mocking, "Is the honey good, uncle, which you eat? How do you do? Eat not too much, I beseech you. Pleasant things are apt to surfeit, and you may hinder your journey to the court. When Lanfert cometh (if your belly be full) he will give you drink to digest it, and wash it down your throat."

And having thus said, he went towards his castle. But by this time, Lanfert, finding the bear fast taken in the tree, he ran to his neighbors and desired them to come into his yard, for there was a bear fast taken there. This was noised through all the town, so that there was neither man, nor woman, nor child but ran thither, some with one weapon, and some with another — as goads, rakes, broom-staves, or what they could gather up. This army put Bruin into a great fear, being none but himself to withstand them, and hearing the clamor of the noise which came thundering upon him, he wrestled and pulled so extremely, that he got out his head, but he left behind him all the skin, and his ears also; insomuch that never creature beheld a fouler or more deformed beast. For the blood covering all his face, and his hands leaving the claws and skin behind them, nothing remained but ugliness. It was an ill market the bear came to, for he lost both motion and sight — that is, feet and eyes. But notwithstanding this torment, Lanfert, the priest, and the whole parish came upon him, and so becudgelled him about his body part, that it might well be a warning to all his misery, to know that ever the weakest shall still go most to the wall. This the bear found by experience, for every one exercised the height of their fury upon him. Even Houghlin with the crooked leg, and Ludolf with the long broad nose, the one with a leaden mall, and the other with an iron whip, all belashed poor sir Bruin, not so much but sir Bertolf with the long fingers, Lanfert and Ortam did him more annoyance than all the rest, the one having a sharp Welsh hook, the other a crooked staff well leaded at the end, which he used to play at stab ball withal. There was Birkin and Armes Ablequack, Bane the priest with his staff, and Dame Jullock his wife; all these so belabored the bear, that his life was in great danger. The poor bear in this massacre sat and sighed extremely, groaning under the burden of their strokes, of which Lanfert's were the greatest and thundered most dreadfully; for Dame Podge of Casport was his mother, and his father was Marob the steeple-maker, a passing stout man when he was alone. Bruin received of him many showers of stones till Lanfert's brother, rushing before the rest with a staff, struck the bear in the head such a blow, that he could neither hear nor see, so that awaking from his astonishment the bear leaped into the river adjoining, through a cluster of wives there standing together, of which he threw divers into the water, which was large and deep, amongst whom the parson's wife was one; which the parson seeing how she floated like a sea-mew, he left striking the bear, and cried to the rest of the company, "Help! oh, help! Dame Jullock is in the water; help, both men and women, for whosoever saves her, I give free pardon of all their sins and transgressions, and remit all penance imposed whatsoever." This heard, every one left the bear to help Dame Jullock, which as soon as the bear saw, he cut the stream and swam away as fast as he could, but the priest with a great noise pursued him, crying in his rage, "Turn, villain, that I may be revenged of thee;" but the bear swam in the strength of the stream and respected not his calling, for he was proud that he was so escaped from them. Only he bitterly cursed the honey tree and the fox, which had not only betrayed him, but had made him loose his hood from his face, and his gloves from his fingers. In this sort he swam some three miles down the water, in which time he grew so weary that he went on land to get ease, where blood trickled down his face; he groaned, sighed, and drew his breath so short, as if his last hour had been expiring.

Now whilst these things were in doing, the fox on his way home stole a fat hen, and threw her into his mail, and running through a bypath that no man might perceive him, he came towards the river with infinite joy; for he suspected that the bear was certainly slain: therefore said to himself, "My fortune is as I wished it, for the greatest enemy I had in the court is now dead, nor can any man suspect me guilty thereof." But as he spake these words, looking towards the river, he espied where Bruin the bear lay and rested, which struck his heart with grief, and he railed against Lanfert the carpenter, saying, " Silly fool that thou art, what madman would have lost such good venison, especially being so fat and wholesome, and for which he took no pains, for he was taken to his hand; any man would have been proud of the fortune which thou neglectest." Thus fretting and chiding, he came to the river, where he found the bear all wounded and bloody, of which Reynard was only guilty; yet in scorn he said to the bear, "*Monsieur, Dieu vous garde.*"

" O thou foul red villain," said the bear to himself, " what impudence is like to this ? "

But the fox went on with his speech, and said, " What, uncle ? have you forgot anything at Lanfert's, or have you paid him for the honeycombs you stole ? If you have not, it will redound much to your disgrace, which before you shall undergo, I will pay him for them myself. Sure the honey was excellent good, and I know much more of the same price. Good uncle, tell me before I go, into what order do you mean to enter, that you wear this new-fashioned hood? Will you be a monk, an abbot, or a friar? Surely he that shaved your crown hath cropped your ears; also your foretop is lost, and your gloves are gone; fie, sloven, go not barehanded, they say you can sing *peccavi* rarely."

These taunts made Bruin mad with rage, but because he could not take revenge, he was content to let him talk his pleasure. Then after a small rest he plunged again into the river, and swam down the stream, and landed on the other side, where he began with much grief to meditate how he might get to the court, for he had lost his ears, his talons, and all the skin off his feet, so that had a thousand deaths followed him, he could not go. Yet of necessity he must move, that in the end compelled by extremity, he set his tail on the ground, and tumbled his body over and over, so by degrees, tumbling now half a mile, and then half a mile, in the end he tumbled to the court, where divers beholding his strange manner of approach, they thought some prodigy had come towards them; but in the end the King knew him, and grew angry, saying, "It is sir Bruin, my servant; what villains have wounded him thus, or where hath he been that he brings his death thus along with him?"

"O my dread Sovereign Lord the King," cried out the bear, "I complain me grievously unto you; behold how I am massacred, which I humbly beseech you revenge on that false Reynard, who, for doing your royal pleasure, hath brought me to this disgrace and slaughter."

Then said the King, "How durst he do this? now by my crown I swear I will take the revenge which shall make the traitors tremble!"

Whereupon the King sent for all his council, and consulted how and in what sort to prosecute against the fox, where it was generally concluded that he should be again summoned to appear and answer his trespasses ; and the party to summon him they appointed to be Tibert the cat, as well for his gravity as wisdom ; all which pleased the King well.

[*The further adventures of Reynard the Fox, how he was tried and sentenced, and by his wit cheated the gallows, and how he was afterwards received into the King's favor, may be found in many other books.*]

ANDROCLES AND THE LION

THERE was a certain slave named Androcles, who was so ill treated by his master that his life became insupportable. Finding no remedy for what he suffered, he at length said to himself: "It is better to die than to continue to live in such hardships and misery as I am obliged to suffer. I am determined, therefore, to run away from my master. If I am taken again, I know that I shall be punished with a cruel death; but it is better to die at once than to live in misery. If I escape, I must betake myself to deserts and woods, inhabited only by beasts; but they cannot use me more cruelly than I have been used by my fellow-creatures; therefore I will rather trust myself with them than continue to be a miserable slave."

Having formed this resolution, he took an opportunity of leaving his master's house, and hid himself in a thick forest, which was at some miles distance from the city. But here the unhappy man found that he had only escaped from one kind of misery to experience another. He wandered about all day through a vast and trackless wood, where his flesh was continually torn by thorns and brambles : he grew hungry, but could find no food in this dreary solitude. At length he was ready to die with fatigue, and lay down in despair in a large cavern which he found by accident.

He had not lain long quiet in the cavern before he heard a dreadful noise, which seemed to be the roar of some wild beast, and terrified him very much. He started up with the intention of escaping, and had already reached the mouth of the cave, when he saw coming towards him a lion of immense size, who prevented any possibility of retreat. Androcles now believed his death to be inevitable ; but, to his great astonishment, the beast advanced towards him with a gentle pace, without any sign of enmity or rage, and uttered a kind of mournful wail, as if he wanted the assistance of the man.

Androcles, who was naturally of a resolute disposition, acquired courage from this circumstance to examine his strange guest. He saw, as the lion approached him, that he seemed to limp upon one of his legs, and that the foot was extremely swelled, as if it had been wounded. Acquiring still more fortitude from the gentle demeanor of the beast, he went up to him, and took hold of the wounded paw as a surgeon would examine a patient. He then perceived that a thorn of uncommon size had penetrated the ball of the foot, and was the cause of the swelling and lameness which he had observed. Androcles found that the beast, far from resenting this familiarity, received it with the greatest gentleness, and seemed to invite him to proceed. He therefore extracted the thorn, and, pressing the swelling, discharged a quantity of matter, which had been the cause of so much pain.

As soon as the beast felt himself thus relieved, he began to testify his joy and gratitude by every expression within his power: he jumped about like a spaniel, wagged his enormous tail, and licked the feet and hands of his physician. Nor was he contented with these demonstrations of kindness — from this moment Androcles became his guest; nor did the lion ever go forth in quest of prey without bringing home the produce of his chase, and sharing it with his friend. In this savage state of hospitality did the man continue to live for several months. At length, wandering through the woods, he met with a company of soldiers sent out to apprehend him, and was by them taken prisoner and conducted back to his master. The laws of that country being very severe against slaves, he was tried and found guilty of having fled from his master, and, as a punishment for his pretended crime, he was sentenced to be torn in pieces by a furious lion, kept many days without food, to inspire him with additional rage.

When the fatal day arrived, the unhappy man was exposed, unarmed, in the midst of a spacious arena, enclosed on every side, round which many thousand people were assembled to view the mournful spectacle. Presently a dreadful yell was heard, which struck the spectators with horror; and a monstrous lion rushed out of a den, which was purposely set open, and darted

forward with erected mane and flaming eyes, and jaws
that gaped like an open sepulchre. A mournful
silence instantly prevailed. All eyes were directly
turned upon the victim, whose destruction now appeared inevitable. But the pity of the multitude was
soon converted into astonishment when they beheld the
lion, instead of destroying his defenceless prey, crouch
submissively at his feet,
fawn upon him as a faith-
ful dog would do upon
his master, and rejoice

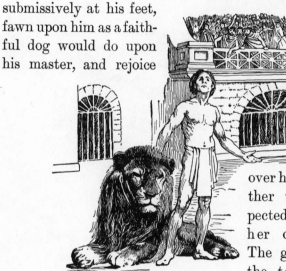

over him as a mo-
ther that unex-
pectedly recovers
her offspring.
The governor of
the town, who
was present, then
called out with a loud voice, and ordered Androcles to
explain to them this mystery.

Androcles then related to the assembly every circumstance of his adventures in the woods, and concluded
by saying that the very lion which now stood before
them had been his friend and entertainer in the woods.
All the persons present were astonished and delighted
with the story, to find that even the fiercest beasts are
capable of being softened by gratitude and moved by

humanity; and they all asked for the pardon of the unhappy man from the governor of the place. This was immediately granted to him, and he was also presented with the lion, who had in this manner twice saved the life of Androcles.

MY LION FRIEND

By MONSIEUR GERARD.

IN February, 1846, Monsieur de Tourville, commander of Ghelma, sent for me, and told me that the tribe of Beni-Bughal requested my assistance to free them from the ravages of a lioness, which, with her cubs, had established her headquarters within the pasture-grounds of their tribe. I immediately mounted my horse, and rode with the sheik to the tent-village of the tribe, encamped at the foot of the Jebel Mezrur.

At dawn, I reconnoitred the wood in which the lioness and her cubs usually hid themselves; and in the thicket, upon a carefully-arranged heap of leaves, I found a small female cub, about one month old, not larger than a cat. I took it up in my burnoose, carried it to the tents, and again went back to the neighborhood of the lair, to await there the return of the lioness. When I reached the forest the sun was setting. I hastened to find the thicket, and sat down under a cork-tree. But now I observed that the thicket was so dense as to afford me no room to take aim with my rifle; I had therefore to cut the branches of the trees with my double-edged dagger to the extent of the length of my rifle.

My plan of attack was simple. When the lioness showed her head between the bushes I intended at once to blow out her brains. Night came on, and I listened attentively to every noise around. A bear passed me first; I nearly mistook him for the lioness, but his slow, unwieldy steps soon undeceived me. Again, a jackal glided to the lair, and snuffed about for the provisions of the lion-cubs. But now there was no mistake possible; I thought I heard distinctly my expected victim breaking the bones of a sheep with its teeth, and leisurely feeding upon the carcass which I had noticed in the thicket. For two hours I waited in strong excitement, and still I was deceived. My arm grew stiff; I could no longer keep my rifle to my shoulder; I leant against the tree, waiting till I should see the eyes of the lioness shining through the darkness.

It may have been eight o'clock when I suddenly heard the sound of heavy steps and the rustling of the branches. I could not doubt that it was the lioness. The noise ceased at about twenty yards' distance. I apprehended that she might have observed me, and that, with one sudden leap, she might clear the distance which separated us. I jumped up, in the hope of seeing perhaps her eyes. Leaning against the tree, the rifle in readiness, I fixed my glance upon the bushes, which rose before me as dense as a wall; but I neither saw nor heard anything. My imagination, excited by the recollection of former adventures, pierced

through the darkness and the obstacles which ob-
structed my sight, and presented to me the lioness,
with neck strained, ears back, and body trembling,
ready to spring. I got nervous. Though it was
bitingly cold I felt the perspiration on my forehead,
when a sudden thought restored my presence of mind
and calmed my nerves. Why, thought I, have I not
climbed the tree, instead of posting myself under it?
— why should I not seize one of the branches, and in a
few seconds be thirty feet above ground, in perfect
safety? But I recollected that in the daytime I should
not have thought of the tree, and should have believed
it unworthy of myself to seek such a refuge. This
thought restored my self-possession and self-reliance.

But what was my rage and surprise when, instead of
the terrible roar of a lioness, maddened by the loss of
her cub, I heard the whine of a young lion crying for
his absent nurse! I cannot help laughing when I
recollect the excitement into which this little fellow
had put me. The lioness not coming forth, I caught
hold of the cubs. I put them into my pocket, and returned in the direction of the tents. Straggling for
three hours through woods and ravines, and often fancy-
ing I heard the roar of the lioness following the scent
of her cubs, I arrived at last at the Duar — Arab tent-
village — guided by the barking of the dogs.

Settled here, the first thing I did was to compare the
two cubs. The male was about a third larger than his
sister, and a very fine animal he was. I gave him the
name of Hubert, in honor of the patron saint of the
chase. While the little lioness avoided men, and
scratched whosoever dared to touch her, Hubert re-

mained quite quiet at the hearth, and looked about
with an astonished but not savage stare.   The Arab
females were never tired of petting him, and rewarded

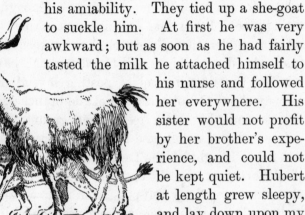

his amiability.   They tied up a she-goat
to suckle him.   At first he was very
awkward; but as soon as he had fairly
tasted the milk he attached himself to
his nurse and followed
her everywhere.   His
sister would not profit
by her brother's expe-
rience, and could not
be kept quiet.   Hubert
at length grew sleepy,
and lay down upon my
burnoose as quietly as
if he had been with his mother.

The next day, I reconnoitred the ravines and hills of
the neighborhood, followed by the Arabs.   In the
evening I partook of a meal in the tent of a shepherd,
and returned to my former ambush.   I waited in vain
till dawn — the lioness did not appear.   I was told
afterwards that on the loss of her two cubs, she had
left the country with a third.   The disappearance of
the dreaded beast restored calm in the tribe Beni-
Bughal, and I left them with my two adopted pets to
proceed to Ghelma.   But the young lioness soon died
in teething, which is always a critical, and often fatal,
period to lion-cubs.

As to Hubert, he did very well, and was growing so
fast that the milk of three goats was scarcely sufficient
for him.   He became the pet of all the camp, especially

of Lehman the trumpeter, Bibart the blacksmith, and poor Rustan the spahi, who, one year after, was terribly maimed by the lions of Medjez Ammar. A register was opened for Hubert, in which his services were entered: he was originally put down as a horseman of the second class, waiting for advancement. I extract from the register, in which every fact and service of Hubert was faithfully recorded, the following feats:

"*April* 20, 1846. — When Hubert was three months old, the squadron stood this day in the courtyard of the headquarters, ready to proceed to the drill-ground; the trumpeter sounded the call; and horseman Hubert, shut up in his room on the second floor, leaps to the window, and shouts, 'Here!' but he is not heard, and he is set down as absent. The captain orders — *March;* the trumpeter sounds; and Hubert, jumping from the window down into the courtyard, appears with the squadron. For such excellent conduct, the entry that he was absent at the call is cancelled.

"*May* 15. — Hubert kills his nurse, the old goat, and is therefore nominated a horseman of the first class.

"*Sept.* 8. — He makes a sortie on the market-place; puts the Arabs to flight; kills several sheep and a donkey; fells a guardsman to the ground; and surrenders only to his friends Lehman, Bibart, and Rustan. For this gallantry he is promoted to be a non-commissioned officer; gets an iron chain of honor round his neck; and is attached to the door-posts of the stable as permanent sentinel.

"*Jan.* 16, 1847. — A Bedouin was prowling about the stables; Hubert, suspecting him to be a robber, breaks the chain, seizes the Arab, and keeps him on the ground till the officer comes, to whom he delivers up his prisoner in a wretched condition. For this feat Hubert is made a color-sergeant, and gets two chains of honor round his neck. In April he kills a horse and fells two soldiers; and thus rises to be an officer, and is put into a cage."

Poor Hubert! And I, his best friend, was ordered to imprison him! The authorities, lenient to him because he was so amiable, could not longer ignore his escapades; he could not but be sentenced to death or to imprisonment for life.

My first idea was to let him escape; but I feared that, accustomed to intercourse with men, he might return to the camp and be killed. During the first months of his punishment I sometimes came at night and opened his cage. He leaped out with delight, and we played at hide-and-seek. But one evening, when he was in his best spirits, he hugged me so fondly that he would certainly have strangled me had not my comrades come and delivered me from his caresses. It was the last time we played together. Nevertheless, I must confess that he had no bad intentions : he did not make use either of his claws or of his teeth, and always behaved kindly and gently to his friends. Still, displeased that he could not leave the cage without a heavy chain fastened to the irons, he became sad and often excited. His character changed for the worse; I began to think that I must part with him. An officer offered me 3000 francs, on behalf of the king of Sardinia; but I could not sell my friend Hubert as I sell the skins of the lions I kill. The Prince of Aumale had been kind to me. I offered Hubert to him, requesting that he would provide for him in the Zoölogical Gardens at Algiers.

Hubert left Ghelma in October, 1847, to the great distress of the ladies, towards whom he had displayed the utmost politeness, and of all the soldiers, who loved him nearly as much as I did myself. Lehman and Bibart got drunk intentionally, in order to bear more easily the pangs of parting; still, they were so overwhelmed with grief at taking leave, and made such a row, that they had to be given into custody to enable Hubert to be got off.

At Algiers they found Hubert too tall and magnificent to remain in the Zoölogical Gardens; he was to be sent to Paris, and I was ordered to accompany him to France. Poor animal! Indeed he was tall — a horse-collar was scarcely big enough for his neck — and far too magnificent for the wretched life to which he was doomed.

The captain of the vessel in which Hubert was transported across the sea allowed me to open his cage while he took his meals; the passengers being kept away beyond the reach of his chain. As soon as I opened the door he darted forth, thanked me in his way, and took a walk as far as the chain permitted him to go. Now a beef-steak was brought, of about eight to ten pounds. He ate it, and lay down in the sun for digestion. After his hour of recreation was past, he crept back into his cage, allowed himself to be pulled by the ears, and waited patiently for his next meal. Thus passed the last pleasant days between us. At Toulon we parted. He was sent to Marseilles, and I went on a visit to my family at Cuers. In a few weeks I came likewise to Marseilles; but, although so short a time had elapsed, my friend was no longer the same. Joy, indeed, lighted up his fine face, but he seemed suffering and worn out. His eyes appeared to ask with reproach: "Why hast thou forsaken me? Where am I? Whither am I to be carried? Wilt thou remain with me?" I was grieved at his unhappy looks; and scarcely was I out of sight when I heard him roaring, and shaking furiously the bars of the cage. I returned; and when he saw me he became calm, and clung to the railing that I might pat him. A few minutes afterwards he fell asleep. I retreated slowly, not to disturb his slumber. Sleep is forgetfulness for the animal as well as for man.

In three months after I was in Paris. My first visit, of course, was to M. Leo Bertrand, editor of the journal for sportsmen; my second to the Jardin des Plantes. Coming to the gallery of the wild beasts, I was surprised by the smallness of the cages, and displeased by the bad smell, easily endured by hyænas and jackals, but which must kill lions and panthers, to which cleanliness is life.

Under such disagreeable impressions I arrived at the cage of my lion-friend, who, half-dozing, looked indifferently at the crowd before him. Suddenly he raised his head, his eyes sparkled, the muscles of his face throbbed, the top of his tail moved : he had seen the regimentals of a spahi, but did not yet recognize his old comrade. I came nearer; and, unable to control my emotion, I put my hand through the rails. It was really a most touching meeting for myself and all who  witnessed it. Hubert's eyes were riveted on my features; now he put his nose to my hand; his eyes became clearer and fonder; he guessed that it was his friend. One word, I knew, would dispel all uncertainty.

"Hubert, old fellow!" I said. This was enough. With a terrible leap he jumped against the bars, so that they nearly broke. My friends fled in terror, and

tried to drag me away. Noble animal! even by your
joy you inspire fear! Hubert stood erect, his neck on
the railing, which he shook with his paws as if he
wished to break through every obstacle that separated
us. He looked glorious, roaring for joy and anger.
His red tongue licked my hand with delight, and he
tried to put his enormous paws out of the cage to hug
me. Some strangers came nearer — he became wild
and furious; but when we were left alone he again
grew calm and caressing. I cannot tell how trying it
was for me to part. Twenty times I came back, to
make it understood to Hubert that I should return;
but as often as I left him the whole gallery trembled
with his furious leaps and roars.

I often visited the poor prisoner, and we remained
together for hours; but I soon saw that he became
sadder and more weary. The officers of the garden
thought that my visits brought nostalgia upon him,
and I determined not to see him so often. On one of
the days of May I came as usual, and the keeper said:
"Sir, do not come any more: Hubert is dead." I hastened away; but now I often go to the gardens to in-
dulge in thoughts of my poor friend.

Thus died Hubert, born for freedom and for the air
of the mountains. Civilization killed him. But, oh ye
lionesses of the Atlas, never shall I again steal your
cubs! Better for them to be killed at once, as if by
lightning, in the forest, under the free sky of their
home, than to linger in captivity. The lead of the
hunter is preferable to consumption in a cage.

A LION STORY

(From Cast Up by the Sea.)

By SIR SAMUEL BAKER.

IT was on a bright moonlight night that Ned had determined to start. At about one A.M., when the people of the village were asleep, Ned strapped the small saddle-packs upon Nero, and with knapsacks upon their backs and double-barrelled guns in their hands, he and Tim forsook the comfortable hut, and struck into the depths of the forest. They marched till daylight upon a narrow footway that resembled the run of sheep. This was already well known to them for a distance of about six miles, as they had often travelled upon the route during their shooting excursions, but beyond that limit all was unexplored. When day broke Ned found himself in a dense forest, where giant trees rose to the height of upward of a hundred feet, springing from a thick and tangled underwood, through which it would have been impossible to penetrate except by the narrow path already mentioned. They had marched five hours when the sun rose at six o'clock; thus Ned calculated that they had made fifteen miles : he accordingly determined to push on until eight at the same rate of three miles per hour.

The night had been cool, and they had marched almost without fatigue until sunrise, but the last two hours had been extremely hot, and Ned was thankful when he suddenly arrived on the banks of a clear stream that rippled over a bed of pebbles between two over-hanging cliffs. It was a lovely spot, shaded by the dark foliage of the tamarind-trees that grew in the deep clefts among the rocks, and Ned had no sooner arrived than he unstrapped Nero's load, and quickly throwing off his own clothes he plunged into a pool of cool water that formed a natural basin in the river's bed. The dog followed his master, together with Tim, and all revelled in the luxury of the morning bath.

After bathing Ned arranged the packs upon some bare rocks beneath the shade of a large tamarind-tree, and all being extremely hungry he looked despairingly at the bag of biscuits which formed their scanty fare. Tim had already lighted a fire, although there was nothing to cook, when Ned suddenly listened to a distant sound, and, jumping up, he took his gun, which he loaded with shot instead of ball, and started along the bed of the stream in quest of guinea-fowl that he had heard cackling in the distance. He was followed by Nero, and after a rough scramble among the rocks in the bed of the winding stream he arrived close to the sound. As he carefully turned a corner in the river he observed a large number of guinea-fowl sitting close together upon the branches of a tree, from which they kept up an incessant cackling at a falcon which, having captured one of their party, was now eagerly devouring its prey upon a high rock above the stream. Creeping through the bushes while the attention of the guinea-fowl was attracted by the falcon, Ned arrived unseen within thirty yards of the tree, and aiming at the centre of the flock he fired. To his delight five birds fell to the ground, one of which being only winged would have escaped in the thick bushes had not Nero at once secured it; they were in exceedingly good condition, and as Ned felt their fat breasts with satisfaction, he tied their legs together with a strip of tough bark, which he tore from the stem of a mimosa, and then joyfully returned to breakfast. They had now sufficient for the evening, as the birds were so large that even their appetites could hardly manage two for breakfast; therefore the pot was placed upon the fire, and two were boiled, while three were stuck upon spits for roasting. Tim was a good hand at jungle cookery; thus he placed a straight bamboo across two forked sticks which rested in the ground close to the fire; against this he laid his spits, with one end fixed in the earth; these he occasionally turned when they required it, and in about forty minutes the fowls were beautifully roasted. Breakfast was ready. They wisely determined to eat the boiled fowls and to carry the roast upon the afternoon march, as they would better support the heat of the journey. A few biscuits stewed up with the soup of the boiled fowls,

together with the bones left from breakfast, afforded
Nero a hearty meal, and both Ned and Tim lay down
beneath a shady tree, against the stem of which they
placed their guns. In a short time the whole party,
including the dog, were sound asleep.

They had slept for about four hours when Ned was
suddenly awoke by a low growl from Nero, and sitting
up he saw the dog rush into the jungle and bark
furiously at some object unseen; but almost at the
same instant Ned felt himself seized from behind, and
before he had time to offer the slightest resistance, or
even to discover the cause of attack, his arms were
firmly bound, and he was entirely helpless. Tim had
been secured in the same manner. A loud yell was
now raised, and Ned was surrounded by a party of
naked savages armed with spears and bows. Nero
upon hearing the noise came bounding back from the
man whom he had attacked in the jungle, and seeing
Ned he immediately took his stand by his side.

All this happened so suddenly and unexpectedly that
Ned could hardly believe his eyes; but putting a bold
face upon the matter he smiled as the leader of the
party confronted him, at the same time he made signs
that the twisted palm-leaves that confined his arms
caused him much pain. This man was an immensely
powerful negro, with a ferocious expression of countenance, but upon seeing Ned smile he examined him
closely with surprise; he then looked at the dog and
at Tim, as though completely puzzled at the nature of
his prisoners. In the meantime Nero was growling
fiercely, although restrained from attack by Ned's
voice.

Having satisfied himself that the party consisted of only two persons and the dog, the negro chief gave an order to his men, who at once prepared two long forked sticks, about the thickness of a man's arms. In a few minutes Ned found his neck firmly secured in the fork by means of a cross-piece of wood that was lashed across the points. Tim was fettered in a similar manner; a rope was then attached to the extremity of the handle, and thus led by two powerful negroes, both Ned and Tim found themselves in the possession of a gang of slave-hunters. Without further delay several men took possession of the guns, knapsacks, and various effects that lay upon the ground, and they marched rapidly forward for about an hour, until they arrived at a narrow path which turned to the west, upon which they hurried without once halting until nearly sunset.

Ned was suffering severely from thirst and fatigue; the heat was excessive, and upon arrival at a considerable stream he made signs to the man who led him that he wished to drink. At that moment the party halted, and the negro descended to the river, and having slaked his own thirst, he returned with a large gourd-shell full of clear water. Never had Ned enjoyed a draught of water with such delight, and he drained every drop from the gourd. He now made signs that they should release him from the yoke, and that he would not attempt to escape. Upon this a consultation was held, which ended by the approach of the leader of the party, who with violent threats and gesticulations, explained that, should Ned attempt to desert, he would be immediately put to death. He then drew a knife from a sheath slung upon his arm above the left elbow, with which he cut the rope that

secured Ned's neck in the fork; at the same time he
released his arms.

Ned was so stiff that he could scarcely raise his hands
to his forehead in gratitude for his freedom; but having
performed this simple act of courtesy to the negro chief,
he explained by signs that Tim should also be released.
Without further delay Tim's bonds were cut; at the
same time he was given a gourd full of water. Having
taken a long draught Tim stretched his stiffened arms,
and then rubbed his elbows as he sat down by the side
of Ned, who, tired out, had thrown himself at full length
upon the ground.

" Dis is a pretty kettle ob fish, Massa Ned ! " exclaimed
Tim. " Pity Massa Ned didn't marry all de ole chief's
gals ! Now we run away we got into bad bus'ness.
Tim knows dis work ; not de fust time Tim had his
neck in de fork. Dese black fellers big blackguards,
Massa Ned ; catched we for slaves. Tim knows dis
work ; catched Tim before now."

Tim's former experience had been severely practical,
and he rightly surmised that both he and Ned were
captured for the purpose of being sold to some neighboring tribe; thus they might be handed about from
one to the other as slaves for the remainder of their
existence. At the same time, when he had reflected upon
Ned's want of diplomacy in refusing the old chief's
daughters, he in no way faltered in his allegiance, as
he was thoroughly prepared to suffer any misery so
long as he could share the lot of his young master; but
it was Ned's misfortune that he regretted.

"Do you think they mean to sell us, Tim?"
asked Ned.

"Yes, Massa Ned, p'r'aps sell Tim to one man; sell Massa Ned to anoder."

"Brutes!" exclaimed Ned; "this slave-trade is, indeed, an accursed traffic!"

"Yes, Massa Ned," rejoined Tim, "very bad bus'ness —almost bad like King George's bus'ness."

"What do you mean, Tim?" asked Ned.

"I say," replied the practical Tim, "de black nigger fellers almost bad as de press-gang fellers, only not quite. King George's fellers steal de boys to let de Frenchmen shoot 'em; de black niggers steal 'em, make 'em do de work; press-gang more bad, take de white slaves, let de Frenchmen kill 'em."

Ned would not question Tim's logic. There was no doubt of their situation; the tribes were at perpetual warfare with each other for the purpose of capturing slaves, some of which were exchanged for ivory with distant countries, while others were transported to Zanzibar, which was the great Portuguese depot for the trade. One fact was clear, that it was necessary to find favor in the eyes of their captors, and to trust in Providence for their future guidance. Determined upon this policy, although stiff and tired, Ned rose from the ground, and assisted the party in collecting wood for the night fires that were necessary to protect them from wild animals. There was a large quantity of fallen timber in the forest, and in a short time the united efforts of the people had collected numerous trunks and branches of dead trees, which were arranged in several piles. All being completed, a negro commenced the tedious operation of producing fire by the friction of two pieces of wood. He first produced a stick, in which he cut a notch; he then selected a piece of straight and dry wood about as thick as the little finger; this he sharpened to a point which he inserted in the notch, and holding this firmly upon the ground with his toes, he rapidly twirled the upper stick between the palms of his hands, so that the point revolved within the notch as though it were a drill. In about three minutes it began to smoke, but as the success in producing fire by this method depends upon the quality of the wood, much labor was vainly expended, and the friction brought no spark, as the wood was of the wrong kind. Ned immediately produced a flint and steel from his pocket with a piece of tinder formed of canvas; with this he at once struck a light, to the astonishment of the natives, who crowded round him to witness the extraordinary operation. For at least ten minutes he was obliged to continue the performance of producing a shower of sparks by the blow of the flint and steel, to the intense delight of the natives, who vainly attempted it, but only succeeded in knocking the skin off their knuckles.

It was nearly dark, and the forest appeared in deep gloom as the pile of dry wood blazed brightly and illumined the trees upon the bank of the river where the party had bivouacked. The chief accompanied by one of his men, had been some time absent in the search for wild yams, which abounded in the forest, and climbed like gigantic convolvuli around the stems of trees. Tim had already placed his pot upon the fire, and the water was boiling, in expectation of the supply of vegetables, when suddenly a loud shriek was heard in the dense wood at no great distance. This was almost

immediately succeeded by a terrific roar; another loud
cry of alarm was heard, and all the men rushed to their
arms, crying, " The lion! the lion! "

In an instant Ned seized the gun loaded with ball,
and without the slightest hesitation he rushed toward
the spot through the thick bushes, followed by Nero and
the entire party. In the excitement of the moment his
stiffness and fatigue had vanished, and he dashed forward with a speed that was hardly equalled even by the
naked negroes who accompanied him. In less than a
minute they heard a rush in the jungle before them.
Ned immediately cocked his gun, but in that instant the
figure of the powerful negro chief appeared, flying
toward them as he shouted the dreaded name, " The
lion! "

A loud roaring and growling was now distinctly heard
within a hundred paces of them, and the negroes hesitated to advance. Ned resolutely pushed forward, followed by Tim and Nero; and presently the dog, who
had heard the terrible sound, dashed from his master's
side, and rushing toward the spot was heard barking
loudly at the lion. In a few moments Ned arrived at a
small open glade in the middle of the forest, in which
to his horror he saw the lion upon the body of a man
whom he seized by the throat, while Nero stood within
a few yards baying him furiously. Upon Ned's arrival
in the open spot the lion angrily shook the neck of the
man as a dog would shake a rat, and then slowly
dragged the body toward the thick bush. Ned rushed
forward, and stood within ten paces of the immense
brute, who, seeing himself thus challenged, turned, and
releasing his hold on the neck of his victim, he placed

one of his paws upon the chest, and crouched upon the ground, facing and glaring upon his unexpected adversary. At this moment Nero sprung toward him and barked loudly; this diverted his attention, and the lion turned his shaggy head toward the dog. Profiting by the opportunity, Ned took a steady aim at the temple, a little in front of the ear, and fired.

At the report of the

gun the lion rolled over upon his back, and convulsively stretched out his prodigious paws, which trembled in the palsy of death, as the ball had passed through his brain. Hardly had the smoke cleared when Nero rushed in and seized the lion by his hairy throat, which he shook and tore in desperate fury, at the same time he received a deep scratch from one of the claws that contracted in the death struggle.

At the report of the gun the natives had rushed back in terror, but now that they witnessed its effect they crowded around Ned, and taking his hand they kissed the palm and embraced him after their fashion, by raising both his hands three times above his head. The ferocious-looking negro, who was their chief, also drew near in the ecstasy of the moment, and throwing up his arms, he shouted an address of admiration, which was succeeded by a loud yell of praise from all present. The dead body of the negro who had been killed was then drawn upon one side, and left for the beasts of prey that would devour it during the night, while with exciting shouts of victory the negroes dragged the lion through the forest, and laid it by the night fire that was brightly blazing at the place of bivouac.

It appeared that the chief and the deceased negro were returning from their search after yams, when the lion suddenly sprang upon them from the thick jungle, and seizing the man by the throat, he quickly strangled him. The chief had thrown his spear without effect, as it had glanced from the stem of a tree; he had then shouted for help, which had been so quickly and courageously given by Ned.

For several hours after the moon rose the conversation continued upon the recent event, and there was a general feeling of astonishment and admiration at Ned's courage and the power of the gun. Nero also shared in

the praise, as the negroes were delighted that the dog
had flown so directly at the lion's throat when the
fatal shot was fired.   While the exciting topic was dis-
cussed by the blazing fires the heroes of the night, Ned,
Tim, and Nero, were stretched upon some dry grass fast
asleep, tired out with the long day's march; they had
gone supperless to rest, as sleep was more desired than
food; in the meantime the natives, having carefully
skinned their late enemy, made use of Tim's cooking-
pot, and feasted on the lion.

A NARROW ESCAPE FROM A TIGER

By ROBERT COCHRANE.

SOME time ago I was shooting in the Kimidy district with my friend Jack Waldron, an officer in a regiment of Madras Native Infantry. Kimidy is a little native town in the north of the Madras Presidency, and is situated among some jungly hills.

Kimidy was in some respects an excellent place for a holiday. Living was wonderfully cheap. You could purchase a whole sheep for a shilling and a fowl for fourpence. Milk, butter, and eggs could be obtained for the merest trifle.

Then the thick jungle that closely encircled the place was full of game, both great and small. One was often awakened in the morning by the crowing of the wild jungle-cocks and the screams of the pea-fowl in the immediate vicinity of the station. Wild hogs would enter the gardens of the officers at night, and commit sad havoc with the English vegetables that were planted there.

Spotted deer and the Indian elk were very numerous

upon the jungly hills about the place ; and a bear could generally be found within ten minutes' walk of the station by those who cared to look for him with beaters. Lastly, there were tigers and leopards in these teeming jungles ; but such animals were not often met with close at hand, they preferred to reside at a little distance from the military.

In such a paradise of sport it might be supposed that the time would pass very pleasantly for men who were fond of shooting ; but there was a serious drawback to the delights of life at Kimidy — there was the danger of contracting fever.

Pooree, upon the eastern coast of India, was the usual place to which invalids from Kimidy betook themselves, and a very miserable place it was ; but then it was the sea-side, and that was everything. Let the reader picture to himself a great waste of glaring yellow sand, and he will have a fair idea of Pooree.

Well, Jack Waldron and I got rather tired, after a time, of shooting bears and pea-fowl ; and before our month's leave of absence had expired we proposed to visit the famous temple of Juggernaut near Pooree. Besides this, I was feeling rather unwell, and feared an attack of jungle-fever ; and as Pooree is no great distance from Kimidy, we settled to go down there one night in palanquins we had brought with us from the south.

It was the Indian cold weather at this time, and the air was sufficiently chilly to make a blanket agreeable at night. Jack and I looked forward to a comfortable sleep as we got into our palanquins about eight o'clock in the evening. We had made a very comfortable dinner, and we felt in very good-humor when the bearers took the palanquins on their shoulders and set off for Pooree.

Waldron's palanquin went first, and mine followed. It was pitch-dark, but the moon was expected to rise about midnight, and, in the meantime, we were provided with two men carrying torches of burning rags, on which they threw oil from time to time. I lay awake for an hour or so, smoking, and watching the curious effects of the light thrown by the torches on our party and on the jungle skirting the roadside. Then I fell asleep, to dream that I was on my way to England in a steamer, which was rolling hard, as I thought, in the very middle of the Bay of Biscay.

I was awakened by a chattering among the bearers, and, looking at my watch, saw that it was ten minutes past twelve, and that the moon was rising. We had stopped at a public bungalow by the roadside, and close to a village, in which there seemed to be a great deal of *tom-toming* and noise going on. Waldron had got out of his palanquin, and was talking to the bearers, who were greatly excited.

Just then he came to me with a very grave face. "This is awkward," he said; "there is cholera very bad in the village, and our bearers are in such mortal terror that I am afraid they will run back to Kimidy. What is to be done?"

"We must get on at any price," I replied; "it would never do to stop here all night. Here! Lift the palanquins and go on quick," I cried to the men in their own tongue. But, in spite of all our threats and entreaties, the bearers would not lift the palanquins from the ground until we consented to give them a present of one rupee each. Even then three or four of them disappeared, and were seen no more, leaving us short-handed for the next stage of the journey.

At last we got on our way once more, the bearers grumbling greatly all the time. We still maintained our old order of march, and, whatever my companion's feelings may have been, I know that I was very glad indeed when we passed the village and heard the last of the tom-toms and cholera-horns with which the poor villagers were striving to drive the demon of pestilence out of their borders.

Our way lay through a beautiful bamboo jungle, and for some time I was interested in watching the graceful, waving forms of the gigantic canes, as we slowly passed them. Then I composed myself to sleep again.

I don't think I could have slept more than half-an-hour, when I was awakened by the clamor of the bearers, who were chattering in great excitement about the door of my palanquin, which they had allowed to fall roughly on the ground. At first, half-asleep as I was, I could not make out what they wanted; but when I gathered that my friend Waldron was seized with cholera I was alarmed indeed, and crawled out of the palanquin as speedily as I could to render him assistance.

The bearers were all as frightened and helpless as a flock of sheep with a wolf in their midst, and I could see that they were perfectly panic-stricken. On reaching Waldron's palanquin, which was a hundred yards or so ahead of mine, I found my friend, as I thought, very ill, and, as he faintly assured me, suffering from all the symptoms of cholera.

What was to be done? We had no medicine but quinine, and I gave him a good dose of it. Then I ran back to call the bearers to go on without an instant's delay; but imagine my dismay when I discovered that they had, one and all, disappeared! I shouted and called without effect. There was no answer. I ran back upon our road for some distance at my best speed, but could see no one; I shouted again and again, threatened and entreated by turns, but only to the trees of the forest, for not a bearer was to be seen.

At last I was obliged to own to myself that we were deserted, and, in no little anxiety, returned to my sick friend. He appeared to be worse, and could scarcely speak, and yet I could do nothing for him. Suddenly the thought flashed across my mind that I might return to the village we had left, and, with the aid of the head-man, compel another set of bearers to accompany me.

I told Waldron of this at once; and my poor friend, who was by this time so nervous and weak as scarcely to be able to understand what I said, silently squeezed my hand, a gesture I accepted as an assent. There was no time to be lost. I wrapped a blanket round him, and set off upon my lonely errand by the flickering light of the moon.

At first I was too much engrossed by poor Waldron's state to think much of my surroundings; and I had gone over perhaps half the distance that divided us from the last stage we had left when I became painfully aware that I was in a very awkward situation myself. It was that part of the road where the bamboos grew thickly, and I was passing a great cluster of canes whose feathery leaves obscured the light when I

tripped over a stone and fell flat on the road.

I was not much hurt. I had only bruised my knee; but in getting up again I happened to look back, and a strange feeling of awe came over me at what I saw: *there was a tiger following me.* At first I would not believe it; I reasoned with myself that such a thing was impossible.

"I am nervous, tired, anxious, and have, perhaps, an attack of fever coming on," I said to myself; "and that dark thing there in the road, that I fancy is a tiger crouching, is no tiger at all, but only a shadow or a stone. It's all nonsense. Think of Waldron, and step out."

I did so, encouraging myself, while I walked as fast as I could, by such thoughts as these, although I felt by no means comfortable. Remember, I had no rifle, gun, or even pistol with me, and was quite at the mercy of the tiger, if tiger it was. Perhaps for one hundred yards or so I restrained my curiosity to look round again, but at last this overcame my sense of prudence, and I stopped short, and faced round.

There could be no mistake this time. Not thirty paces from me, standing full in the moonlight, was a large tiger, which crouched to the ground directly I turned. I do not know what another person would have done; for myself, I felt for the moment mad with mingled rage and terror. To be *followed* thus was cruel and irritating, and there must be an end to it.

I cursed the tiger in my heart, as if he were a reasonable being opposing my wishes, and in a fit of desperation I threw up my arms suddenly and shouted with all my strength. I knew it was a fearful risk; but my joy was greater than I can express when I saw the tiger rise and slink into the jungle. He did this so silently and smoothly that I had to look hard at the place where he had been to feel assured he was really gone.

Happily, I had my cigar-case and lights in the pocket of my coat; and, to reassure myself a little, I drew out a cigar, and, with trembling fingers, succeeded in lighting it.

My courage now revived, and I even had the boldness to throw a good-sized stone into the bush where my enemy had disappeared. " He is gone for good," I said to myself, " and joy be with him," for there was

no response to this insult; and, the thought lending
me renewed vigor, I stepped out briskly again. " The
beast evidently took me for a deer or something of
that sort, and bolted when he heard the human voice
divine. Hullo! As I live, there he is again."

The cigar dropped from my mouth as I muttered
these last words under my breath; and I stood trans-
fixed, as it were, gazing at the long, stealthy form of
the tiger as he passed across a glade in the jungle. He
was much closer than before, not twenty paces distant,
I fancy; and the horrible thought came coldly over
me that he was keeping me company until a good
chance offered for a spring.

Again I shouted aloud, and again there was no
response. I summoned all the courage I could muster,
and walked on, keeping as near to the other side of
the path as the jungle permitted, and peering cautiously into the bushes as I advanced. Still I could
see no tiger. I had got over another hundred yards
or so, all my nerves strung to the utmost, when again
I beheld the same dreadful form gliding across a moonlight glade.

This time I saw the animal so plainly that the
marks on his skin were clearly visible. It was evident the animal was stalking me, and I paused to
consider what was to be done. To return was as bad
as to stand still, and to go on looked very like venturing on certain death.

Nowhere was there a tree I could climb for safety.
The bamboos grew in thick clumps, with so much
undergrowth about their stems as to render it hopeless
to try to penetrate it without making much noise in

the attempt, and I felt that such noise would be in the highest degree dangerous. I might run at my best pace ahead, and for a second I thought of doing so; but, then, again, the tiger could easily outstrip me, and would not running encourage him to follow?

There was nothing for it but to walk on as I had been doing; and accordingly, affecting a courage I was far from feeling, I went on my way. I could hear nothing as I walked but the sound of my footsteps and the faint rustling of the leaves in the bamboos overhead; but this silence of the night only rendered the glimpses I caught of my enemy the more appalling, as he slunk like a shadow from bush to bush, but always on a line with me, and, as I fancied, nearer and nearer to the roadside.

I do not know how long this continued. I was in such a state of mind as to take no count of time, and my only idea was to get on as fast as possible to the village for assistance. It was just then, and when I was plodding along over the ruts and stones in the path, that I heard, or fancied I heard, the sound of bearers' voices borne faintly towards me on the night breeze.

The sound seemed to be wafted to me from afar, like a song of deliverance, and I stopped for a moment to be sure that my ears had not deceived me. But those feelings of joy were premature; for, when I again looked about me, there was the tiger, *and this time in front of me.*

The tiger must have passed ahead while I stopped to listen; and he now lay crouched in the very middle of the path, about twenty paces in front of me. The

moon was shining very brightly at the moment, not
a cloud was near it; and I could distinctly make out
every limb of the animal, even to his tail, which was
moving from side to side with a rapid whisking
motion.

Instinctively I stepped a few paces backwards, fully
expecting to see the tiger pounce upon me in one or
two of those great bounds peculiar to the animal; but
he just sneaked a little nearer, and so stealthily that I
only could tell that he had moved by his preserving the
same distance from me as before. Not daring to look
round, I stepped back again, supported to some extent
by the cries of the palanquin bearers in the distance,
that were now drawing rather closer to me.

It was a palanquin coming along the road from
Pooree, and if it came quickly I might be saved. This
was the question: would the tiger devour me before it
could arrive, or not? I could not think upon it; my
brain swam, and I believe for a time I must have been
unconscious of anything about me.

The last thing I remember was an attempt I made
to shout, although whether I did shout or not I cannot
say, and then I awoke to find myself in the arms
of a stranger, who was bending over me, and holding
a flask to my lips. There was a crowd of attendants
standing round, and two palanquins, one of which was
Waldron's.

In a few words the stranger explained everything.
He held a post in a neighboring district, and was
travelling on duty from Pooree when he came to the
place where poor Waldron lay on the road all alone.
Luckily, he had a medicine-chest with him, and was

something of a doctor. He prescribed for my friend on the spot, and ordered a few of his many attendants to take up the sick man's palanquin and follow him.

They travelled at their best speed, or I might not have lived to tell the tale. The civilian went on to tell me that he was aroused a second time by his servants who ran ahead shouting out "Tiger! Tiger!" and by the excitement among his bearers, who nearly allowed the palanquin to fall on the ground. He seized his rifle, which lay loaded beside him; but when he jumped out of the palanquin the tiger was gone, and there remained in its place, to his great astonishment, myself.

That a European should be found in a faint on such a road, and in such a place, was a mystery to him

until I told my story, when, seeing how fatigued and excited I was, he insisted upon my getting into his palanquin, while he walked alongside it. My own palanquin, I should say, was being brought slowly after us by two or three of my new friend's servants.

There is little more to tell. Waldron's illness did
not prove to be very severe. Perhaps I was the
greater invalid of the two, for I suffered much from
fever, brought on, no doubt, by the exposure and
excitement of the previous night. But the sea air of
Pooree soon restored us to our usual health.

The gentleman who rescued us said that he would
certainly beat up my friend the tiger. Not long afterwards he sent me a tiger-skin which he had no doubt
was the coat of the very beast that went so near eating
me up. It was the only tiger that haunted that
particular road, he said, and it was killed by a native
sportsman for the sake of the government reward.

TRAPPING A LEOPARD

By ROBERT COCHRANE.

MANY years ago, soon after my arrival on the east coast of Africa, I used to amuse myself by setting traps for the antelopes which abound in the forest-jungles of the lower portion of that beautiful coast. I was not very successful; I caught several of the tiny Pete, which are graceful little things, miniature antelopes not exceeding a hare in size; but nothing larger came my way for a long time. At last, one morning, on reaching the spot where the trap had been set, I found it gone; and, on searching about, I discovered traces of an antelope having dragged it down the steep incline towards the brook, which, lined with dense bushes, separated the jungle from the open beyond. These traces I followed for some distance, until they entered the thicket by the stream, when, finding it very difficult to force my way through it, I skirted along it outside, under the hope that I might find the track as it came out, or at least make myself sure that the antelope was still inside. I had perhaps gone fifty yards when there was a sudden rustle among the leaves on my left hand, and, with a low growl, the long, spotted body of a leopard sprang out, and, crossing a few yards in front of me, was soon lost to view among the tangle of weepers which hung in festoons from every tree.

A suspicion at once seized my mind that if I opened the bushes from which the leopard had emerged I should find what I was in search of, and on doing so I saw that I was right; for there, with the trap still fastened to its leg, lay the body of a spotted ante-lope (*Tragela-phus sylvaticus*), un-marked save by four deep gashes in the neck and throat. On seeing it I determined that I would go no nearer, nor touch it, but would go back for my gun, and set it as a trap for the great cat, which would certainly return to its prey. As I had never killed a leopard, the chance of now doing so prompted me not to touch the bait.

I therefore returned, with a native to help me, and after some trouble — as I had had no experience in gun-setting — we succeeded in laying the trap so that, if the leopard returned, it could hardly escape.

About eleven o'clock that night, my brother, who had been smoking outside, came in and said: " Your gun's gone off; I heard it just before I came in. Let's go down with a lantern and see if the brute is dead."

I made no objection. A leopard was, as yet, only a big cat to me, and I did not know the danger we incurred. So we took the only other gun there was — at least Harry did — and I took the lantern, with about an inch of candle in it, and we set off for the place together. We had not far to go — not more than half a mile — and on getting to the brook, just across where the gun had been set, I proceeded to strike a light, for, though the night was a fine one, in the jungle it would be all but pitch dark ; and after doing so, and closing the lantern, we proceeded to wade across, but unluckily dropped the matches into the water on the way. We now forced our way through the thick bushes until we reached the spot ; and, fortunately for us — for we had just walked to the place without the slightest caution, and had the leopard been there we must have come right on the top of it — we found it gone. A glance sufficed to show that the bait was still untouched; and then, by the light of the lantern, we examined the ground; and in a few minutes we discovered plenty of evidence, in the shape of blood and fragments of bone, that the gun had not been set in vain.

" Let's follow him ! " said Harry ; " he can't have gone far in that state ; " and, without answering him, I immediately set to work to track the blood-spots — no difficult task — by the lantern's light, while my brother walked behind with the gun. I have often since thought what a picture it would have made : the black, silent jungle all round, the weird-like trunks of the trees with their tracery of creepers dimly visible by the light of the solitary candle, myself holding it and stooping down the better to see the tracks. My companion, his gun carried anyhow, walked behind, grumbling aloud at the loss of the matches. He wanted to light his pipe, and I would not give him the candle to do so, lest he should put it out; both of us quite careless and utterly ignorant of the terrible danger we ran. No animal, not even a lion, is so much to be dreaded as a wounded leopard which had taken refuge in thick jungle; and here were we tracking one in the middle of the night, in utter darkness, but armed with a lantern and a single-barrelled gun, as innocently as if it were but a harmless antelope!

We had easily followed the blood-besprinkled path for fifty or sixty yards when the candle began to flame and flicker and to show signs of coming to an end, causing me to stoop the closer down over my task. Suddenly Harry exclaimed: "What's that in front? It looks like a beast's eyes." And as he spoke, and I raised my head to look, the candle gave a last flare and went out; but the momentary light had sufficed to show me the still form of a leopard crouched under a tree about five or six paces beyond, seemingly all inanimate save those two balls of fire glaring at us out of the darkness. Just as I said, "It's alive!—give me the gun; I can shoot it from here," and as he was in the act of handing me the weapon, I heard it give a low, snarling growl; and in a second more it had fixed itself on my shoulder, and had my left arm in its mouth. Fortunately, neither of us lost his presence of mind. I had dropped the gun when the brute sprang upon me, and Harry was hunting for it about my feet, I directing him as best I might, while I tried to strangle or choke off my assailant, which was struggling to maintain its position on my shoulder. At last, after what had seemed an age to me, I heard my brother utter an exclamation of satisfaction, and then coming close, in a whisper asked me how he should fire. "Feel for its head," said I; "it can't bite; it's got my arm in its mouth." Of course, we were in pitch darkness all this time, and the great danger was lest Harry would shoot me. However, there was no time to lose, and, feeling his way with his hands, he thrust the muzzle of the gun past me and pulled the trigger. The brute struggled convulsively and fell at our feet. It was not however dead, as its half-choked snarls and violent efforts to rise showed; and, fearing lest it should recover and again attack us, we hurried away from the spot as fast as we could. Nor were we a moment too soon, for a second afterwards the animal was on its legs; and, though we could see nothing, we heard its menacing growl of rage and the rustling of the bushes as it passed parallel to us, while the continued sound showed that it was going in the same direction as ourselves.

The position in which we were thus placed was anything but an agreeable one. Before us was the wounded and enraged animal, upon which we might at any instant stumble in the mirk darkness; while, for the same reason, we had not the faintest idea of which direction we ought to take to get out of the jungle, though we knew we were near its edge. To make things worse, the injuries which I had received from the leopard began to be so excessively painful that I felt quite faint and hardly able to keep up with Harry.

However, we stumbled on for some time in the direction which Harry thought was the right one, until it suddenly occurred to me that the gun had never been reloaded; and as I had noticed that he had brought a shot-belt, I told him to pull up and load. Hardly had we stopped, and he was still employed in fumbling about for his powder-flask, when we heard the soft, silky footfall which characterizes all the cat tribe, and an occasional rustling among the dead leaves : the sound seemed to be coming towards us, nearer and nearer, until it appeared to be within two or three yards of us, when it suddenly ceased. Although we afterwards found that this must have been another leopard, possibly disturbed by our shot, at the time it never occurred to either of us that it could be other than the wounded one; and our feelings as we stood there in the dark, expecting it to spring on us every second, may perhaps be more easily imagined than described.

We did not dare to stir, and fully five minutes must have passed while we stood perfectly still, hardly breathing, listening intently, and our eyes in vain trying to pierce the gloom which surrounded us; the leopard, which had no doubt heard or smelt us, remaining equally motionless. Then a lower and more subdued sound seemed to indicate that it was trying to steal away unheard. When this died away by degrees, Harry completed loading his gun; and after another quarter of an hour spent in wandering through the jungle, we suddenly, and much to our delight, caught the sound of running water; and in a few minutes more found ourselves on the bank of the stream, after which we had no further difficulty in finding our way home. My wounds, though painful and long in healing, turned out to be less serious than we had imagined; my arm was not broken, though severely bitten, and the worst scratch I had was on the thigh. I was unable to join the party which started anew next morning; but, as they found the leopard dead within a few yards of where it had attacked me, I had not much to regret on that account.

It turned out to be a male of unusual size; and we found that the first shot, owing to the string having been set too tightly, had struck the point of the shoulder, smashing the bone but not inflicting a mortal wound. Harry's charge had gone into his throat close to the head, severing the jugular vein and causing the almost immediate death of the animal from loss of blood.

THE GRIZZLY BEAR

(FROM ASTORIA.)

By WASHINGTON IRVING.

THE grizzly bear is the only really formidable quadruped of North America. He is the favorite theme of the hunters of the Far West, who describe him as equal in size to a common cow, and of prodigious strength. He makes battle if assailed; and often, if pressed by hunger, is the assailant. If wounded he becomes furious, and will pursue the hunter. His speed exceeds that of a man, but is inferior to that of a horse. In attacking, he rears himself on his hind legs and springs the length of his body. Woe to horse or rider that comes within the sweep of his terrific claws, which tear every thing before them.

At the time we are treating of, the grizzly bear was still frequent on the Missouri and in the lower country; but, like some of the broken tribes of the prairies, he has gradually fallen back before his enemies, and is now chiefly to be found in the upland regions, in rugged fastnesses like those of the Black Hills and the Rocky Mountains.   Here he lurks in caverns or holes which he has digged in the sides of hills, or under the roots and trunks of fallen trees.   Like the common bear he is fond of fruits and mast and roots, the last of which he will dig up with his fore-claws.   He is carnivorous also, and will even attack and conquer the lordly buffalo, dragging the huge carcass to the neighborhood of his den that he may prey upon it at his leisure.

The hunters, both white and red men, consider this the most heroic game.   They prefer to hunt him on horseback, and will venture so near as sometimes to singe his hair with the flash of the rifle.   The hunter of the grizzly bear, however, must be an experienced hand, and know where to aim at a vital part; for of all quadrupeds he is the most difficult to be killed.   He will receive repeated wounds without flinching, and rarely is a shot mortal unless through the head or heart.

That the dangers apprehended from the grizzly bear at this night encampment were not imaginary was proved on the following morning.   Among the hired men of the party was one William Cannon, who had been a soldier at one of the frontier posts, and entered into the employ of Mr. Hunt at Mackinaw.   He was an inexperienced hunter and a poor shot, for which he was much bantered by his more adroit comrades. Piqued at their raillery, he had been practising ever since he had joined the expedition, but without success. In the course of the present afternoon he went forth by himself to take a lesson in venery, and, to his great delight, had the good fortune to kill a buffalo.   As he

was a considerable distance from the camp he cut out
the tongue and some of the choice bits, made them into
a parcel, and slinging them on his shoulders by a strap
passed round his forehead, as the voyagers carry pack-
ages of goods, set out all glorious for the camp, antici-
pating a triumph over his brother hunters. In passing
through a narrow ravine he heard a noise behind him,
and, looking round, beheld to his dismay a grizzly bear
in full pursuit, apparently attracted by the scent of the
meat. Cannon had heard so much of the invulner-
ability of this tremendous animal that he never attempted to fire ; but, slipping the strap from his forehead,
let go the buffalo meat and ran for his life. The bear
did not stop to regale himself with the game, but kept
on after the hunter. He had nearly overtaken him
when Cannon reached a tree, and, throwing down his
rifle, scrambled up it. The next instant Bruin was at
the foot of the tree ; but as this species of bear does
not climb, he contented himself with turning the chase
into a blockade. Night came on. In the darkness
Cannon could not perceive whether or not the enemy
maintained his station, but his fears pictured him rigor-
ously mounting guard. He passed the night, therefore, in the tree, a prey to dismal fancies. In the
morning the bear was gone. Cannon warily descended
the tree, gathered up his gun, and made the best of his
way back to the camp without venturing to look after
his buffalo meat.

While on this theme we will add another anecdote
of an adventure with a grizzly bear, told of John Day,
the Kentucky hunter, but which happened at a different
period of the expedition. Day was hunting in com-

pany with one of the clerks of the company, a lively youngster, who was a great favorite with the veteran, but whose vivacity he had continually to keep in check. They were in search of deer, when suddenly a huge grizzly bear emerged from a thicket about thirty yards distant, rearing himself upon his hind-legs with a terrific growl, and displaying a hideous array of teeth and claws. The rifle of the young man was levelled in an instant, but John Day's iron hand was as quickly upon his arm. " Be quiet, boy ! be quiet ! " exclaimed the hunter between his clenched teeth, and without turning his eyes from the bear. They remained motionless. The monster regarded them  for a time ; then, lowering himself on his forepaws, slowly withdrew. He had not gone many paces before he again turned, reared himself on his hind legs and repeated his menace. Day's hand was still on the arm of

his young companion; he again pressed it hard, and kept
repeating between his teeth, "Quiet, boy!—keep quiet!
— keep quiet!" though the latter had not made a
move since his first prohibition. The bear again low-
ered himself on all-fours, retreated some twenty yards
farther and again turned, reared, showed his teeth, and
growled. This third menace was too much for the
game spirit of John Day. "I can stand this no longer,"
exclaimed he, and in an instant a ball from his rifle
whizzed into the foe. The wound was not mortal; but
luckily it dismayed instead of enraging the animal, and
he retreated into the thicket. Day's young companion
reproached him for not practising the caution which he
enjoined upon others. "Why, boy," replied the veteran,
" caution is caution, but one must not put up with too
much even from a bear. Would you have me suffer
myself to be bullied all day by a varmint ?"

THE GIRLS, THE BEAR, AND THE ALLIGATORS

By ROBERT COCHRANE.

OME years ago two Floridan girls concluded to take a day's hunt in the Great Aurantula Hammock, the upper edge of which touches the river some miles below. Starting out early they made good progress, and by nine o'clock were in the midst of the wild hammock. During the forenoon they had luck — killing a deer, a wild cat, ten big gray squirrels, and several enormous snakes. After taking a noon-day lunch, they decided to cross over Alligator Creek, a wide but shallow stream that crosses the hammock, emptying into the Withlacochee. Just before reaching the creek they had to pass through a dense canebreak. When about halfway through one of their dogs that had lingered behind came rushing up, yelping lustily, while close on its heels was a big black bear, fierce and ugly as it could be. The path was so narrow that they had no chance to fight the animal, and in fact the dog and bear came in on them so suddenly that little time was allowed for reflection. Miss Josie slung her rifle around and fired at the beast, but in the confusion only wounded him. The girls then ran ahead, intending to get out on to the open bank by the water's edge, so as to get a fair ground to battle old Bruin. But the infuriated animal, aroused to madness by the rifle ball, pursued them so closely that only scientific dodging saved them from a close hug. Emerging from the path, they noticed the dug-out used to cross the creek lying right in front of them, and both of the girls, struck with the same idea, sprang into the boat, their impetus carrying it out into the creek.

The dog was unable to get into the boat, but he bit at Bruin's heels so sharply that the latter had to stop his pursuit of the girls and endeavor to punish his four-footed assailant. But the dog was too wary, and kept out of Bruin's reach; the girls called him, and, plunging in, he swam out to them. Meanwhile the hungry denizens of the creek, whose numbers gave it its name, were awakened by the tumult, and they began to show themselves. As the dog jumped in, the splash attracted scores of the ugly reptiles from all directions, and the water was dotted by the black snouts of the hungry alligators. The girls noticed this, and called encouragingly to their dog, who seemed to be fully aware of his danger. Several black noses were already pointed in his direction, and it looked as if the alligators might get a meal. But Wilda seized the pole lying at the bottom of the canoe, and by a skilful push sent the boat close to the dog. Josie was waiting, and as the dog swam up she helped him to clamber over the side, almost upsetting the frail vessel. And it was just in time too; for, just as the dog's legs slipped out of the water, a huge pair of jaws rose out of the depths with an ominous snap. With a souse the disappointed saurian sank.

While this was going on Bruin stood on the bank growling and snarling in impotent rage at the dog and girls thus escaping.   Seeing the dog in the canoe seemed to render him still more furious, and with a deep growl he dashed into the water and began swimming towards the boat.   Between the bear and the alligators the girls began to think their hands would be full.   Wilda picked up her gun and made a snap-shot at the animal; but a movement of the dog disconcerted her aim, and the load of buckshot flew to one side, only a small number striking the bear.   But this angered him the more, and, with a snarl, he almost leaped out of the water in his mad eagerness to reach the boat. Wilda dropped her gun, and picking up the pole, soon placed the boat a rod ahead of the pursuing animal. Josie had again reloaded her gun, and she turned to deliver his quietus to the animal.   But the commotion in the water and the bear's evident disquietude put a new face on matters, and she withheld her fire.

The dog's yelping and the bear's growling had evidently awakened the scaly denizens of the creek to a realizing sense that it was meal-time.   Missing the dog, they were not averse to bear-meat.   Bruin, in his hurry to catch his first prey, had paid little attention to what might befall him in the creek.   But now he began to notice the increasing number of black spots on the water all turning towards him, and probably instinct told him that hungry alligators in their own element were a foe not to be despised.   With an uneasy whine he attempted to turn and regain the shore, but now it was too late.   With a rush, a big black form was seen to dart up against him, and in a second he was seized

and dragged under. The old fellow was game, however, and now that he had gotten into the fight he
proved no mean antagonist. With an immense effort
he plunged away from the attacking alligator and
dashed forward for the shore. The water shoaled, and
it seemed as if he would escape. A big bull saurian
dashed forward and seized
the bear by one of his
hind legs, while two
others attempted to
cut off his retreat.
With a deep roar of

rage the bear turned on the one
that seized him, and with one
stroke of his paw clawed out
the alligator's eye. The latter
bellowed with pain, and, thrashing the water madly,
plunged forward at Bruin. Other alligators joined in,
and the poor animal was beset on all sides. Sitting on
his haunches, with the blood flowing from a gaping
wound in his hind leg, the bear snapped, clawed, and
bit at his savage antagonists; but they were too many

for him.   Another seized one of his legs in its powerful
jaws, and with a strong effort drew the bear off into
deeper water; others dashed at him from all sides,
snapping at him from every point.   The water splashed
high, and was churned into snowy whiteness by the
furious efforts of the fighters save where the red blood
told the tale.   But a few moments longer did the un-
equal struggle last.   Bruin strove to regain his feet,
but the cruel jaws of the reptiles closed on his legs,
sides, and wherever a hold could be secured, and with
one mighty, agonizing roar the bear disappeared, while
the furious struggle continued under water for several
seconds.

The girls gazed on the fight spellbound, but now
they were rudely aroused to their own peril.   The dog
had barked loudly during the savage fight going on so
near, and the alligators who missed bear-meat seemed
to be after dog's flesh.   The canoe rocked, almost over-
turning, and the startled girls saw a monstrous pair of
open jaws close to the side of their small craft.   Josie
pushed her rifle barrel in the alligator's mouth and
pulled the trigger, sending a bullet where it evidently
did not agree, judging from the reptile's sudden sinking and thrashing about.   A moment later a huge tail
came flying over the bow of the boat, and, striking the
dog, who stood there barking, knocked him into the
water.   A big pair of wide-open jaws was just about
to close on the tempting morsel when Wilda stooped
down, and catching the dog's fore-paws, by a sudden
effort drew him into the boat, the saurian's jaws closing with a snap that indicated a great disappointment.
The dog cowered down on the bottom of the boat, while

the girls attended to the other alligators, who seemed
to manifest an inclination to get into the canoe.   Several shots were fired at the scaly reptiles, but their
taste of blood had made them fearless.   For the next
few minutes the brave girls had all they could do in
urging the canoe to shore.   As it touched the sand both
leaped out; none too soon, either, for a big pursuing
alligator threw itself forward, crushing in the sides of
the dug-out.   The girls had had enough hunting for
that day, and returned home by another route.   The
next day, on a party of them going down to the scene
of the struggle, they saw several dead alligators in the
creek.

A FIGHT BETWEEN A LION AND A CROCODILE

(FROM SHE)

BY H. RIDER HAGGARD.

SHORTLY after this the moon came up, and notwithstanding every variety of roar that echoed over the water to us from the lions on the banks, thinking ourselves perfectly secure, we began to doze.

I do not quite know what it was that caused me to lift my head from the friendly shelter of the blanket, perhaps because I found that the mosquitoes were biting through it. Anyhow, as I did so I heard Job whisper, in a frightened voice —

"Oh, my stars, look there!"

Instantly we all of us looked, and this was what we saw in the moonlight. Near the shore were two wide and ever-widening circles of concentric rings rippling away across the surface of the water, and in the heart and centre of these circles appeared two dark and moving objects.

129

"What is it?" asked I.

"It is those blamed lions, sir," answered Job, in a tone which suggested an odd mixture of a sense of personal injury, habitual respect, and acknowledged fear, "and they are swimming here to heat us," he added nervously, picking up an " h " in his agitation.

I looked again : there was no doubt about it; I could catch the glare of their ferocious eyes. Attracted either by the smell of the newly killed waterbuck meat or of ourselves, the hungry beasts were storming our position.

Leo already had a rifle in his hand. I called to him to wait till they were nearer, and meanwhile found my own. Some fifteen feet from us the water shallowed on a bank to the depth of about fifteen inches, and presently the first of them — it was the lioness — waded to it, shook herself, and roared. At that moment Leo fired ; the bullet travelled down her open mouth and out at the back of her neck, and down she dropped, with a splash, dead. The other lion — a full-grown male — was some two paces behind her. At this second he set his forepaws on the bank, when something happened. There was a rush and disturbance of the water, such as one sees in a pond in England when a pike takes a little fish, only a thousand times fiercer and larger, then suddenly the lion uttered a terrific snarling roar and sprang forward on to the bank, dragging something black with him.

" Allah ! " shouted Mahomed, " a crocodile has got him by the leg ! " and sure enough he had. We could see the long snout with its gleaming lines of teeth and the reptile body behind it.

Then followed a most extraordinary scene. The lion managed to struggle on to the bank, the crocodile half standing and half swimming, still nipping his hind leg. He roared till the air quivered with the sound; then, with a savage, shrieking snarl, he turned and clawed hold of the crocodile's head. The reptile shifted his grip, having as we discovered afterwards, had one of his eyes torn out, and ad-

vanced slightly; whereon the lion took him by the throat and held it, and over and over they rolled upon the bank, struggling hideously. It was impossible to follow their movements, but when next we had a clear view the tables were turned, for the crocodile, whose head seemed to be a mass of gore, held the lion's body in his iron jaws just above the hips, and was squeezing him, shaking him to and fro. For his part, the tortured brute, roaring in agony, clawed and bit madly at his enemy's scaly head, and fixing his great hind claws in the softer skin of the crocodile's throat, ripped it open as one would rip a glove.

Then, of a sudden, the end came. The lion's head fell forward on the reptile's back, and with an awful groan he died, and the crocodile, after standing for a minute motionless, slowly rolled over on to his side, his jaws still fixed across the carcass of the lion, which, as we found, he had bitten almost in halves.

This duel to the death was a wonderful and a shocking sight, and one that I suppose few men have seen. And thus it ended.

SAGACITY OF THE ELEPHANT

By ROBERT COCHRANE

THE elephant may well be considered the head of the menagerie. Young and old are never tired of watching these wonderful creatures; they are so knowing, so loving, yet so terrible in their anger. An elephant can tear off huge branches of trees with his trunk, or stamp the life out of a tiger with his great feet; yet, after training, the same trunk can pick up a pin, and the mighty feet tread gingerly over the recumbent forms of sleeping or intoxicated keepers. Strange as it may appear, an elephant's skin is very sensitive; mosquitoes annoy him greatly, and a beating is a terrible punishment. Courageous as he is, an elephant is very nervous; he will fight any other huge beast, yet a mouse is said to make him shake with apprehension and trumpet with terror.

Elephants are very mischievous and inquisitive; they raise latches, open doors, and enjoy immensely their own practical jokes, though so ready to resent indignities to themselves. Sensitive as regards insult, their affection is warm and lasting, and dogs, horses, and other animals are often the objects of their attachment. Elephants are pleased with gay colors, delight in sweet perfumes, are dainty in their tastes, and revel in the water like an Englishman in his bath. They practise theft with the ingenuity of the " Artful Dodger " himself, are as meddlesome as monkeys, have the caution and the cunning of a diplomatist and the memory of a Magliabechi.

When born, a baby-elephant stands about three feet high, and is not considered grown-up until thirty years old. Accidents excepted, he is likely to live about one hundred and fifty years, if not longer. Though delicate in his tastes, an elephant likes quantity as well as quality, and at his meals makes nothing of bales of hay and gallons of water. His ingenuity in trying to cater for himself is astonishing, and often amusing. An American showman saw an elephant pull up a stake to which he was chained, go to a feed-bin containing oats, wrench off the lock, raise the lid, eat all he wanted, put down the lid again, return to his place, poke the stake back into the same hole and stamp it down with his foot ; and when his keeper came looked as innocent as a lamb. A twinkle in his cunning eyes showed his enjoyment of the situation when the man stormed and raged on discovering the robbery.

An incident of an elephant's memory is said to have occurred some years since when Wombwell's menagerie was exhibiting at Bolton. Four years before, the same collection was in the town, and on that occasion, on being released from its van, a large elephant walked across the town-hall square to a public-house and protruded its trunk into the lobby. The barmaid supplied the animal with refreshments; and the keeper, who had been in search of his charge, then conducted him back to his den. On being released at the breaking up of the show on the second visit, the same elephant broke away at a brisk trot in the direction of the hostelry, and the unwonted charge upon the premises greatly alarmed the inmates. The former barmaid, now the landlady, arrived on the scene, and recognizing her old friend, once more regaled him to his heart's content. The elephant then submitted to be led away by his keeper.

Their sagacity is indeed marvellous. In an Indian town, an elephant, during his keeper's absence, was one day amusing himself with his chain in an open space, when a thief who was pursued by a crowd of people ran for protection under the huge animal. Seemingly pleased with the poor wretch's confidence, the creature instantly faced about, erected his trunk, threw his chain in the air, and became so furious in defence of the criminal that neither the surrounding multitude, nor even the mahout, to whom he was greatly attached, could prevail with him to give up the hunted man. This strange scene had continued for several hours when at length the governor arrived, and was so pleased at the elephant's generous perseverance that he pardoned the criminal. The poor man expressed his gratitude by kissing and embracing the proboscis of his kind benefactor, who appeared so sensible of what had happened that he became tame and gentle in an instant, and suffered his keeper to lead him away without the least resistance.

No circus, however small, could hope to exist without an elephant. Whole herds form parts of several shows there; and the eagerness of Barnum some years ago to obtain a white elephant is easily understood, that animal being considered by showmen the greatest attraction in the country.

Although elephants will not submit to abuse they are not difficult to teach, and at first are fond of going through their tricks on their own account. Performing-elephants in Rome were taught to dance by the association of music and a hot floor. A block and pulley is now sometimes used in training an elephant to assume various positions, and the word of command given as if it was doing the trick of its own accord. Good treatment with firmness is necessary in teaching them, and any rebelliousness must be checked by the whip. They cry out when subdued, and the trouble is then over for the time. Even wild elephants are said to be easily taught when once subdued.

Most of us have admired the wonderful agility of such clumsy-looking animals in balancing themselves on inverted tubs and so forth. At Astley's, elephants used to delight thousands with their performances. These huge creatures were made to stand on their hind legs with their forefeet poodle-wise, dangling in the air. Another stood on its head with his hind legs raised perpendicularly. Placed on pedestals, they wheeled round rapidly or balanced themselves on two side-legs only, and gave various other evidences of wonderful training. Well-trained baby-elephants are great favorites. One was taught to sit at table, fan herself, and do numerous tricks to delight children and their elders too. The two clever baby-elephants, "Jock" and "Jenny," were marvellously trained. They made their bow to the audience, and then one of them walked on the tops of a double row of bottles. On a plank placed over a trestle they see-sawed like a couple of children, guessing the required equilibrium with almost human exactitude. Playing on an organ and drum and dancing in time to the jingles of bells were amongst their other accomplishments.

The habitual caution of these intelligent creatures is illustrated when they are travelling from show to show. Should several be in a car together, one of their number will remain awake on guard while the others are sleeping.

Some years ago experiments were made in the transport of elephants by railway. One of the ordinary

cattle-wagons of the East India Railway was fitted up
for the purpose, and the animal was placed in the
centre space of the wagon between six shafts and a
breast and back bar, secured in addition by anklets on
the fore and hind feet, united by couplings transversely
and longitudinally, and further by four diagonal moor-
ing-chains passing through holes and lashed round the
corner pillars of the wagon. The first elephant loaded,
having his head free, took the opportunity to remove
with his trunk a portion of the roof of the truck; it
was therefore found necessary to put a collar round the
neck of the elephant, with a vertical chain leading
through and secured to the floor. In this way a successful experiment was made to Pundooah and back,
the animal showing no signs of fear or making any
attempt to free himself.

Many interesting and famous elephants have been
favorites of the circus-going public. One of these,
known as " Canada," was a desperate character. When
in one of his tantrums, " he did as much mischief as a
tornado " — to use an American showman's words —
tossing hacks into the air and tearing down signs and
lamp-posts. He was sent with the rest of a menagerie
to a farm, and when there had one of his mad fits.
Rushing into the stable-yard, " in a few minutes he
killed two buffaloes, a sacred cow, a couple of elks,
several horses, and a camel. He would seize an
animal, toss it in the air, catch it on his tusks, and then
either jam or trample the life out of it." He then
sallied out for the town, and the popular excitement
can be imagined. " A trap was set with a long ponderous chain with an enormous corner-stone at its end

to entangle the animal's legs, and hold him." A man
then ran out in sight of Canada, and the elephant
instantly rushed after him. "The trap was successful
so far as making the chain and stone fast to him; but
he kept right on, and would have caught the man, who
was a fast runner, had the latter not jumped down
into an unfinished cellar of a new house, and ran up
a narrow flight of steps on the opposite side. The
elephant jumped down after him as easily as a dog
would, with the big stone clattering behind him." Fortunately, the stone was large enough to stick wedged
against the walls on each side of the stairway, and
Canada was fast; but it was a close shave for the man.
They managed to secure the savage animal with more
chains, and then went to work to conquer him. As
the account graphically describes it, "they wore out
big clubs on him, fired loads of buckshot into his trunk
and ears, and beat and tortured him for hours until he
howled in token of surrender." The moment he was
loose, however, he gave a yell of rage, dashed out of
the cellar, and started to kill. Every one flew for his
life; but he was tired, and took up his position under
cover of three haystacks, hunting all who ventured
near him. "Buckshot fired into his head only checked
his wild rushes, and whenever he thought people were
on the other side of a stack from him he tried his best
to topple the hay over on them. The fight went on
for three days and nights, during which time he had
not a bite to eat — for he was too angry even to take
any of the hay around him — and not a drop of water."
At length, despairing of saving him, the shot-guns
were exchanged for heavy rifles, and several big bullets
at close range finally put an end to him.

The interest in Jumbo, the Zoo favorite which was sold to Barnum in 1882, and died in a railway accident, was subsequently transferred to Barnum's so-called white elephant. In spite of generally expressed disappointment at its appearance, and doubts as to its "sacredness," this arrival attracted thousands of people in London, and was also viewed by still greater numbers in America.

Elephants being so powerful and intelligent, are worse than any wild animal when in one of their sudden fits of ungovernable rage. The amount of killing they take is incredible. Heavy rifles often have little effect in stopping their wild charges; and in one instance, in India, even a field-piece fired repeatedly failed for a considerable time to put an end to the career of a mad elephant.

WORKING ELEPHANTS AT RANGOON

(FROM FOUR HUNDRED ANIMAL STORIES.)

By ROBERT COCHRANE.

THE elephants there are beauties, fine, powerful, well-trained animals. It is both interesting and amusing to watch them working the timber. The government have nine elephants employed at the depot, and there are other animals belonging to natives at work there also. I often take my seat on a teak-log — picking out the cleanest and softest for the purpose — light a cheroot, and watch the performance. Elephants are pretty much like men; I don't mean in personal appearance, but in character. I can pick out "characters I have met" quite easily among the group of sixteen or eighteen all working there together sometimes. There are willing workers and there are skulkers; there are gentle tempers, and there are others "as dour as a door-nail." Some of them will drag a log two tons in weight without a groan; while others, who are equally powerful but less willing, will make a dreadful fuss over a stick that is, comparatively speaking, nothing.

There are a good many female elephants employed. Some belong to the government; but most

141

of them are owned by Karens, who bring them in from
the jungle when work is obtainable. They are not so
powerful as the males; and the want of tusks is rather
against them, because they have to do the pushing or
"ounging" part of the work, as the natives call it, with
their trunks. These they roll up in a coil, and just at
the place where the trunk and the head unite they
press against the log and roll it over.

The legs were very nearly knocked from under a
man two days ago by a lively female who was rolling
over a log in this way. She had discovered by experience that it was easier to move a heavy log by a violent jerk than by slow, steady pushing; and when the
man on her neck called out "Oung!" and pushed her
ear forward with his foot — the equivalents in elephant-
driving for "Go along, old lady!" — she stood for a
moment motionless, then in an instant up coiled the
trunk, down went the head, and away rolled the log,
one end of it coming round with a sweep which all but
made an "Aunt Sally" of the innocent spectator. He
sprang from the ground as if he had received an electric
shock, and saved himself; after which he received the
congratulations of the by-standers for being an ass to
stand like that in the way of an elephant.

The highly-trained male elephants with tusks manage
the "ounging" part of their work very skilfully. The
trunk is used as a pad or buffer between the ivory and
the wood, and the pushing is done steadily. An
average log weighs about a ton and a half. When it
has to be pushed into the river the elephant feels the
end of it with his trunk, and, having ascertained where
he can place his tusks with most advantage, adjusts

the buffer, and starts off pushing the log steadily before him.   Should it happen to be an extra heavy one, he stops occasionally to take breath; and as it slides down the muddy bank towards the water he gives it a finishing slap, as if to say : " There, you're afloat at last! "   Sometimes the logs are awkwardly jammed up together, so that the ends have to be raised in order to get the dragging-chains fastened.   This he does by putting his tusks underneath ; and passing his trunk over the log to keep it steady, lifts it up to the required height.   When it is a very heavy lift, he will go down on his knees to get a better purchase. He stacks the timber most skilfully also by lifting the end of the log as much as nine or ten feet in this m a n n e r, places it on

the top of the pile, then goes to the other end and pushes it forward till he gets it quite flush with the rest.   In all this he is of course directed by his rider, the mahout, who uses certain words which the elephant has been accustomed to hear, and signs the meaning of which he knows perfectly.   A push of the foot behind the right or left ear makes him answer the driver's wish as a boat answers the rudder, and a nudge behind the neck means " straight ahead."

A highly-trained elephant, however, will work among timber by *verbal* directions as intelligently almost as a collie will among sheep. The finest and best-trained animals are reserved for employment in the saw-mills, where they work amongst the machinery with sagacity and precision. Strangers have sometimes been so much impressed with their admirable qualities in this respect that they have carried away slightly exaggerated impressions on the subject. One case I remember in which a spectator was so profoundly overcome by the careful manner in which he saw the elephant laying planks and slabs on the travelling benches to be cut, that he gravely reported the circumstance in an Indian newspaper, remarking that the animal shut one eye when it looked along the bench to make sure the timber was laid on for the saw accurately !

MOTI GUJ — MUTINEER

By RUDYARD KIPLING.

ONCE upon a time there was a coffee-planter in India who wished to clear some forest land for coffee-planting. When he had cut down all the trees and burned the underwood, the stumps still remained. Dynamite is expensive; and slow fire is slow. The happy medium for stump clearing is the lord of all beasts, who is the elephant. He will either push the stump out of the ground with his tusks, if he has any, or drag it out with ropes. The planter, therefore, hired elephants by ones and twos and threes, and fell to work. The very best of all the elephants belonged to the very worst of all the drivers or mahouts; and this superior beast's name was Moti Guj. He was the absolute property of his mahout, which would never have been the case under native rule: for Moti Guj was a creature to be desired by kings, and his name, being translated, meant the Pearl Elephant. Because the British government was in the land, Deesa, the mahout, enjoyed his property undisturbed. He was dissipated. When he had made much money through the strength of his elephant, he would get extremely drunk and give Moti Guj a beating with a tent-peg over the tender nails of the fore-feet. Moti Guj never trampled the life out of Deesa on these occasions, for he knew that after the beating was over, Deesa would embrace his trunk and call him his love and his life and the liver of his soul, and give him some liquor. Moti Guj was very fond of liquor — arrack for choice, though he would drink palm-tree toddy, if nothing better offered. Then Deesa would go to sleep between Moti Guj's forefeet, and as Deesa generally chose the middle of the public road, and as Moti Guj mounted guard over him, and would not permit horse, foot, or cart to pass by, traffic was congested till Deesa saw fit to wake up.

There was no sleeping in the daytime on the planter's clearing : the wages were too high to risk. Deesa sat on Moti Guj's neck and gave him orders, while Moti Guj rooted up the stumps — for he owned a magnificent pair of tusks ; or pulled at the end of a rope — for he had a magnificent pair of shoulders — while Deesa kicked him behind the ears and said he was the king of elephants. At evening time Moti Guj would wash down his three hundred pounds' weight of green food with a quart of arrack, and Deesa would take a share, and sing songs between Moti Guj's legs till it was time to go to bed. Once a week Deesa led Moti Guj down to the river, and Moti Guj lay on his side luxuriously in the shallows, while Deesa went over him with a coir swab and a brick. Moti Guj never mistook the pounding blow of the latter for the smack of the former that warned him to get up and turn over on the other side.

Then Deesa would look at his feet and examine his eyes, and turn up the fringes of his mighty ears in case of sores or budding ophthalmia. After inspection the two would " come up with a song from the sea," Moti Guj, all black and shining, waving a torn tree branch twelve feet long in his trunk, and Deesa knotting up his own long wet hair.

It was a peaceful, well-paid life till Deesa felt the return of the desire to drink deep. He wished for an orgy. The little draughts that led nowhere were taking the manhood out of him.

He went to the planter, and " My mother's dead," said he, weeping.

" She died on the last plantation two months ago, and she died once before that when you were working for me last year," said the planter, who knew something of the ways of nativedom.

" Then it's my aunt, and she was just the same as a mother to me," said Deesa, weeping more than ever. " She has left eighteen small children entirely without bread, and it is I who must fill their little stomachs," said Deesa, beating his head on the floor.

" Who brought you the news ? " said the planter.

" The post," said Deesa.

" There hasn't been a post here for the past week. Get back to your lines ! "

" A devastating sickness has fallen on my village, and all my wives are dying," yelled Deesa, really in tears this time.

" Call Chihun, who comes from Deesa's village," said the planter. " Chihun, has this man got a wife ? "

" He ? " said Chihun. " No. Not a woman of our

village would look at him. They'd sooner marry the elephant."

Chihun snorted. Deesa wept and bellowed.

"You will get into difficulty in a minute," said the planter. "Go back to your work!"

"Now I will speak Heaven's truth," gulped Deesa, with an inspiration. "I haven't been drunk for two months. I desire to depart in order to get properly drunk afar off and distant from this heavenly plantation. Thus I shall cause no trouble."

A flickering smile crossed the planter's face. "Deesa," said he, "you've spoken the truth, and I'd give you leave on the spot, if anything could be done with Moti Guj while you're away. You know that he only will obey your orders."

"May the light of the heavens live forty thousand years. I shall be absent but ten little days. After that, upon my faith and honor and soul, I return. As to the inconsiderable interval have I the gracious permission of the heaven-born to call up Moti Guj?"

Permission was granted, and in answer to Deesa's shrill yell, the mighty tusker swung out of the shade of a clump of trees where he had been squirting dust over himself till his master should return.

"Light of my heart, protector of the drunken, mountain of might, give ear!" said Deesa, standing in front of him.

Moti Guj gave ear, and saluted with his trunk.

"I am going away," said Deesa.

Moti Guj's eyes twinkled. He liked jaunts as well as his master. One could snatch all manner of nice things from the roadside then.

"But you, you fussy old pig, must stay behind and work."

The twinkle died out as Moti Guj tried to look delighted. He hated stump-hauling on the plantation. It hurt his teeth.

"I shall be gone for ten days, oh, delectable one! Hold up your near forefoot and I'll impress the fact upon it, warty toad of a dried mud-puddle." Deesa took a tent-peg and banged Moti Guj ten times on the nails. Moti Guj grunted and shuffled from foot to foot.

"Ten days," said Deesa, "you will work and haul and root the trees as Chihun here shall order you. Take up Chihun and set him on your neck!" Moti Guj curled the tip of his trunk, Chihun put his foot there, and was swung on to the neck. Deesa handed Chihun the heavy *ankus* — the iron elephant goad.

Chihun thumped Moti Guj's bald head as a paver thumps a curbstone.

Moti Guj trumpeted.

"Be still, hog of the backwoods! Chihun's your mahout for ten days. And now bid me good-by, beast after mine own heart. Oh, my lord, my king! Jewel of all created elephants, lily of the herd, preserve your honored health; be virtuous. Adieu!"

Moti Guj lapped his trunk round Deesa and swung him into the air twice. That was his way of bidding him good-by.

"He'll work now," said Deesa to the planter. "Have I leave to go?"

The planter nodded, and Deesa dived into the woods. Moti Guj went back to haul stumps.

Chihun was very kind to him, but he felt unhappy and forlorn for all that. Chihun gave him a ball of spices, and tickled him under the chin, and Chihun's little baby cooed to him after work was over, and Chihun's wife called him a darling; but Moti Guj was a bachelor by instinct, as Deesa was. He did not understand the domestic emotions. He wanted the light of his universe back again — the drink and the drunken slumber, the savage beatings and the savage caresses.

None the less he worked well, and the planter wondered. Deesa had wandered along the roads till he met a marriage procession of his own caste, and, drinking, dancing, and tippling, had drifted with it past all knowledge of the lapse of time.

The morning of the eleventh day dawned, and there returned no Deesa. Moti Guj was loosed from his ropes for the daily stint. He swung clear, looked round, shrugged his shoulders, and began to walk away, as one having business elsewhere.

"Hi! ho! Come back, you!" shouted Chihun. "Come back and put me on your neck, misborn mountain! Return, splendor of the hillsides! Adornment of all India, heave to, or I'll bang every toe off your fat forefoot!"

Moti Guj gurgled gently, but did not obey. Chihun ran after him with a rope and caught him up. Moti Guj put his ears forward, and Chihun knew what that meant, though he tried to carry it off with high words.

"None of your nonsense with me," said he. "To your pickets, devil-son!"

"Hrrump!" said Moti Guj, and that was all — that and the forebent ears.

Moti Guj put his hands in his pockets, chewed a branch for a toothpick, and strolled about the clearing, making fun of the other elephants who had just set to work.

Chihun reported the state of affairs to the planter, who came out with a dog-whip and cracked it furiously. Moti Guj paid the white man the compliment of charging him nearly a quarter of a mile across the clearing and "Hrrumphing" him into his veranda. Then he stood outside the house, chuckling to himself and shaking all over with the fun of it, as an elephant will.

"We'll thrash him," said the planter. "He shall have the finest thrashing ever elephant received. Give Kala Nag and Nazim twelve foot of chain apiece, and tell them to lay on twenty."

Kala Nag — which means Black Snake — and Nazim were two of the biggest elephants in the lines, and one of their duties was to administer the graver punishment, since no man can beat an elephant properly.

They took the whipping chains and rattled them in their trunks as they sidled up to Moti Guj, meaning to hustle him between them. Moti Guj had never, in all his life of thirty-nine years, been whipped, and he did not intend to begin a new experience. So he waited, waving his head from right to left, and measuring the precise spot in Kala Nag's fat side where a blunt tusk could sink deepest. Kala Nag had no tusks; the chain was the badge of his authority; but for all that, he swung wide of Moti Guj at the last minute, and tried to appear as if he had brought the chain out for amusement. Nazim turned round and went home early.

He did not feel fighting fit that morning, and so Moti Guj was left standing alone with his ears cocked.

That decided the planter to argue no more, and Moti Guj rolled back to his amateur inspection of the clearing. An elephant who will not work and is not tied up is about as manageable as an eighty-one-ton gun loose in a heavy seaway. He clapped old friends on the back and asked them if the stumps were coming away easily ; he talked nonsense concerning labor and the inalienable rights of elephants to a long " nooning " ; and, wandering to and fro, he thoroughly demoralized the garden till sundown, when he returned to his picket for food.

" If you won't work, you sha'n't eat," said Chihun, angrily. " You're a wild elephant, and no educated animal at all. Go back to your jungle."

Chihun's little brown baby was rolling on the floor of the hut, and stretching out its fat arms to the huge shadow in the doorway. Moti Guj knew well that it was the dearest thing on earth to Chihun. He swung out his trunk with a fascinating crook at the end, and the brown baby threw itself shouting, upon it. Moti Guj made fast and pulled up till the brown baby was crowing in the air twelve feet above his father's head.

" Great Lord ! " said Chihun. " Flour cakes of the best, twelve in number, two feet across and soaked in rum, shall be yours on the instant, and two hundred pounds' weight of fresh-cut young sugar cane therewith. Deign only to put down safely that insignificant brat who is my heart and my life to me ! "

Moti Guj tucked the brown baby comfortably between his forefeet, that could have knocked into tooth-

picks all Chihun's hut, and waited for his food.   He
ate it, and the brown baby crawled away.   Moti Guj
dozed and thought of Deesa.   One of many mysteries
connected with the elephant is that his huge body needs
less sleep than anything else that
lives.   Four or five hours in the night
suffice — two just before midnight,
lying down on one side ; two just after
one o'clock, lying down on the other.
The rest of the silent hours are filled
with eating and fidget-
ing, and long grumbling
soliloquies.

At midnight, therefore, Moti Guj strode out of his
pickets, for a thought had come to him that Deesa
might be lying drunk somewhere in the dark forest with
none to look after him.   So all that night he chased
through the undergrowth, blowing and trumpeting and

shaking his ears.   He went down to the river and blared across the shallows where Deesa used to wash him, but there was no answer.   He could not find Deesa, but he disturbed all the other elephants in the lines, and nearly frightened to death some gypsies in the woods.

At dawn Deesa returned to the plantation.   He had been very drunk indeed, and he expected to get into trouble for outstaying his leave.   He drew a long breath when he saw that the bungalow and the plantation were still uninjured, for he knew something of

Moti Guj's temper, and reported himself with many lies and salaams.   Moti Guj had gone to the pickets for breakfast.   The night exercise had made him hungry.

"Call up your beast," said the planter; and Deesa shouted in the mysterious elephant language that some mahouts believe came from China at the birth of the world, when elephants and not men were masters. Moti Guj heard and came.   Elephants do not gallop. They move from places at varying rates of speed.   If an elephant wished to catch an express train he could

not gallop, but he could catch the train.   So Moti Guj
was at the planter's door almost before Chihun noticed
that he had left his pickets.   He fell into Deesa's arms
trumpeting with joy, and the man and beast wept and
slobbered over each other, and handled each other from
head to heel to see that no harm had befallen.

" Now we will get to work," said Deesa.   " Lift me
up, my son and my joy ! "

Moti Guj swung him up, and the two went to the
coffee-clearing to look for difficult stumps.

The planter was too astonished to be very angry.

EXPLOITS OF SAMSON

(From Four Hundred Animal Stories.)

By ROBERT COCHRANE.

SOME male elephants have no tusks. These are called *hines* by the Burmese. The most powerful animal I ever had was one of them. He was very tall, and in strength a perfect Samson among elephants. An incident in his history is worth relating here. In the month of January the male elephants sometimes give trouble. Samson had fallen into a capricious mood, and in a fit of jealousy he frightened all the others so thoroughly one night that they broke their fetters and made a bolt of it out of the timber-yard, with Samson in pursuit. One unfortunate member who was on the sick-list at the time and had an impediment in his walk was bowled over and trampled on several times, and was never fit for anything but the hospital afterwards. The others took to the jungle, and it cost some money to recover them. Samson remained in possession of the timber-yard for three whole days, no living thing daring to venture near him.

I have watched a fowl, that had thoughtlessly gone to scrape for its morning meal on the accustomed spot in the rear of the elephant-shed, run for its bare life, with Samson after it at full speed, trunk and tail extended! Crowds of people used to collect daily, most of them at a highly respectful distance, however, to witness the giant keeping the world at bay. Sometimes an adventurous native, out of pure mischief, would approach within thirty yards or so of him, spear in hand, when Samson would thump his trunk upon the ground and rush at the intruder, who soon disappeared under the nearest veranda. The poor animal was helpless against such tactics. They were to him what the deprivation of sight was to his prototype; but the desire for revenge was there still, and he tried his strength upon the posts of the building, attempting to push them down. When he had failed in this, he deliberately set about unroofing it with his trunk; whereupon the tormentor pricked his legs from underneath the house with his spear and made him desist. After carrying on this game till he got tired, he walked off with his companion one night to the jungle, and selected a spot for his future residence close to a mud-pool.

For some days he made raids upon the adjoining gardens, eating up the fruit-trees without compunction; and in revenge for some opposition he met with from a market-gardener who did not appreciate his new neighbor's high-handed way of doing things, levelled his hut to the ground. Things were beginning to get serious. Claims for damages now became unpleasantly frequent; so it was absolutely necessary to put a stop to his depredations. Accordingly, I sent out a deputation of elephants to wait upon him, with picked men as drivers and attendants, for the purpose of bringing him to reason. There were ten elephants altogether, the senior member being a very patriarchal-looking animal with an immense pair of tusks — the one, in fact, who was always employed to settle difficulties among the juniors; and in this capacity he had been uniformly successful.

When the deputation arrived at the spot, Samson was enjoying his morning bath in the mud, and they surrounded him. The patriarch, with the chief mahout driving, and another good man and true behind him for the purpose of supplying any lack of moral courage that might manifest itself under trying circumstances, was taken nearest to the renegade. The moment Samson realized the situation he made a rush from the bath at the patriarch, who, forgetting his wonted dignity of manner, turned tail and bolted. The hook and the spear with which the drivers were armed alike failed to restore courage to the leader. On he went, tearing through the jungle, the branches of trees and thorny creepers making sad havoc with the persons of the men on his back. His bad example demoralized the whole force; they fled for their lives every one of them.

At last it came to be a race between Samson and the patriarch, the other elephants having made lateral tracks for themselves and got clear of danger. When it came to close quarters between the two, the mahout, thinking discretion the better part of valor, laid hold of the branch of a tree as he passed and held on, leaving the other man to his fate. In a very short time he too was unseated, but in an involuntary manner; the elephant shot under the branch of a tree which did not afford space for the man to pass under as well, and he was swept to the ground. He was able, however, to elude the pursuer, who was so eager to get at the four-footed fugitive that he took no notice of the fallen rider as he crawled along into the thick jungle.

Fortunately no life was lost in this most exciting adventure. Even the patriarch got off scot-free. When tired of the pursuit, Samson returned to his rural retreat. The deputation got home in the evening, more frightened than hurt. We administered chlorodyne with much success to those whose bruises and lacerations bespoke a sleepless night; and it has since been regarded as a specific for patients suffering from cutaneous diseases and nervous excitement.

But we have not done with Samson yet. He was a valuable elephant, and I was most anxious to recover him. I offered a reward of two hundred rupees (say $100.00) to any one who would bring him in; and a few days afterwards he came marching into the timber-yard as gentle as a lamb, with a young lad astride on his neck. This youth was the son of the man from whom I had purchased him, and the boy had been familiar with the animal from his childhood. Hearing of the reward that was offered for the apprehension of his old pet, he set off in quest of him. When he found him, he made use of the terms with which Samson had formerly been familiar. There was no longer any difficulty. The youth took him by the ear, told him to give him a leg up — the usual way for mahouts to mount their steeds — and immediately Samson was himself again. Next day he was on duty, looking as if nothing had happened, and his little friend was the possessor of a reward which to him was a small fortune.

Such is the affinity between God's creatures which the law of kindness establishes. The little fellow had really more power in the tones of his voice over the huge animal than a phalanx of its own species under the direction of a score of men!

A MAD ELEPHANT

(FROM TENT LIFE IN TIGER-LAND.)

BY MR. JAMES INGLIS.

T HE cry was raised, " Run, run, Sahibs, the Tusker has gone ' must ' (or mad). He has broken loose. "
We all started to our feet. George had just gone down to the bank of the river to where the cooking was going on, which lay nearer the mad elephant's picket. By this time the terror-stricken servants were flying in all directions. The huge brute, with infinite cunning, had all along been making mighty efforts to wrench up the stake to which he was bound. This at last he had succeeded in doing. With the first desperate bound, or lurch forward, the heavy ankle-chains, frayed and worn in one link, had snapped asunder; and with the huge stake trailing behind him, he charged down on the camp with a shrill trumpeting scream of maddened excitement and savage fury. The men with the spears waited not for the onset. One poor fellow, bending over his pot of rice trying to blow the smouldering embers of his fire into a flame, was seized by the long, flexible trunk of the infuriated brute, and had but time to utter the terrible death-

scream which had startled us ere his head was smashed like an egg-shell on the powerful knee of the maddened monster. He next made a rush at the horses that, excited and frightened by the clamor around them, were straining at their ropes, and buried his long, blunt tusks in the quivering flanks of one poor Caboolee horse that had struggled in vain to get free.

All this was the work of a moment. Poor George, who was bending over some stewpan wherein was simmering some delicacy of his own concoction, was not aware of the suddenly altered aspect of affairs till the huge, towering bulk of the elephant was almost over him. Another instant and he would have shared the fate of the hapless mahout had he not, with admirable presence of mind, delivered the hissing-hot stew, with quick dexterity and precision, full in the gaping mouth of the furious brute. His next sensation, however, was that of flying through the air, as the brute, with one swing of its mighty trunk, propelled him on his aërial flight, and he fell souse in the middle of the stream, with the saucepan still tightly clutched in his hand.

Over the river we could see the brute, who had thus scattered us, in a perfect frenzy of rage, kneeling on the shapeless heap of cloth, furniture, poles, and ropes, and digging his tusks with savage fury into the hangings and canvas, in the very abandonment of mad, uncontrollable rage. We had little doubt but that poor Mac lay crushed to death, smothered beneath the weight of the ponderous animal, or mangled out of all likeness to humanity by the terrible tusks that we could see flashing in the clear moonlight. It seemed an age, this agony of suspense. We held our breaths, and dared not look into each other's faces : everything showed as clear as if it had been day. We saw the elephant tossing the strong canvas canopy about as a dog would worry a door-mat. Thrust after thrust was made by the tusks into the folds of cloth. Raising his huge trunk, the brute would scream in the very frenzy of his wrath; and at last, after what seemed an age to us, but which in reality was but a few minutes, he staggered to his feet and rushed into the jungle.

Just then a smothered groan struck like the peal of joy-bells on our anxious ears, and a muffled voice from beneath the folds of the tent in Mac's well-known tones groaned out : " Look alive, you fellows, and get me out of this, or I'll be smothered ! "

In trying to get out of the way of the first rush of the elephant, his foot had caught in one of the tent-ropes, and the whole falling canopy had then come bodily upon him, hurling the camp-table and a few cane chairs over him. Under these he had lain, able

to breathe, but not daring to stir, while the savage
beast had behaved as has been described. His escape
had been miraculous. The cloth had several times
been pressed so close over his face as nearly to stifle
him.   The brute in one of its savage, purposeless
thrusts had pierced the ground between his arms and
his ribs, pinning his Afghan *choga* or dressing-gown
deep into the earth ; and he said he felt himself sinking
into unconsciousness, what with tension of nerve and
brain and semi-suffocation together, when the brute had
happily got up and rushed off.

" How did you feel ? " I asked.

" Well, I can hardly tell you."

" It must have grazed your ribs ? "

" It did.   After that, I seemed to turn quite uncon-
cerned.   All sorts of funny ideas came trooping across
my brain. I couldn't for the life of me help feeling
cautiously about for my pipe, which had dropped somewhere near when I tripped on the ropes. I seemed,
too, to have a quick review of all the actions I had
ever done, and was just dropping off into a dreamy
unconsciousness, after pulling a desperate race against
Oxford with my old crew, when your voices roused me
to sensation once more."

MONKEY STORIES

(FROM FOUR HUNDRED ANIMAL STORIES.)

BY ROBERT COCHRANE.

SOME VERY HUMAN TRAITS IN MONKEYS

SIR GORE OUSELEY, diplomatist and travel-ler, gives a remarkable instance of the " ex-quisite sensibility " of the monkey. On board the man-of-war which took him out as ambassador to Persia, there was a pet mon-key of the captain's, a peculiarly affection-ate, gentle, amiable creature, which was a favorite with the whole ship's com-pany. But it was not without the mischievous propensities of its kind. There was a milch-goat kept on board specially for the ambassador's use. One morning the monkey lashed the goat to the tackle of a gun, and milked it into a marine's hat — the headgear of the marines at that time was a stiff glazed hat. Caught red-handed, the monkey was brought before the captain, who sentenced him to be sent to Coventry for a week, any one taking the slightest notice of the culprit during that period to forfeit his grog. The monkey went about wistfully seeking the attentions to which he had been accustomed, but none of his old friends had a kind look or word for him. In vain he put on his most coaxing and engaging airs; they were wasted. For two days he bore his punishment; but on the morning of the third, finding himself still in disgrace, his sensitive heart broke under the strain of misery. He sprang on the bulwarks, and placing both hands over his head, gave one pitiful cry, then leaped into the sea and was seen no more.

The following story, too, shows a similar trait in the simian character. On board one of Her Majesty's ships on the West Indies station there were two monkeys, a big one and a little one, both great favorites. Dressed in the uniform of middies, the two would parade the deck, gravely salute the captain, and imitate every action of the officer of the watch. The pair were sworn friends and confederates. Both were arrant thieves; but the big one did the actual stealing, whilst the little one bolted with the stolen goods and hid them. On one occasion the captain's gold snuff-box was missing. That the monkeys had stolen it was obvious, for both of them were seized with convulsions of sneezing; but the minutest search failed to find the box, till the smaller monkey was seen surreptitiously peering into a middy's chest, and there beneath the linen was found the missing box. When the ship was at anchor in Kingston harbor, Jamaica, the big monkey stole a bottle of Madeira, which he emptied without sharing a drop with his "pal," who sat and looked at him reproachfully. The wine made the bibulous monkey very drunk. He jumped on the bulwarks, and got so excited at the sight of a shark which was swimming round the ship that at last, after a great deal of jabbering and gesticulation, he sprang into the water, perhaps with some vague idea of playing with the fish. It was a fatal mistake. The shark turned over on its back, opened its huge jaws, and — exit monkey. His little comrade watched the tragedy in agony; his screams were painful to hear. His grief was inconsolable, and the next day he jumped overboard and joined his dead mate. After reading this, who will deny that monkeys have their feelings, and very human feelings too?

The conformity to the requirements of society is something marvellous in the monkey tribe, resulting apparently from their wonderful faculty for imitation. A ludicrous instance of this power is related by Mrs. Loudon. Father Casaubon had a Barbary ape, which was so attached to him that it tried to follow him wherever he went. One day, when the reverend father proceeded to church, the monkey contrived to escape from his fastenings, and silently followed his master. On arrival at the place of worship, the ape climbed up to the sounding-board, and lay there quiet until Casaubon began his sermon. Then it perched itself just above his head and watched his actions; and as the holy father gesticulated, it mimicked his gestures to the best of its capabilities. The congregation tittered;

and Casaubon, shocked at the ill-timed levity, administered a severe rebuke, suiting his actions to his words,
and being all the while most grotesquely imitated, so far
as gestures went, by his silent pupil. This was too
much for the congregation; a roar of laughter greeted
the competitors, as some friendly person kindly pointed
out to the exasperated pastor the cause of the
general hilarity.

Amusing as this anecdote is, it affords very little idea
of the highly polished condition to which our monkey
friends can be brought when in contact with civilized
beings. Every naturalist can give instances. Buffon

 tells of a chimpanzee
which " always walked
on its hind-legs, even
when carrying heavy
burdens. I," he says,
" have seen this animal
present its hand to con-
duct the company to
the door, or walk about
with them through the
room; I have seen it
sit at table, unfold its
napkin, wipe its lips,
make use of a spoon
or fork to carry its
victuals to its mouth, pour out its drink into a glass,
touch glasses when invited, go for its cup and saucer,
carry them to the table, pour out its tea, sweeten and
leave it to cool; and all this without any other insti-
gation than the signs or commands of its keeper, and

sometimes even of its own accord. It was gentle and inoffensive; it even approached you with a kind of respect, and as if only seeking for caresses."

As a rule, so far as our experience goes, the mischievousness of monkeys is not purely wanton, but is prompted by a motive. Sometimes the motive is revenge, as in the following case. A retired colonel at Bath had a pet monkey. His next-door neighbor was a widow lady with three mischievous and troublesome boys, who, when they were home for the holidays, made that unhappy monkey's life a burden to him by throwing lighted squibs and crackers at him, and giving him nuts filled with pepper or  mustard. When his tormentors went back to school, the monkey, from a respectful distance, watched them depart, then came down, crept cautiously along the balcony to the widow's drawing-room window, and seeing that there was no one about, entered, got hold of a bottle of ink, and liberally sprinkled its contents over the carpet and furniture. He was caught, handed over to his master, and soundly whipped — but he had had his revenge.

In another curious case jealousy of a quite human type prompted revenge. A nobleman, well-known as a

prominent member of the Royal Yacht Club, had a pet
monkey, which used to accompany him on his yachting
cruises, and was accustomed to receive a great deal of
attention from every one on board.　Among the guests
on the yacht on one occasion was a beautiful girl, who
attracted general admiration ; but, as she professed a
dislike for monkeys, Master Pug's presence was not
encouraged.　The monkey felt himself aggrieved and
neglected.　But when the party landed to inspect some
caves, he contrived to slip into the boat unobserved and
accompany them.　Watching his opportunity, he seized
a large crab, and placed it against the heel of the young
lady, which it gripped with its huge claw so fiercely
that she screamed with pain.　Unfortunately for the
monkey, he had been detected in the act, and he
suffered for it.

But most of the mischievous pranks of which monkeys
are guilty proceed from no worse motive than a desire
to imitate the actions of their masters.　And if imitation be the sincerest form of flattery, the mischief of
the monkey should be regarded more leniently than it
generally is.　And yet it must have been difficult for
a late royal academician to appreciate this subtle form
of flattery when his pet monkey, taking advantage of
the master's absence from the studio, calmly seated
himself on a stool before a nearly finished canvas, and
with mahl-stick, palette and brush, proceeded to lay on
the colors with a recklessness and dash worthy of a
latter-day "impressionist."

Nor were the inmates of a Suffolk vicarage, on returning from morning service on Sunday, altogether
pleased to find that in their absence the pet monkey

had removed the table-cloth, which had been laid for dinner, with all the appurtenances, from the table to the floor, where it was set out with a scrupulous atten-tion to details which showed how carefully the lesson had been learned.

One of the drollest instances of the monkey's keenness of obser-vation and power of mimicry that we have met with is the following. A retired admiral and his wife liv-ing at Chelten-ham had a favo-rite monkey. One day the lady, hearing a strange noise in the din-ing-room, looked in to see what it

was. The sight which met her eyes was a ludicrous one. Seated in the arm-chair, with the admiral's smoking-cap on his head, and the admiral's spectacles on his nose, was the monkey; and in his hand was the open newspaper, which he shook and patted, whilst he jabbered and gesticulated with great emphasis at the

cat which lay blinking on the hearthrug. It was a
clever and carefully-studied imitation of the testy old
admiral's tone and manner when reading to his wife
some passage from the newspaper which excited his
wrath or indignation.

It is strange that so little attempt is made to utilize
this strong imitative faculty in monkeys. They might
easily be trained to perform as athletes and acrobats.
Some fifty years ago an Italian count, who had a villa

on the shore of Lake Albano, kept a monkey which he
had taught both to row and sail a small skiff. The
monkey used to navigate this tiny craft with great
skill; but, unfortunately, one day, when climbing the
mast, he capsized the boat and was drowned.

Possibly the reason why monkeys have been so little
on the stage is that their appearance there would
emphasize too strongly the striking similarity between
man and monkey. Something of the sort, indeed, was
tried in London in 1753, and " Mrs. Midnight's Animal

Comedians " for a brief space took the town by storm.
A trained troupe of dogs and monkeys took part in a
ballet, dressed in the costume of the day, and their
dancing is said to have been clever and graceful. The
ballet was followed by a stirring battle-piece. The
monkeys defended and the dogs assaulted a mimic
fortress. Everything was *en règle* — uniforms, arms,
and all the paraphernalia of war. The stormers with
scaling-ladders dashed gallantly to the assault. The
monkeys received them with a withering fire of mus-
ketry. After a fierce struggle the ramparts were
carried. Then the firing ceased, and when the smoke
cleared away, the gallant foemen were seen drawn up
side by side, waving their shakos, whilst the band
played " God save the King." If this sort of spectacle
could be produced successfully a hundred and fifty
years ago, why not now?

Herr Brehm tells the following droll story: " A
female baboon which I brought up in my family got
hold of a kitten with the intention of making a pet
of it and mothering it, but was scratched by the terrified foundling. The monkey carefully examined the
kitten's paws, pressed the claws forward, looked at
them from above, from beneath, and from the side, and
then bit them off to secure itself against further
scratches."

This tendency of monkeys to make pets of other
animals is curiously illustrated by an instance in our
own experience. In this case the monkey had a mania
for nursing, or " mothering," as Herr Brehm has it,
pets both animate and inanimate; sometimes it was
a doll, sometimes a guinea-pig, sometimes a white rat.

This craze, however, brought the monkey to an untimely end. He had fixed covetous eyes upon a litter of young pigs, and resolved to steal one to make a pet of it. He popped over the wall of the stye and seized a sucking grunter. He leapt with his prize on the door of the stye; it was rickety, and, giving way with his weight, precipitated him back right into the jaws of the infuriated sow, who quickly made an end of him.

From Graaf-Reinet, South Africa, comes the strange story of a monkey signalman. A correspondent of *Chambers's Journal* writes: "As regards monkeys, we have several varieties here. I think the Cynocephalus is the most sagacious. We had a remarkably intelligent baboon here a few years ago. He was a giant of his species. His master and trainer had the misfortune to have both his legs cut off in a railway accident, and on his leaving the hospital, the Cape government gave him a berth as signalman, near the terminus here. He taught this baboon not only to work the signals, but to place the wheels of a little trolley on the line, and then the bed on the wheels. His master would then seat himself on the trolley, and Jackoo would push him along to his house, about two hundred yards down the line. He would then detach the pieces of the trolley and clear them off the line. He would also lock the door of the signal-box and take the key to his master. When he died I obtained the body, and sent it to the Albany Museum at Grahamstown, but the taxidermist informed me that the body was too decomposed for preservation. I believe his skeleton has been afforded a place in the Museum. A picture has been printed of poor Jackoo and his master, showing the former working the railway signals as hundreds of people have seen him.

When Mr. Mayhew was writing his book on "London Labour and London Poor," he did not forget to interview and question one of the owners of performing monkeys. The man gave information freely in broken English and French, but somewhat timidly, as he had a frightened impression that in the streets of the town the monkey was "defended" (meaning *défendu*, "forbidden") and that his information might get him into trouble. He never did "play de monkey" in town, he said; he went out "vare dere is so many donkey up a top at dat village." He stated that performing monkeys were becoming scarce; there were not a dozen "wot play in Angleterre," for the reason that "monkey is 'defended' in the streets." He himself was making about twelve shillings a week, sometimes three shillings a day, sometimes sixpence, sometimes nothing. He had had his monkey three months, having bought him for thirty-five shillings.

"I did teach a him all he know. I teach a him vid de kindness, do you see. I must look rough for tree or four times, but not to beat him. I mustn't feed him ven I am teaching him. Sometimes I buy a happorth of nuts, to give him after he has done wot I want him to do."

Then he alluded mournfully to this monkey's accomplished predecessor, who could use the sword, dance, and play the drum and the fiddle. "Ah! but he don't play de fiddle like de Christian, you know, but like de monkey!" On this prodigy of a monkey he had lavished his care and affection, teaching him to waltz with time and step regulated by jerks of the string, and rewarding him with "biled raisins." But just as the *artiste* was conquering the difficulties of the waltz, he indulged in an imprudent meal of red paint, and, as the old epitaphs say, "physicians were in vain," and he and his tricks came to an end.

A French paper relates a good story about a merchant in Marseilles who wrote to a correspondent on the coast of Africa asking him to send him at his convenience two or three monkeys of the rarest and most valuable species. As chance would have it, the merchant, in stating the number, wrote the *ou* (or) between the figures two and three with a very small *o* and a diminutive *u*. How great events may issue from small causes will appear from the sequel. A few months passed over, when at last a messenger was sent from the harbor to inform the merchant that his menagerie had landed. "My menagerie!" was the astonished reply. "Yes, a menagerie; in fact, a whole cargo of monkeys has come for you." The merchant could not believe the man until a letter was delivered to him from his friend in Africa, a person of the most scrupulous exactness, in which he gravely apologized for his having been unable, notwithstanding all his efforts, to procure more than one hundred and sixty monkeys instead of two hundred and three as ordered, but promised to forward the remainder as soon as possible. Imagine the feelings of the merchant on going down to the port to convince himself with his own eyes of the existence of his one hundred and sixty monkeys, which were all comfortably housed and which grinned at him through the bars of their cages.

Monkeys in Confinement.

Monkeys in confinement are not wholly destitute of good qualities. Observation proves that the curiosity, petulance, and mischief so frequently ascribed to these creatures in general, are as foreign to some tribes as are repulsive habits and ferocity common to others. Most apes are naturally gentle, grateful, and affectionate, even towards their jailers, and although when teased they grow sullen or peevish, they can rarely be provoked to violent passion. Generally, they wear an aspect of melancholy; due, doubtless, to the unnatural circumstances in which they are placed; but their eyes are bright, and their looks full of intelligence. The gravity and deliberation with which they act are most impressive, and cause one to regard with a kind of respect the opinion prevalent among many uncivilized peoples that monkeys can talk. Thus, a traveller, writing about Java, says: "The Sultan of Djokjokarta entertained us by the exhibition of a curious collection of monkeys and apes. Some were of huge proportions, full four feet in height, and looking as fierce as if just captured from their native jungles. The orang-outangs and long-armed apes had been trained to go through a variety of military exercises; and when one of us expressed surprise at their seeming intelligence, the Sultan said gravely: 'They are as really *men* as you and I, and have the power of speech if they choose to exercise it. They do not talk, because they are unwilling to work and be made slaves of.' This strange theory is generally believed by the

Malays, in whose language *orang-outang* is simply 'man
of the woods.' "

Darwin mentions an anecdote, strongly illustrative of
our contention, that the characters of monkeys are as
varied as those of men. " A man who trains monkeys
to act," says the eminent naturalist, " used to purchase
common kinds from the Zoölogical Society at the price
of five pounds each; but he offered to give double the
price, if he might keep three or four of them for a few
days, in order to select one. When asked how he could
possibly so soon learn whether a particular monkey
would turn out a good actor, he answered that it all
depended on their power of attention. If, when he
was talking and explaining anything to a monkey, its
attention was easily distracted, as by a fly on the wall,
or other trifling object, the case was hopeless. If he
tried by punishment to make an inattentive monkey
act, it turned sulky. On the other hand, a monkey
which carefully attended to him could always be
trained."

My Pet Ape.

My office in the last port where I was stationed
looked over the sea, and had a veranda outside it,
which of course was kept sacred. I was sitting
one day in my office-chair, looking out over the bay
beyond, to collect my thoughts for a despatch then
in hand, when I espied a Celestial coming along the
veranda with some dark object in his arms, the dark
object showing its appreciation of the attention it
was receiving by placing two arms of inordinate length

round the man's neck. I naturally rose up to see what this phenomenon was, and having been told that it was a rare animal, I at once made overtures for its purchase. As soon as negotiations were concluded, I fastened my purchase — a black gibbon — to my copying-press, instead of sending him up to my house, being anxious to introduce him myself to my two dogs and to Joseph the cat. I could not entrust a rare animal to my servants, lest the introduction through their agency to Joseph and the rest might result in some disaster.

When I fastened the gibbon to the press I took no account of the length of the animal's arms, and I was therefore not a little surprised when a black hand took possession of a red-and-blue pencil and a black mouth began to eat it. Nature is said, in her beneficence, to instruct the lower animals what to eat and what to avoid. That, no doubt, applies to an animal in the wild state, such animal being directed by instinct where to find an antidote to anything deleterious which it may have eaten. An animal in captivity must, however, be treated differently, and must not be allowed to do as it likes. So I reasoned; and as I had no herb ready to correct the

evil which I knew would result from eating a pencil,
I proceeded to recover the stolen article. Though my
new pet did not mind being touched, though he would
jump into your lap and make himself at home, he
strongly objected to part with anything which he had
once got hold of, and a good deal of diplomacy had to
be used before I repossessed myself of the pencil.

Scarcely was this fun at an end before some black
fingers were dipped into the ink; and when the ink
was removed out of reach, the gum-bottle was next
turned over, the gum being particularly appreciated.
Thinking that the animal might be thirsty, I put a
saucer of water before him; but though easy to put
the saucer down, it was impossible to pick it up again,
even though there was not a drop of water left in it.
It seemed to me, on reflection, that I had made a bad
purchase.

At first, the name of "Sambo" was given to the
gibbon, on account of its jet-black color; then this was
changed in course of time to "Samuel," the little fellow
becoming too respectable to be called Sambo. At the
last port at which I was stationed the lower windows
of my dwelling-house were provided with iron bars
— about five inches apart — as a protection against
thieves. These bars were a great convenience to me,
as I could attach Sam to them at meal-times, thus
keeping him out of mischief, whilst giving him plenty
of freedom. The question of feeding Sam was not an
easy one to tackle. If we sat down and began eating
before he was served, the most noisy protests were
made; and when the saucer of rice was put down,
there was no one courageous enough to recover the

empty saucer. The point was often settled by Sam himself, who, having finished his rice, would throw the saucer into the air a few times — catching it very cleverly — and then hurl it away from him. A wooden bowl was found to answer better; but this also received much rough usage, and had to be repeatedly renewed.

One very noticeable feature about Sam was his extreme jealousy. If I stroked the cat in his presence, he used to get into a paroxysm of rage and make great efforts to bite me. He would be almost as much vexed if I patted the dogs. When a guest came to luncheon he was so angry at the intrusion that he often had to be removed. He would absorb all the conversation until removal, it being quite impossible to keep him quiet. He had a singular objection to anything being removed by the servants; and had he been fastened to my chair instead of the window, no plate once put on the table could have been taken away. When in the drawing-room with me — and he was often there — he would even fly at my wife if she attempted to touch the tea-things. At this date he has sobered down a good deal; but even now, though a servant may bring me a letter, he must not take away a reply if Sam is with me. He objects to any one coming near me; and if my wife shakes my coat, or even touches my shoulder, he catches hold of her, though now perhaps more in play than in anger.

His disposition has naturally changed during his long captivity, and I am therefore obliged to speak of his actions in the past tense. Sitting up, Sam measures sixteen and a half inches; but his arms are twenty-

three inches long. He is jet black all over, has fur as
thick as that of many animals which live in cold
climes, and the hair on the top of his head grows up
into a point, which naturally enhances his personal
appearance. His nose is flat, and is doubtless more
useful than ornamental. He has a good voice, and
whether he calls out for his food or expresses his
delight at seeing you, his notes are equally agreeable.
When I take him his bread and milk at half-past six
every morning, he shows his gratitude in a queer way :
prostrating himself, he makes what no doubt are elo-
quent speeches in his own language. After he has
spoken for some time and made numerous faces, he
takes hold of my hand and hugs it. Until he has gone
through this elaborate performance, he will not touch
his food. Though his diet should consist of rice and
fruit only, he often has bread and jam, and often, too,
a slice of cake. He has no objection, moreover, to
either rice-pudding or plum-pudding. When his appetite shows signs of weakness, an egg beaten up in milk
revives him ; and symptoms of fever call for a little
quinine mixed with sugar. I never give Sam tea.
Tea makes such animals nervous, and has other deleterious effects on their constitutions which need not be
particularized here. Orang-outangs taken to Britain
are generally dosed with tea on arrival, and are given
an inordinate quantity of fruit to eat. Very little
fruit is required, and care should be taken not to give
too much water. In their wild state gibbons no doubt
eat a large quantity of fruit ; but then nature comes to
their aid if ill effects arise, and points out to them the
herb which will cure them. In captivity they do not

get much exercise, and science can do very little for them when bodily ailments occur.

If Sam breaks loose in the summer, he helps himself liberally to bananas : if his rope gives way in the winter, he makes his way to the drawing-room ; there he warms himself, and having done this, he jumps on the sofa, pulls an antimacassar over him, and goes to sleep.

When I go into the garden, I release him altogether. He jumps from tree to tree to the great amazement of the Celestials, who watch his movements from hillocks outside my grounds, and occasionally he comes down to have a game with my two pups. It is not a common sight to see a gibbon loose, nor can you always get a picture of a gibbon and a dog rolling over and over each other in play. Perhaps some of my readers may at one time or another have kept gibbons. If they have, they must have been struck with the singular way in which gibbons quench their thirst. The young gibbon does not put his mouth to the water he wants to drink ; he dips his left hand into it and sucks the back of his fingers, the hair which is on them taking up half a tablespoonful of water at a time. As he grows older he shakes off this youthful folly, and then dips his head into the water and sucks the fluid up in the same way that a horse does. What the gibbon lives on in his native wilds it is impossible to say; but he evidently has a predilection for spiders' webs. My pet clears away all webs within his reach, and apparently not liking to leave the owners of them homeless, he devours them too. He is very fond of hard-backed beetles ; but these

delicacies are now strictly forbidden, as they are not
calculated to agree with bread and jam or with rice-
pudding.

It was not an easy matter to keep Sam alive in the
tropics ; now that he is not only well out of the tropics
but in a region where the winters are severe, one may
well despair of being able to preserve him. During
the twenty-seven months which he has now spent with
me, he has been my constant companion. He went
with me to the office when I was in the south of
China : he goes with me now that I am in the north.
In the south he used to pull the hats of my chair-
coolies off : here he continues this play, varying it by
pulling my hat off and throwing it away. At the
office he constitutes himself my special guardian,
making strong protests against any one approaching
my desk. He will allow a stranger to go up to him
and scratch his head ; but he makes the noisiest
demonstrations possible if any one ventures to shake
hands with me or touch anything on my desk.

If I leave my house in the morning without him, he
speedily lets me understand how sore in spirit he is,
and I have eventually to take him. Sometimes I am
reluctant to take him, as he pulls things about at the
office, and on the way to the office he swoops down on
any fruit which may be within range. If he captures a
pear or an apple, he returns with it in great triumph,
showing as much pleasure in his face, and making as
much noise as a child does when given a piece of cake
of more than ordinary richness or a lollipop of extra
quality. I became so well-known that itinerant fruit-
vendors knew where to apply for compensation for

thefts committed. There was no ill-feeling created;
indeed there were roars of laughter when the "black
monkey," as they termed Sam, made a good seizure.
I had to keep a string of "cash" at the office to pay
for Sam's depredations.

THE EARLY DAYS OF BLACK BEAUTY

(FROM BLACK BEAUTY.)

BY ANNA SEWELL.

THE first place that I can well remember was a large pleasant meadow with a pond of clear water in it. Some shady trees leaned over it, and rushes and water-lilies grew at the deep end. Over the hedge on one side we looked into a ploughed field, and on the other we looked over a gate at our master's house, which stood by the roadside; at the top of the meadow was a grove of fir trees, and at the bottom a running brook overhung by a steep bank.

Whilst I was young, I lived upon my mother's milk, as I could not eat grass. In the daytime I ran by her side, and at night I lay down close by her. When it was hot, we used to stand by the pond in the shade of the trees, and when it was cold, we had a nice warm shed near the grove.

As soon as I was old enough to eat grass, my mother used to go out to work in the daytime, and come back in the evening.

There were six young colts in the meadow besides me; they were older than I was; some were nearly as

large as grown-up horses. I used to run with them,
and had great fun; we used to gallop all together
round and round the field as hard as we could go.
Sometimes we had rather rough play, for they would
frequently bite and kick as well as gallop.

One day, when there was a good deal of kicking, my
mother whinnied to me to come to her, and then she
said, —

" I wish you to pay attention to what I am going to
say to you. The colts who live here are very good
colts, but they are cart-horse colts, and of course they
have not learned manners. You have been well-bred
and well-born; your father has a great name in these
parts, and your grandfather won the cup two years at
the Newmarket races; your grandmother had the sweet-
est temper of any horse I ever knew, and I think you
have never seen me kick or bite. I hope you will grow
up gentle and good, and never learn bad ways; do
your work with a good will, lift your feet up well when
you trot, and never bite or kick even in play."

I have never forgotten my mother's advice; I knew
she was a wise old horse, and our master thought a
great deal of her. Her name was Duchess, but he
often called her Pet.

Our master was a good, kind man. He gave us good
food, good lodging, and kind words; he spoke as kindly
to us as he did to his little children. We were all fond
of him, and my mother loved him very much. When
she saw him at the gate, she would neigh with joy, and
trot up to him. He would pat and stroke her and say,
" Well, old Pet, and how is your little Darkie ? " I was
a dull black, so he called me Darkie; then he would

give me a piece of bread, which was very good, and sometimes he brought a carrot for my mother. All the horses would come to him, but I think we were his favorites. My mother always took him to the town on a market day in a light gig.

There was a ploughboy, Dick, who sometimes came into our field to pluck blackberries from the hedge. When he had eaten all he wanted, he would have, what he called, fun with the colts, throwing stones and sticks at them to make them gallop. We did not much mind him, for we could gallop off; but sometimes a stone would hit and hurt us.

One day he was at this game, and did not know that the master was in the next field; but he was there, watching what was going on; over the hedge he jumped in a snap, and catching Dick by the arm, he gave him such a box on the ear as made him roar with the pain and surprise. As soon as we saw the master, we trotted up nearer to see what went on.

"Bad boy!" he said, "bad boy! to chase the colts. This is not the first time, nor the second, but it shall be the last. There — take your money and go home; I shall not want you on my farm again." So we never saw Dick any more. Old Daniel, the man who looked after the horses, was just as gentle as our master, so we were well off.

Before I was two years old, a circumstance happened which I have never forgotten. It was early in the spring; there had been a little frost in the night, and a light mist still hung over the woods and meadows. I and the other colts were feeding at the lower part of the field when we heard, quite in the distance, what sounded like the cry of dogs. The oldest of the colts raised his head, pricked his ears, and said, "There are the hounds!" and immediately cantered off, followed by the rest of us to the upper part of the field, where we could look over the hedge and see several fields beyond. My mother and an old riding horse of our master's were also standing near, and seemed to know all about it.

"They have found a hare," said my mother, "and if they come this way we shall see the hunt."

And soon the dogs were all tearing down the field of young wheat next to ours. I never heard such a noise as they made. They did not bark, nor howl, nor whine, but kept on a "yo! yo, o, o! yo! yo, o, o!" at the top of their voices. After them came a number of men on horseback, some of them in green coats, all galloping as fast as they could. The old horse snorted and looked eagerly after them, and we young colts wanted to be galloping with them, but they were soon away into the fields lower down; here it seemed as if they had come to a stand; the dogs left off barking, and ran about every way with their noses to the ground.

"They have lost the scent," said the old horse; "perhaps the hare will get off."

"What hare?" I said.

"Oh! I don't know *what* hare; likely enough it may be one of our own hares out of the woods; any hare they can find will do for the dogs and men to run after;" and before long the dogs began their "yo! yo, o, o!" again, and back they came all together at full speed, making straight for our meadow at the part where the high bank and hedge overhang the brook.

" Now we shall see the hare," said my mother; and just then a hare wild with fright rushed by, and made for the woods. On came the dogs; they burst over the bank, leapt the stream, and came dashing across the field, followed by the huntsmen. Six or eight men leaped their horses clean over, close upon the dogs. The hare tried to get through the fence; it was too thick, and she turned sharp round to make for the road, but it was too late; the dogs were upon her with their wild cries; we heard one shriek, and that was the end of her. One of the huntsmen rode up and whipped off the dogs, who would soon have torn her to pieces. He held her up by the leg torn and bleeding, *and all the gentlemen seemed well pleased.*

As for me, I was so astonished that I did not at first see what was going on by the brook; but when I did look, there was a sad sight; two fine horses were down, one was struggling in the stream, and the other was groaning on the grass. One of the riders was getting out of the water covered with mud, the other lay quite still.

" His neck is broke," said my mother.

" And serve him right, too," said one of the colts.

I thought the same, but my mother did not join with us.

" Well, no," she said, " you must not say that; but though I am an old horse, and have seen and heard a great deal, I never yet could make out why men are so fond of this sport; they often hurt themselves, often spoil good horses, and tear up the fields, and all for a hare, or a fox, or a stag, that they could get more easily some other way; but we are only horses, and don't know."

Whilst my mother was saying this, we stood and looked on. Many of the riders had gone to the young man; but my master, who had been watching what was going on, was the first to raise him. His head fell back and his arms hung down, and every one looked very serious. *There was no noise now ; even the dogs were quiet, and seemed to know that something was wrong. They carried him to our master's house.* I heard afterwards that it was young George Gordon, the Squire's only son, a fine, tall young man, and the pride of his family.

There was now riding off in all directions to the doctor's, to the farrier's, and no doubt to Squire Gordon's, to let him know about his son. When Mr. Bond, the farrier, came to look at the black horse that lay groaning on the grass, he felt him all over, and shook his head ; one of his legs was broken. Then some one ran to our master's house and came back with a gun ; presently there was a loud bang and a dreadful shriek, and then all was still ; the black horse moved no more.

My mother seemed much troubled ; she said she had known that horse for years, and that his name was " Rob Roy ; " he was a good horse, and there was no vice in him. She never would go to that part of the field afterwards.

Not many days after, we heard the church-bell tolling for a long time ; and looking over the gate we saw a long strange black coach that was covered with black cloth and was drawn by black horses ; after that came another and another and another, and all were black, while the bell kept tolling, tolling. *They were carrying young Gordon to the churchyard to bury him. He would*

*never ride again.   What they did with Rob Roy I never
knew ; but 'twas all for one little hare.*

I was now beginning to grow handsome ; my coat
had grown fine and soft, and was bright black.   I had
one white foot, and a pretty white star on my forehead.
I was thought very handsome ; my master would not
sell me till I was four years old ; he said lads ought
not to work like men, and colts ought not to work like
horses till they were quite grown up.

When I was four years old, Squire Gordon came to
look at me.   He examined my eyes, my mouth, and
my legs ; he felt them all down ; and then I had to
walk and trot and gallop before him ; he seemed to like
me, and said, " When he has been well broken in, he
will do very well."   My master said he would break
me in himself, as he should not like me to be frightened
or hurt, and he lost no time about it, for the next day
he began.

Every one may not know what breaking in is, therefore I will describe it.   It means to teach a horse to
wear a saddle and bridle, and to carry on his back a
man, woman, or child ; to go just the way they wish,
and to go quietly.   Besides this, he has to learn to
wear a collar, a crupper, and a breeching, and to stand
still whilst they are put on ; then to have a çart or a
chaise fixed behind, so that he cannot walk or trot without dragging it after him ; and he must go fast or slow,
just as his driver wishes.   He must never start at what
he sees, nor speak to other horses, nor bite, nor kick,
nor have any will of his own ; but always do his master's will, even though he may be very tired or hungry ;
but the worst of all is, when his harness is once on, he

may neither jump for joy nor lie down for weariness.
So you see this breaking in is a great thing.

I had of course long been used to a halter and a
headstall, and to be led about in the field and lanes
quietly, but now I was to have a bit and bridle; my
master gave me some oats as usual, and after a good
deal of coaxing he got the bit into my mouth, and the
bridle fixed, but it was a nasty thing! Those who
have never had a bit in their mouths cannot think how
bad it feels; a great piece of cold hard steel as thick
as a man's finger to be pushed into one's mouth, between one's teeth, and over one's tongue, with the ends
coming out at the corner of your mouth, and held fast
there by straps over your head, under your throat,
round your nose, and under your chin; so that no way
in the world can you get rid of the nasty hard thing;
it is very bad! yes, very bad! at least I thought so;
but I knew my mother always wore one when she
went out, and all horses did when they were grown
up; and so, what with the nice oats, and what with
my master's pats, kind words, and gentle ways, I got
to wear my bit and bridle.

Next came the saddle, but that was not half so bad;
my master put it on my back very gently, whilst old
Daniel held my head; he then made the girths fast
under my body, patting and talking to me all the time;
then I had a few oats, then a little leading about; and
this he did every day till I began to look for the oats
and the saddle. At length, one morning, my master
got on my back and rode me round the meadow on the
soft grass. It certainly did feel queer; but I must say
I felt rather proud to carry my master, and as he con-

tinued to ride me a little every day, I soon became accustomed to it.

The next unpleasant business was putting on the iron shoes; that too was very hard at first. My master went with me to the smith's forge, to see that I was not hurt or got any fright. The blacksmith took my feet in his hand, one after the other, and cut away some of the hoof. It did not pain me, so I stood still on three legs till he had done them all. Then he took a piece of iron the shape of my foot, and clapped it on, and drove some nails through the shoe quite into my hoof, so that the shoe was firmly on. My feet felt very stiff and heavy, but in time I got used to it.

And now having got so far, my master went on to break me to harness; there were more new things to wear. First, a stiff heavy collar just on my neck, and a bridle with great side-pieces against my eyes called blinkers, and blinkers indeed they were, for I could not see on either side, but only straight in front of me; next, there was a small saddle with a nasty stiff strap that went right under my tail; that was the crupper. I hated the crupper, — to have my long tail doubled up and poked through that strap was almost as bad as the bit. I never felt more like kicking, but of course I could not kick such a good master, and so in time I got used to everything, and could do my work as well as my mother.

I must not forget to mention one part of my training, which I have always considered a very great advantage. My master sent me for a fortnight to a neighboring farmer's, who had a meadow which was skirted on one side by the railway. Here were some sheep and cows, and I was turned in amongst them.

I shall never forget the first train that ran by. I was feeding quietly near the pales which separated the meadow from the railway, when I heard a strange sound at a distance, and before I knew whence it came, — with a rush and a clatter, and a puffing out of smoke, — a long black train of something flew by, and was gone almost before I could draw my breath. I turned and galloped to the further side of the meadow as fast as I could go, and there I stood snorting with astonishment and fear. In the course of the day many other trains went by, some more slowly; these drew up at the station close by, and sometimes made an awful shriek and groan before they stopped. I thought it very dreadful, but the cows went on eating very quietly, and hardly raised their heads as the black frightful thing came puffing and grinding past.

For the first few days I could not feed in peace; but as I found that this terrible creature never came into the field, or did me any harm, I began to disregard it, and very soon I cared as little about the passing of a train as the cows and sheep did.

Since then I have seen many horses much alarmed and restive at the sight or sound of a steam engine; but thanks to my good master's care, I am as fearless at railway stations as in my own stable.

Now if any one wants to break in a young horse well, that is the way.

My master often drove me in double harness with my mother, because she was steady and could teach me how to go better than a strange horse. She told me the better I behaved the better I should be treated, and that it was wisest always to do my best to please my master; "but," said she, "there are a great many kinds of men; there are good, thoughtful men like our master, that any horse may be proud to serve; and there are bad, cruel men, who never ought to have a horse or dog to call their own. Beside, there are a great many foolish men, vain, ignorant, and careless, who never trouble themselves to think; these spoil more horses than all, just for want of sense; they don't mean it, but they do it for all that. I hope you will fall into good hands; but a horse never knows who may buy him, or who may drive him; it is all a chance for us; but still I say, do your best whatever it is, and keep up your good name."

A PARROT WHICH ANSWERED QUESTIONS

(From Memoirs of What Passed in Christendom from 1672 to 1679.)

By SIR WILLIAM TEMPLE.

I HAD a mind to know from Prince Maurice's own mouth the account of a common but much credited story that I had heard so often from many others of an old parrot he had in Brazil, during his government there, that spoke and asked and answered questions like a reasonable creature; so that those of his train there generally concluded it to be witchery or possession. He accordingly asked Prince Maurice about the matter, who told him that having heard of the parrot, he sent for it; and that when it was brought into the room where he was, with a great many Dutchmen about him, it presently exclaimed, "What a company of white men are here!" They asked what it thought that man was, pointing to the Prince. The parrot answered: "Some general or other." When they brought it close to him, he asked it, "Whence come you?" It answered, "From

197

Marinnan." The Prince then said, "To whom do you belong?" The parrot replied, "To a Portuguese." The Prince asked, "What do you do there?" The parrot said, "I look after the chickens." The Prince laughed, and said, "You look after the chickens?" The parrot replied, "Yes; and I know well enough how to do it;" and began to cluck like a hen calling chickens. This parrot appears only to have been a well-trained bird, accustomed to say certain things, and ready to say them, but them only, on occasions such as arose from the presence of the Prince and his attendants and the questions addressed to it.

SOME PARROTS I HAVE KNOWN

(From Four Hundred Animal Stories.)

By ROBERT COCHRANE.

T HE first parrot whom it was my privilege to know resided in the house where I was born. He was an extremely handsome bird, and his plumage was always in beautiful condition. He was, moreover, blessed with an exceedingly good temper. It is true that tradition said that in his early days he had been addicted to swearing — a habit picked up during his voyage to this country from his sailor companions — but words of such a character had happily quite faded from his memory by the time when I first made his acquaintance. By that time, indeed, he had got so far as to occasionally become pious, so pious that he had to be removed from the room at the time of family prayers, as he was prone to exclaim " Let us pray " at inopportune moments, and would occasionally even repeat about half of the Lord's Prayer. The indignity of banishment from the dining-room to the hall on such occasions weighed heavily upon him; he resorted to a mean revenge, which proved so successful that he must often have chuckled over it himself. One night, in the middle of the evening devotions, the sound of the street door latch being unfastened, caused the hasty exit, amid general alarm, of the family. No one was at the door, but some nights later the alarm was repeated; it became common at prayer time, and it was not until some time afterwards discovered that the prayerful exile had endeavored by this very successful ruse to draw attention to the indignity of his position.

Parrots are not above availing themselves of artificial means, when they think it necessary, for the proper reproduction of a particular voice or sound. For instance, in order to obtain the resonance of tone required for the successful imitation of the deep voice possessed by the master of the house, this particular bird would invariably put his head into his empty or half-empty seed-tin, a method of voice production he was never known to adopt at any other time, or for the imitation of any other voice or sound. He thus succeeded in producing a very perfect imitation, and his orders (always most peremptorily proclaimed) were occasionally mistaken for those of his master.

On one occasion a friend had arrived unexpectedly from the country, when the family were out of town; only the master of the house was at home, and he was also going away the very evening his friend arrived. The visitor was, however, asked to remain for the night, an offer which he accepted. The following morning, to the disgust of the servant who was engaged in her work, he appeared early upon the scene, inquiring for her master. "Master went away last night," she answered. "Impossible! Why, I heard him call for his hot water and his boots this morning," cried the astonished guest. "Oh sir, that was the parrot," answered the servant.

The bird sometimes uttered words in season. His owner was a clergyman with a curacy at the East End of London. When the rector made his first call, he was shown into a room where for some minutes he and the bird were alone together. On the entrance of the lady of the house, her visitor at once remarked: "There is no occasion for me to ask your husband's views, as your parrot has just greeted me with the words 'No Popery for Polly.'" The bird had, perhaps not unnaturally, an ecclesiastical turn of mind; he would constantly exclaim, in a burst of enthusiasm, "Long life to Canterbury." The word "Archbishop" he left out; it was too much for him. At the same time he could be critical, and when dissatisfied with the views expressed upon religious questions, would state his opinion warmly. At the time of the great controversy respecting the Maynooth grant, when party spirit ran high, several clergymen met one evening to discuss at the house where the bird lived the burning question of the hour. Polly was covered over, according to custom, after it became dark, and no notice was taken of him. A heated discussion took place, but after a time a slight momentary pause occurred in the conversation, whereupon a stern voice was heard angrily ejaculating from the covered cage, "Stuff! Pack of nonsense! Rubbish!"

This parrot much enjoyed being placed on the balcony of the portico of the house, where he would remain for

hours, much to the amusement of the boys in the street;
but from this coign of vantage the cage had to be removed, as he hailed the passing omnibuses, and per-
sisted in calling for cabs.

All the parrots I have known have been accustomed
to pass the night in their swings. From this upper or
bedroom story the bird one evening fell suddenly down
to the floor of the cage. Though he was not in any
way injured by the fall, the shock drew from him the
exclamation, " Oh, good gracious ! "

A friend living in the neighborhood used to pass the
house as he went to and fro to his daily occupation; he
was in the habit of knocking two or three times a day,
and, truth to tell, he became rather a bore. One day
when he was giving his usual double knock, Polly exclaimed in a low and distinct voice, " There's that
Robbins." It appeared, on inquiry, that the cook,
whose duty it was to open the door in the morning,
had become exasperated by his repeated visits, and had
been accustomed to utter these words when she heard
him at the door.

There was an old factotum in our family who used to
sew for us, and who occasionally spent several weeks at
a time at the house. She was somewhat of a character, had been married three times, and to distinguish
her second dear departed, was in the habit of calling
him " my middle husband." The old woman was very
deaf, and much shouting was needed to make her hear.
One day many vain efforts were made to induce her to
do a piece of work in a particular way, but she could
not or would not see what was wanted, and at last in
despair the lady of the house remarked to the nurse,

" Oh, never mind ; when she is gone, it must be altered."
" Ah," remarked the parrot, in a loud clear voice,
" there's no fool like an old fool."

This bird lived with us for about thirteen years, and
his death was caused by a cold. He had accompanied
us for a summer holiday to a cottage in Surrey, and
one day was unwisely hung up in a draught between a
door and a window. The cold ended in inflammation
of the lungs, and after lingering for nearly a week, he
died ; his last words — addressed to his mistress —
were, " Kiss me, Emily." Much grief, I need hardly
say, was felt for his loss : he was carried to his grave
wrapped in a little flannel gown, and carefully buried
under an evergreen at the end of the lawn.

Another bird had belonged to my grandmother, and
after her death spent the last two or three years of his
life with us. The habit, so noticeable in birds of every
description, of remarking the flight of time, was in this
one very remarkable. At six o'clock in the evening, as
soon as the clock struck, his usual habit was to exclaim,
" Put me to bed ; " and if no notice was taken of his
request, he uttered unpleasant screams, and on being
told to be quiet, would reply, " Why don't you put me
to bed ? " The cover having been placed over his cage,
he would immediately exclaim, " Now put little Dicky
to bed." " Little Dicky " was a canary who lived in a
cage which hung above his own. On one occasion, when
placed one summer's day at the open window of his
home, he much offended an old lady who was passing,
by calling out loudly, " Who are you, you old guy ? "
She knocked at the door and scolded the servant, in-
sisting that some one had deliberately insulted her.

The parrot had one morning been given a bath — or, in other words, the garden watering-can had been turned upon him — and was placed in front of the fire to dry.

There were two small kittens who also liked the warmth of the fire, and who were sitting one on each side of the cage. The bird walked first to one side, and looking down out of the corner of his eye, inquired, " Are you a good boy ? "   Then he sidled across to the other end of his perch and said to the other kitten, " And are you a good boy ? "

One day two children of our family visited the house, and when alone amused themselves by mischievously pulling up some tulips, which grew in a pot in the room, by the roots, afterwards carefully replacing them. A little later, Polly's master, to whom the plants belonged, came into the room, and immediately exclaimed, " Oh, look at my tulips ; see how they are growing."   Polly at once uttered two words, and only two — the reader will forgive their rudeness, they were so much to the point ; they were, " You ass ! "   I need hardly say that some time elapsed before the owner of the tulips was

made acquainted with all the particulars of what had
happened.

Our next parrot, in spite of her eighteen years, has
no signs of age about her; she sings, dances, climbs,
and whistles with all the vigor of youth. She is shy
in the presence of strangers, before whom she will very
rarely talk at all; and is more curious in her habits,
taking great fancies to some people, and decided dis-
likes to others. She has an unpleasant habit of sometimes wishing visitors good-by when she does not ap-
prove of them. She also, if she cannot get what she
wants, gives angry whacks and double knocks upon
the tin floor of her cage. Nothing appears to delight
her more than mischief. She positively revels in it,
and to get hold of anything she ought not to have is
unmixed joy. Evidently the bird has been at some
time very cruelly treated: for many months she was
terrified at the sight of a man or a boy, and for years a
broomstick was an object of horror to her. Since getting over this fear she has shown a decided liking for
the sweep and the coalman, and the latter has left the
house with the bird wishing him pleasantly good-by
and affectionately requesting him to kiss her, which
gives rise to the question whether she may have had,
in her African past, a kind negro friend. Any one who
has ever had opportunities of studying the parrot tribe
must have been struck with their extraordinary gift of
memory, so long ago observed by Plutarch.

It is very curious to observe the peculiar way in which
these birds learn their lessons. When a fresh word is
being acquired, at first (though not always) the word is
miscalled, and the parrot will constantly repeat it, just

like a child practising a lesson, becoming perfect by
degrees. Then when quite mastered, the word is put
away, as it were, at the back of its memory, to be
brought forward when required, two or three years
sometimes elapsing before the occasion arises. Some
easy words it is found quite useless to endeavor to
teach the bird; for instance, for years the words
" Thank you " have been said to her when giving her
food, but she never has once uttered them on receiving
it. On one occasion, though, on seeing some delicacy
being given to the cat, she remarked, in a reproving
voice, " Thank you." Good-morning and good-night
are constantly said at the proper times, but a heavy
London fog perplexes her; she hesitates which to say,
sometimes ending the matter on a dark morning by remarking, " Good-night."

Cats have always been a great attraction to her.
One fine fellow, who was a great favorite, by name
" Thomas," she called beautifully, occasionally slightly
altering his name to " Tom Ass." He has been in
his grave eleven years (and here again the curious
power of memory appears at intervals); " Tommy,
Thomas," and " Poor old Tom," as tenderly called,
often in the fond tone of those who grieve for the dear
departed.

A young kitten succeeded Thomas, by name Peter.
In early youth he distinguished himself by various
tricks, always to his cost, such as walking on the top
of the cage when the cover was off, and getting his
paws nipped in consequence. One very weak moment
he ventured to sit down on the top, dangling his fine
tail within the bars. Polly, of course, seized a firm

hold of it, with the disastrous consequence that bird, cat, and cage all fell down to the ground together.

Another time, when on the table, the cage was seen to move about five inches, the bird having secured a firm grip of Peter's tail while clinging tight to the perch. Years have, however, in a degree brought wisdom to Peter, who is able to measure his distance within half an inch. Still, in spite of this harsh treatment, the cat appears really attached to the parrot, guarding her from strangers of his own family on summer days, when they are both basking in the sun in their London garden. This is more than ordinary kindness, for when the cat steals, a warning cry of " Peter! " attracts attention; and once, on puss jumping on to the kitchen table, Polly immediately exclaimed, " Peter you are stealing."

One peculiarity of the bird is the power of distinguishing each member of the family individually, calling them by their respective names, and this, whether or not she is covered over, or is in the dark. Having lived within the sound of " Big Ben " for several years, the parrot is fond of copying him. This she does mostly late in the evenings, when the traffic in the streets is quietest. She booms the note quite correctly, occasionally in the interval between the chimes and the first stroke of the great bell, insinuating perhaps the not unfair idea that " Big Ben " might hurry up.

Parrots are born whittlers; the tearing up of soft wood is to them a great delight. Perhaps exercise keeps them in health. " Give the bird something to do," the attendant at the Zoölogical Gardens wisely advised, and very excellent advice it was. The bird will often demolish a large stick of firewood in one day, but objects strongly to any person seeing the performance. Unless quite alone in the room, she insists on being secluded from view by her cover, and if any one lifts it up to see what is going on, she directly leaves off work, raises her feathers like a turkey cock, and sometimes has demanded in an angry voice, " What do you want?" The sticks which she is destroying are always cleverly placed between the bars, sometimes upright, so as to get a purchase upon them.

The bird is fond of counting, but cannot go beyond seven. Often when cribbage is being played, she joins in with her figures. Laughing, too, appears to give her much pleasure. Unlike the other two birds, this one has always been allowed to come out at feeding hours, and spends some time at the top of the cage, where she flaps her wings, and then usually descends and takes a promenade to see what mischief she can find to do, finally going in when the food is ready for her. If kept waiting longer than she thinks right, she will call her attendant by name, saying, " Come along, here, here." A favorite remark of hers is, " It is all the same," spoken in a reassuring voice. Once when a gentleman was fussing and fuming about some business, she aptly answered, " Don't bother yourself about it." Also another day she observed, " You must prove that."

Here is a curious story of a parrot which became foster-mother to kittens. At Northrepps Hall, near Cromer, the seat of the late Sir Fowell Buxton, a large colony of parrots and macaws had been established, for whom a home had been provided near the house in a

large open aviary, with hutches for them to lay in.
But the birds as a rule preferred the woods, at any rate
during the summer, only coming home at feeding-time,
when, on the well-known tinkling of the spoon on
the tin containing their food, a large covey of gayly
plumaged birds came fluttering down to the feeding-
place, presenting a sight not often to be seen in
England.   The hutches being then practically deserted,
a cat found one of them a convenient place to kitten
in.   While the mother-cat was away foraging, one of
the female parrots paid a chance visit to the place, and
finding the young kittens in her nest, at once adopted
them as her own, and was found by Lady Buxton's man
covering her strange adopted children with her wings.

A PHOTOGRAPHER'S PARROT

(FROM FOUR HUNDRED ANIMAL STORIES.)

BY ROBERT COCHRANE.

I BECAME acquainted with Mr. Truefitt in the summer of 1873, and having occasion to visit him one Saturday afternoon, was invited to drink tea with the family. The only other stranger present was a Mr. Peters, who, like myself, had called on business. He was telling a very wonderful story, which awakened my incredulity, and I happened to express it. There was silence for a moment; and then a voice—I hear it yet—quiet, grave, solemn, but intensely satirical, uttered these memorable words: "MY CONSCIENCE!" I turned round, and found, to my astonishment, that the speaker who had so suddenly and unexpectedly introduced himself was a parrot, which, after having thus expressed itself, sat on the lower bar of its cage, with its head on one side, looking straight across the table at Mr. Peters. "Wonderful!" I ejaculated. Mr. Peters trembled, but could not keep his eyes from the parrot. "Eh, you rascal,"

said Poll; "go to the kitchen. You're a Fenian. That's
what I say." And having thus delivered itself, it
sprang into its ring, and shouted at the pitch of its
voice, "Ring the bell, ring the bell." Mr. Peters
became pale, rose to his feet, called for his hat and
umbrella, and finally said "good-by," and took his
departure.

As the reader may suppose, I was at once an admirer
of Poll. I had heard parrots in a cracked voice
endeavor to say "Pretty Poll;" but what other parrots
had attempted this parrot had achieved, and having
been assured that what he had said was nothing to
what he could say, I was determined to interview him.
This determination I immediately made known to Mr.
Truefitt, who there and then invited me to spend the
following Monday with him, and intimated that, as he
and his mother and sister expected to be engaged
during the day, I should have the bird pretty much
to myself.

According to appointment, I went early, and was
ushered into the dining-room by the servant. Breakfast
was set, but, with the exception of Mrs. Truefitt, no one
had come down-stairs. Poll was in his usual place, and
appeared to be very much excited. I got out my pocket-
book and pencil, to be ready. "We'll take our seats at
the table," said Mrs. Truefitt; and we had no sooner
done so, than Poll perched on one of the bars which ran
across his cage, and looking towards the door of the
room, shouted in a sound, clear, distinct voice, "Peter,
come to breakfast. Polly wants his breakfast. Quick,
you rascal." It being summer-time, there was no coal
in the grate, but lifting the poker, Mrs. Truefitt made a

feint of stirring the fire, when the parrot, in a most pathetic voice, said, "Is it very cold?" When Mr. Truefitt entered the room, Poll more than surprised me by bowing most gracefully, and saying, "Good-morning, Mr. Truefitt; I hope you are well." But when the auntie of the family appeared, the joy of the bird was unbounded. "Auntie," he said, "*comment vous portez-vous?* What news in the *Scotsman* this morning? Come and kiss me, auntie. Come and kiss me, darling. Kiss me, then. Oh, kiss me." This was uttered in a most affectionate voice. I felt astounded, and could scarcely believe my own eyes and ears. Nor would he cease repeating the latter sentence until the auntie approached him and wished him good-morning. What surprised me most was the appropriateness of the bird's words to the circumstances. Of course, this was the result of training; but how could a bird, not possessed of a reasoning faculty, be trained to know, not only *how* to articulate certain words, but *when* to articulate them? This was the question which puzzled me. For example, when the cups were being filled, he looked gravely down to the table and asked, "Are ye wantin' yer tea?" and when we began to eat, he imitated the smacking of lips, and asked, "Is it nice? Is it good — very good?" And after he had partaken of some dainty which Mrs. Truefitt gave him, he again imitated the smacking of lips, and pronounced it "Good, good, nice, nice, very nice." The fact of this appropriateness says much for Mrs. Truefitt, his sole and exclusive teacher; but I confess that I have always felt a difficulty about it.

We had salmon for breakfast, and some one having

asked if it was good, Poll said, "Fine, fine; taste it, taste it;" and again imitated the smacking of lips, as if he were tasting it himself. During the half-hour or so we sat at breakfast he seemed to know that I was there to hear him and report; at least — which is not a usual thing with him so early in the day — he kept dancing about the cage, and firing off such sentences as the following: "Mamma, Polly is going to school. Mamma, he's going to college to learn to be a doctor. Yes, my pretty bird — yes." Here he would pause a little, and then start another theme. Sometimes he shouted like a mariner, "What ship? What ship, ahoy? Mate, there's a man overboard, of the royal navy." This last sentence he articulated most admirably. Then he was a baronet, and a candidate for the suffrages of a constituency. "Vote," he cried, "for Sir Polly Truefitt. I am a member. Major Polly Truefitt of the British army." And that he was interested in passing events was evident from the fact that he asked Mr. Truefitt the following question: "Peter, have you seen the great Shah?" Then, as if he wished me to understand that he was not altogether ignorant of literature, he quoted, "Come on, Macduff, and *coward* be he who first cries hold enough!" "A horse, a horse, my kingdom for a horse!" "Richard is himself again."

He repeated several other quotations, which I neglected to take down, but I remember that at the close he very emphatically, and with a dash of pride, pronounced the author's name — "Shakespeare," and shook his head, as much as to say that he knew what he was about. After a little silence he said in a *waesome* manner, "Poor papa, poor papa; he is up among the little stars." This he had picked up after the death of the late Mr. Truefitt, who was very fond of him. He repeated this several times; and then, naming a terrier that once belonged to the family, he said mournfully, "Poor Blucher, poor Blucher! Blucher is dead." Then sharply, "But Blucher was only a dog;" and very proudly, "But Polly is a good, good, good little boy. Ah, Jock" — this to the new dog — "you are a bad boy. Go to the kitchen, sir. You are a bad boy; yes, yes."

After breakfast I was left alone with the parrot, but not long. An old gentleman called to see Mr. Truefitt in his studio. He had a boy with him about eight years of age, who was put into the dining-room to wait until the old gentleman came downstairs. The boy sat down on the seat nearest the door, directly opposite Poll's cage. A few moments of silence occurred, and then Poll,

pulling himself up, addressed the little stranger thus: "John, attend to your master. John, fetch me a cigar. John, a glass of beer with the chill off. John, put the horses to the carriage; Polly wants a drive in the gardens with Lady Polly. John, brush my coat; quick, you rascal." At the conclusion of this speech, which was delivered with an air of authority, the poor little fellow, whose name happened to be John, was nearly frightened out of his wits, and leaving the room he disappeared up-stairs screaming, " Grandpa, the bird in the room has been speaking to me."

When the old gentleman came down, he would see this wonderful bird; and he had no sooner made his appearance in the dining-room, than Poll very sharply asked, " What's your name, sir?" The old gentleman literally sank into a chair. " My name," continued the parrot, answering his own question — " my name is pretty Polly Truefitt, seventy-two Princess Street" (the number of a previous house). " I'm a volunteer; Captain Polly Truefitt, first Highland company. What corps are you?" Then putting himself into the attitude of a drill-sergeant, he unburdened himself in the following manner: " Attention. Dress. Eyes front, Shoulder arms" (the reader will excuse Polly's order). " Fix bayonets. Rear rank, take open order; right about face; quick, march. *Hooray*, Hurrah for the Prince of Wales! Sergeant-major, right wheel. Make ready, make ready — present — fire." He then continued for some time shouting " toot-oot-oot," etc., in imitation of the firing of rifles.

The old gentleman was thunderstruck, and no wonder — for Poll's pronunciation while delivering himself of these words of drill, the inflection of his voice, and entire attitude are so perfect, that a captain of volunteers told me that the first time he heard him at it he was waiting for Mr. Truefitt in the adjoining drawing-room, and could scarcely believe, even after the truth was made known to him, but that Mr. Truefitt, being a volunteer, had engaged a drill-instructor to post him up for the evening. "Indeed," he added, "I never heard a drill-sergeant whose articulation was to be compared to that of the parrot." After this effort, as if conscious of having done a good morning's work, Poll wished us "good-by," and leaping into his ring, said no more until the one o'clock gun, which is fired from the castle, went off; when, rousing himself up, he made the room ring by crying, "One o'clock, on o'clock; Polly wants his dinner. Jeannie, lay the cloth Polly wants his dinner, with a glass of sherry;" and ceased not until the cloth was laid and the dinner set.

In the evening four ladies were present, and among them a clergyman's wife, who was more than delighted with Poll's singing. As if certain that he would be desired to sing, he made the following request to himself: "Poll," he said, "sing a pretty song to the ladies;" then coughing, like a nervous young lady about to entertain a party, he sang the following verses, giving to each its appropriate tune:

> O dear, what can the matter be?
> Jocky stays long at the fair.
> He promised to buy me a bunch of blue ribbons
> To tie up my bonnie brown hair.
>
> For Poll's a jolly good fellow,
> Poll's a jolly good fellow,
> Poll's a jolly good fellow,
> Which nobody can deny.
>
> Down among the coals,
> Down among the coals,
> Polly is a clever chap,
> Down among the coals.

I wish I was a swell,
A-roving down Pall-Mall,
Upon the street to spread my feet,
I wish I were a swell.
Don't I, rather!

He sang other verses during the evening, such as
"Charlie is My Darling," but of course substituting
"Polly" for "Charlie;" "Up in a Balloon, Boys;"
"My Dear Boys, My Dear Boys, He is a Pal o' Mine;"
and "Champagne Charlie is My Name, up to Every
Little Game, My Boys;" and amused and delighted us
all by dancing to one or two of his tunes. His singing
of "Poll's a Jolly Good Fellow," was inimitable; but
when asked to repeat it by the clergyman's wife, he
very sharply told her to "go to the kitchen." That
he objected to being encored was evident, so we allowed
him to sing, dance, speak, laugh, or be silent just as
he pleased. Polly is a capital laugher. He bends and
unbends, and does it so heartily that it is difficult to
believe that he is not consciously amused. Then he
cries too, most mournfully, and generally indulges in
it when he hears any one speaking in piteous tones.

When the company had dispersed on the evening in
question, he looked as if aware that he had shown
himself off to some advantage, and, indeed, went the
length of saying, "Poll is a very pretty bird. He's
a good little boy." When drawing near to the later
hours, he interrupted an interesting conversation by
saying, "Are you not going to your beddies? Polly is
going to his beddie. Yes. Good-night, good-night."
He then leapt into his ring, and retired for the night,
evidently highly satisfied with the day's performance.

The last time I saw him, he distinctly pronounced my name, after hearing it a few times. He then wished the Duke of Edinburgh much joy, and informed me that he was proud to have the honor of the acquaintance of the Prince of Wales. Indeed, he seems to be extremely fond of Edward VII., and an anecdote illustrative of this trait in his character may very appropriately conclude this paper. When His Royal Highness, accompanied by his beautiful princess, was in Edinburgh laying the foundation stone of the new Infirmary, the royal procession passed along Princess Street, and halted for a few minutes opposite Mr. Truefitt's window, which was open for the occasion. A maiden lady of democratic principles was heard to say very ostentatiously that the people of Edinburgh were very foolish in making such an ado about two common mortals like themselves. Some one very politely told her to hold her tongue; but she would not be put down, until Poll, who was brought to the open window, fairly silenced her by shouting until the procession moved on, " Hurrah for the Prince of Wales ! "

MY PET STARLING

(From Four Hundred Animal Stories.)

By ROBERT COCHRANE.

THE rearing of a nest of star-lings is always a very difficult task, and I found it peculiarly so. In fact one young starling would require half-a-dozen ser-vants at least to attend it. I was not master of those star-lings, not a bit of it; they were masters of me. I had to get out of bed and stuff them with grub at three o'clock every morning. They lived in a band-box in a closet off my bedroom. I had to get up again at four o'clock to feed them, again at five, and again at six; in fact I saw more sunrises during the infancy of that nest of starlings than ever I did before or since. By day, and all day long, I stuffed them, and at intervals the servant relieved me of that duty. In fact it was pretty nearly all stuffing; but even then they were not satis-fied, and made several ineffectual attempts to swallow my finger as well. At length — and how happy I felt! — they could both feed themselves and fly. This last accomplishment was anything but agreeable to me, for no sooner did I open their door than out they would all fly, one after the other, and seat themselves on my head and shoulders, each one trying to make more noise than all the rest and outdo his brothers.

I got so tired of this sort of thing at last, that one day I determined to set them all at liberty. I accordingly hung their cage outside the window and opened their door, and they all flew, but back they came into the room again, and settled on me as usual. "Then," said I, "I'm going gardening." By the way they clung to me it was evident their answer was, "And so are we." And so they did. And as soon as I commenced operations with the spade, they commenced operations too, by searching for and eating every worm I turned up, evidently thinking I was merely working for their benefit and pleasure. I got tired of this. "Oh bother you all!" I cried; "I'm sick of you!" I threw down my spade in disgust; and before they could divine my intention, I had leaped the fence and disappeared in the plantation beyond.

"Now," said I to myself as I entered the garden that evening after my return, and could see no signs of starlings, "I'm rid of you plagues at last;" and I smiled with satisfaction. It was short-lived, for just at that moment, "Skraigh, skraigh, skraigh" sounded from the trees adjoining; and before I could turn foot, my tormentors, seemingly mad with joy, were all sitting on me as usual. Two of them died about a week after this; and the others, being cock and hen, I resolved to keep.

Both Dick and his wife soon grew to be fine birds.

I procured them a large roomy cage, with plenty of sand and a layer of straw in the bottom of it, a dish or two, a bath, a drinking-fountain, and always a supply of fresh green weeds on the roof of their domicile. Besides their usual food of soaked bread, etc., they had slugs occasionally, and flies, and earth-worms. Once a day the cage-door was thrown open, and out they both would fly with joyful "skraigh" to enjoy the luxury of a bath on the kitchen floor. One would have imagined that being only two, they would not have stood on the order of their going; but they did, at least Dick did, for he insisted upon using the bath first, and his wife had to wait patiently until his lordship had finished. This was part of Dick's domestic discipline. When they were both thoroughly wet and draggled, and everything within a radius of two yards was in the same condition, their next move was to hop on to the fender, and flutter and gaze pensively into the fire; and two more melancholy looking, ragged wretches you never saw. When they began to dry, then they began to dress; and in a few minutes Richard was himself again, and so was his wife.

Starlings have their own natural song, and a strange noise they make too. Their great faculty, however, is the gift of imitation, which they have in a wonderful degree of perfection. The first thing that Dick learned to imitate was the rumbling of carts and carriages on the street, and very proud he was of the accomplishment. Then he learned to pronounce his own name, with the prefix "Pretty," which he never omitted, and to which he was justly entitled. Except when sitting on their perch singing or piping, these two little pets were never tired of engineering about their cage, and everything was minutely examined. They were perfect adepts at boring holes; by inserting the bill closed, and opening it like a pair of scissors, lo! the thing was done. Dick's rule of conduct was that he himself should have the first of everything, and be allowed to examine first into everything, to have the highest perch and all the tidbits; in a word to rule, king and priest, in his own cage. I don't suppose he hated his wife, but he kept her in a state of inglorious subjection to his royal will and pleasure. "Hezekiah" was the name he gave his wife; I don't know why, but I am sure no one taught him this, for he first used the name himself, and then it was only to correct his pronunciation.

Sometimes Dick would sit himself down to sing a song; and presently his wife would join in with a few simple notes of melody; upon which Dick would stop singing instantly, and look round at her with indignation. "Hezekiah! Hezekiah!!" he would say; which being interpreted, clearly meant: "Hezekiah, my dear, how can you so far forget yourself as to presume to interrupt your lord and master with that cracked and quavering voice of yours!" Then he would commence anew; and Hezekiah, being so good-natured, would soon forget her scolding and again join in. This was too much for Dick's temper; and Hezekiah was accordingly chased round and round the cage and soundly thrashed. His conduct altogether as a husband, I am sorry to say, was very far from satisfactory. I have said he always retained the highest perch for himself; but sometimes he would turn one eye downwards, and seeing Hezekiah sitting so cosily and contentedly on her humble perch, would at once conclude that her seat was more comfortable than his; so down he would hop and send her off at once.

It was Dick's orders that Hezekiah should only eat at meal-times; that meant at all times when he chose to feed, *after he was done.* But I suppose his poor wife was often a little hungry in the interim, for she would watch till she got Dick fairly into the middle of a song, and quite oblivious of surrounding circumstances, then she would hop down and snatch a meal on the sly. But dire was the punishment for the deceit if Dick found her out. Sometimes I think she used to long for a little love and affection, and at such times she would  jump up on the perch beside her husband, and with a fond cry sidle close to him.

"Hezekiah! Hezekiah!" he would exclaim; and if she didn't take that hint, she was soon knocked to the bottom of the cage. In fact Dick was a domestic tyrant, but in all other respects a dear affectionate little pet.

One morning Dick got out of his cage by undoing the fastening, and flew through the open window, determined to see what the world was like, leaving Hezekiah to mourn. It was before five on a summer's morning that he escaped; and I saw no more of him until, coming out of church that day, the people were greatly astonished to see a bird fly down from the steeple and alight upon my shoulder. He retained his perch all the way home. He got so well up to opening the fastening of his cage-door that I had to get a small spring padlock, which defied him, although he studied it for months, and finally gave it up, as being one of those things which no fellow could understand.

Dick soon began to talk, and before long had quite a large vocabulary of words, which he was never tired of using. As he grew very tame, he was allowed to live either out of his cage or in it all day long as he pleased. Often he would be out in the garden all alone for hours together, running about catching flies, or sitting up in a tree repeating his lessons to himself, both verbal and musical. The cat and her kittens were his especial favorites, although he used to play with the dogs as well, and often go to sleep on their backs. He took his lessons with great regularity, was an arduous student, and soon learned to pipe "Duncan Gray" and "The Sprig of Shillelah," without a single wrong note. I used to whistle these tunes over to him, and it was quite amusing to mark his air of rapt attention as he crouched down to listen. When I had finished he did not at once begin to try the tune himself, but sat quiet and still for some time, evidently thinking it over in his own mind. In piping it, if he forgot a part of the air, he would cry, "Doctor, doctor!" and repeat the last note once or twice, as much as to say, "What comes after that?" and I would finish the tune for him.

"Tse! tse! tse!" was a favorite exclamation of his,

indicative of surprise. When I played a tune on the fiddle to him, he would crouch down with breathless attention. Sometimes when he saw me take up the fiddle, he would go at once and peck at Hezekiah. I don't know why he did so, unless to ensure her keeping quiet. As soon as I had finished he would say, "Bravo!" with three distinct intonations of the word, thus: "Brāvo! doctor; br-r-ravo! brăvo!"

Dick was extremely inquisitive and must see into everything. He used to annoy the cat very much by opening out her toes, or even her nostrils, to examine; and at times pussy used to lose patience, and pat him on the back.

"Eh?" he would say. "What is it? You rascal!" If two people were talking together underneath his cage, he would cock his head, lengthen his neck, and looking down quizzingly, say, "Eh? *What* is it? *What* do you say?"

He frequently began a sentence with the verb "Is," putting great emphasis on it. "Is?" he would say musingly.

"Is what, Dick?" I would ask.

"Is," he would repeat — "Is the darling starling a pretty pet?"

"No question about it," I would answer.

He certainly made the best of his vocabulary, for he trotted out all his nouns and all his adjectives time about in pairs, and formed a hundred curious combinations.

"*Is*," he asked one day, "the darling doctor a rascal?"

"Just as you think," I replied.

"Tse! tse! tse! Whew! whew! whew!" said
Dick; and finished off with "Duncan Gray" and the
first half of the "Sprig of Shillelah."

"Love is the soul of a nate Irishman," he had been
taught to say; but it was as frequently, "Love is the
soul of a nate Irish starling," or, "Is love the soul of a
darling pretty Dick?" and so on.

One curious thing is worth noting: he never pronounced my dog's name — Theodore Nero — once while
awake; but he often startled us at night by calling the
dog in clear ringing tones — talking in his sleep. He
used to be chattering and singing without intermission
all day long; and if ever he was silent then I knew he
was doing mischief; and if I went quietly into the kitchen, I was sure to find him either tracing patterns on a
bar of soap, or examining and tearing to pieces a parcel
of newly arrived groceries. He was very fond of wine
and spirits, but knew when he had enough. He was
not permitted to come into the parlor without his cage;
but sometimes at dinner, if the door were left ajar, he
would silently enter like a little thief; when once fairly
in, he would fly on to the table, scream, and defy me.
He was very fond of a pretty child that used to come
to see me. If Matty was lying on the sofa reading,
Dick would come and sing on her head; then he would
go through all the motions of washing and bathing on
Matty's bonnie hair; which was, I thought, paying her
a very pretty compliment.

When the sun shone in at my study window, I used
to hang Dick's cage there, as a treat to him. Dick
would remain quiet for perhaps twenty minutes, then
the stillness would feel irksome to him, and presently

he would stretch his head down towards me in a confidential sort of way, and begin to pester me with his silly questions.

"Doctor," he would commence, "*is* it, *is* it a nate Irish pet?"

"Silence, and go asleep," I would make answer. "I want to write."

"Eh?" he would say. "*What* is it? *What* d'ye say?"

Then, if I didn't answer:

"*Is* it sugar — snails — sugar, snails, and brandy?" Then, "Doctor, doctor!"

"Well, Dickie, what is it now?" I would answer.

"Doctor — whew." That meant I was to whistle to him.

"Sha'n't," I would say sulkily.

"Tse! tse! tse!" Dickie would say, and continue, "Doctor, will you go a-clinking?" I never could resist that. Going a-clinking meant going fly-hawking. Dick always called a fly a clink; and this invitation I would receive a dozen times a day, and seldom refused. I would open the cage-door, and Dick would perch himself on my finger, and I would carry him round the room, holding him up to the flies on the picture-frames. And he never missed one.

Once Dick fell into a bucket of water, and called lustily for the "doctor"; and I was only just in time to save him from a watery grave. When I got him out, he did not speak a word until he had gone to the fire and opened his wings and feathers out to dry, then he said, "Bravo! B-*r*-ravo!" several times, and went forthwith and attacked Hezekiah.

Dick had a little travelling cage, for he often had to go with me by train; and no sooner did the train start than Dick used to commence to talk and whistle, very much to the astonishment of the passengers, for the bird was up in the umbrella rack. Everybody was at once made aware of both my profession and character, for the jolting of the carriage not pleasing him, he used always to prelude his performance with, "Doctor, doctor, you *r-r*-rascal. What *is* it, eh?" As Dick got older, I am sorry, as his biographer, to be compelled to say he grew more and more unkind to his wife — attacked her regularly every morning and the last thing at night, and half-starved her besides. Poor Hezekiah! She could do nothing in the world to please him. Sometimes, now, she used to peck him back again; she was driven to it. I was sorry for Hezekiah, and determined to play pretty Dick a little trick. So one day when he had been bullying her worse than ever, I took Hezekiah out of the cage, and fastened a small pin to her bill, so as to protrude just a very little way, and returned her. Dick walked up to her at once. "What," he wanted to know, "did she mean by going on shore without leave?" Hezekiah didn't answer, and accordingly received a dig in the back, then another, then a third; and then Hezekiah turned and let him have one sharp attack. It was very amusing to see how Dick jumped, and his look of astonishment as he said, "Eh? *What* d'ye say? Hezekiah! Hezekiah!"

Hezekiah followed up her advantage. It was quite a new sensation for her to have the upper hand, and so she courageously chased him round and round the cage, until I opened the door and let Dick out.

But Hezekiah could not live always with a pin tied to her bill; so, for peace-sake, I gave her away to a friend, and Dick was left alone in his glory.

Poor Dickie! One day he was shelling peas to himself in the garden, when some boys startled him, and he flew away. I suppose he lost himself, and couldn't find his way back. At all events I only saw him once again. I was going down through an avenue of trees about a mile from the house, when a voice above in a tree hailed me: " Doctor! doctor! What *is* it?" That was Dick; but a crow flew past and scared him again, and away he flew — forever.

TALES OF INSTINCT AND REASON

By Lady Julia Lockwood.

Rescued by a Dog.

I N one of the valleys or glens that intersect the Grampian Hills, there lived a shepherd, whose occupation it was to make daily excursions to the different extremities of his pastures in succession, and to turn his flocks back home by the aid of his dog, if they had strayed too near a neighbor's boundaries.

In one of these excursions, the shepherd happened to carry his infant boy, about three years old, along with him, and, after traversing the pastures for some time, with the child in his arms, the shepherd desired to ascend a summit at some distance, to obtain a more extensive view of his range, and put the child down on the grass with a strict injunction not to stir from the spot till he returned to him.

Scarcely had he gained the summit, when the horizon was suddenly darkened by one of those impenetrable mists, which frequently rise so rapidly amongst those mountains, and turn day into night. The poor shepherd, alarmed, instantly hastened back to find his child, but, owing to the unusual darkness, and his own trepidation, he unfortunately missed his way in the descent, and after fruitless search of many hours amongst the dangerous morasses and cataracts with which these mountains abound, he was at length overtaken by night. Still wandering on without knowing whither, he at length came to the verge of the mist, and, by the light of the moon, discovered he had reached the bottom of the valley, and was within a short distance of his own cottage.

It being fruitless to renew the search that night, he entered his cottage, disconsolate, having lost both his child and his dog, his faithful companion for years: but, upon asking his wife, he found the dog had been home, had received his usual piece of cake, and had run off with it instantly.

For several days the shepherd renewed the search for his child, and had returned each evening disappointed, to his home, when his wife always declared to him the

dog had been home and fetched his cake, going off instantly with it in his mouth. Being struck with this singular circumstance, the shepherd remained at home one day, and when the dog came home for his piece of cake, and was departing with it in his mouth, the shepherd resolved to follow, which he did, and the dog, seeing his master follow him, slackened his pace, and led the way to a cataract, at some distance from the spot where the child had disappeared. The banks of the ravine, through which the cataract fell, almost joined at top, yawning over an abyss of immense depth.

Down went the dog, without hesitation, and soon disappeared into a cave, the mouth of which was almost on a level with the bottom of the torrent. The shepherd with difficulty followed, but on entering the cave, what were his emotions, when he beheld his child eating with great satisfaction the cake which the dog had brought to him, whilst the faithful creature stood by watching his young charge with the utmost complacence.

From the situation in which the infant was found, it was supposed that he had wandered to the brink of the precipice, and then scrambled down till he reached the cave, which the fear of the torrent prevented him quitting; and that the dog had traced him by his scent to the spot, and afterwards prevented him from starving by bringing him his own daily allowance of cake. It appeared he had never quitted the child day or night, except when necessary to fetch the food; and when absent on this duty, he ran with his utmost speed, never stopping till he reached his young charge again in safety.

A Sagacious Dog.

Mr. Lefevre possessed a plantation on the very verge of the valley towards the Blue Mountains. He possessed a family of eleven children, and he was greatly

alarmed one morning at missing the youngest, who
was about four years of age — he had disappeared
about ten o'clock.

His distressed parents and family sought after him
in the river, and in the fields, but to no purpose. Terrified to an extreme degree, they entreated their neighbors to assist them in the search. They traversed the
woods and beat them over with the most scrupulous
attention. Thousands of times they called the boy by
name, and were only answered by the echoes of the
wilds. They then assembled themselves at the foot of
the mountains of Chatagniers, without being able to
gain the least intelligence of the child.

After reposing themselves for some minutes, they
formed into different bands, and night coming on, the
parents in despair refused to return home, for their
fright was constantly increased by the knowledge they
had of the mountain cats, an animal so rapacious, that
the inhabitants cannot defend themselves against their
attack.

Then they thought of the wolves, or some other
dreadful animal, devouring their darling child. "Derick, my poor little Derick! where art thou?" frequently exclaimed the mother, in the most heart-rending
tones; but all was of no avail. As soon as daylight
appeared they renewed their search, but as unsuccess-
fully as on the preceding day.

Fortunately an Indian, laden with furs, coming from
an adjacent village, called at the house of Mr. Lefevre,
intending to repose himself there, as he usually did
when travelling through that part of the country. He
was very much surprised to find no one at home but

an old negress, kept to the house by her infirmities. "Where is my brother?" said the Indian. "Alas!" replied the negro woman, " he has lost his little Derick, and all the neighborhood are employed in looking after him in the wood; " it was then three o'clock in the afternoon. "Sound the horn," said the Indian, " and try and call the master home. I will find the child." The horn was sounded ; and as soon as the father returned, the Indian asked him for the shoes and stockings that little Derick had last worn. He then ordered his dog, which he had brought with him, to smell them, and then, taking the house for his centre, he described a circle of a quarter of a mile, ordering his dog to smell the earth wherever he led him. The circle was not completed, before the sagacious animal began to bark. This sound brought some feeble ray of hope to the disconsolate parents. The dog followed the scent, and barked again; the party pursued him with all their speed, but soon lost sight of him in the wood. Half an hour afterwards they heard him again, and soon saw him return. The countenance of the poor dog was visibly altered ; an air of joy seemed to animate him, and his gestures seemed to indicate that his search had not been in vain.

" I am sure he has found the child ! " exclaimed the Indian. But whether dead or alive was at present a cruel uncertainty. The Indian then followed the dog, which led him to the foot of a large tree, where lay the child in an enfeebled state, nearly approaching death.

He took it tenderly in his arms, and hastily carried it to the disconsolate parents. The joy of the father and mother was so great, that it was more than a quarter of an hour before they could express their gratitude to the kind Indian, or the dear sagacious dog. When their thanks were fully expressed, they regaled the Indian and his dog with a plentiful meal before they again set forth on their journey.

A Dog that Punished its Pups.

A small black terrier dog, Vic, and a cat were great friends. Vic was so gentle and kind that the cat never thought of her giving a bite or hurting her in any way. Once Vic had some puppies at the same time that the cat had a little family of kittens. The youngest girl, to whom the cat and kittens belonged, gave one of the kittens to a friend of hers, who lived at a house not very far from where her home was. Vic thought that the tiny kitten was much too young to be sent away from its mother, so she went every day to nurse and feed it herself till she thought the little kitten was old enough to take care of itself. The family Vic belonged to went to stay at a house three miles off, and left Vic and the servants behind. One day she heard them say that her young

master, of whom she was very fond, was coming home
from college that very day, so she jumped out of the
window, and ran off to the other house as fast as she
could go, and got there just in time to receive him as he
arrived at the door.

This clever little Vic often seemed to understand
what she heard, and would wag her tail, and look up
quickly if it was anything
about herself.

While Vic was quite a
small puppy,
she came to

live with her master's
brother and sister, who were
very little children, so they
and Vic grew up together, and I really think if Vic
could only have spoken, she would have said her lessons
often much better than they said theirs, she was such
a clever little dog.

When Vic had puppies she used to dig a deep hole
with her paws in a bank, and then carry in some straw
and make a nice comfortable bed quite at the end, and
put all her little puppies there, and she never let them
come out till they were able to walk, and take care of

themselves, unless the children Vic lived with dug them out before, to see what they were like ; and which they sometimes did, but that was a very great pity, as it was much better to leave them in their earthy nest till they were advanced enough in growth and strength to come out by themselves.

One of the puppies she had was naughty, and teased her very much, so she took it down close to some water, and began playing with it till she got it quite close to the edge of the bank, and then pushed it in, and walked quietly away to her home. I am very much afraid that Vic intended to drown her poor little puppy, and, if so, it was very wrong and unnatural in her; but luckily a gentleman who was standing by a tree not far off saw her wicked act, and went and pulled the poor little puppy out of the water ; though it might have deserved some punishment.

Some Monkey Tricks.

The wonderful arrangements monkeys make when intent upon any of those mischievous tricks which appear to give them more pleasure than anything else they can do, are well authenticated, and frequently witnessed by officers who have been stationed at the Cape of Good Hope, as well as by British residents who have resided there, and been possessed of farms and vineyards.

An engineer officer told me that when the large monkeys had laid their plans together for robbing a vineyard, they collected in great numbers in the neighborhood, and appeared to appoint a leader, or commander-in-chief of their expedition, who made all the necessary arrangements, and gave to each of his chosen friends their orders.

They sent on their spies to see if there were any persons watching the delicious grapes they were coveting ; and if they were pretty sure of safety, they approached the place, carefully posting regular sentinels on every height to keep a lookout for danger, and give intimation of the approach of any one who might injure them.

When this was done, and every precaution taken, the leader and the band of long-tailed brothers made a descent on the coveted grapes, eating as much of the fruit as they could, and then carrying off for the sentries, and for their little ones at home, as large a booty as circumstances permitted.

Should it happen that any early traveller or the owner of the land came near, by whichever way he approached, one watcher instantly gave the alarm, which quickly spread from outpost to outpost, and was communicated to the grand army, who fled to their forest homes, on the tops of high trees, with as much speed as possible.

Monkeys have wondrous powers of climbing, and also of hanging from the branches of trees by their long and supple tails, which give them, in fact, five legs, as they can support themselves by the tail, and use their fore and hind legs for other purposes. The fore feet nearly resemble the human hand, and they are as clever in using them as men are. One of the most singular instances of intelligence recorded of monkeys is the manner in which they have been observed to cross a stream. They go along the banks till they find two trees exactly opposite each other, one on either bank of the river. They then climb one of the highest and strongest branches, when the leader tells the nearest monkey to him to catch hold of his tail, and then, dropping himself off, hangs suspended by the tail. A third monkey now catches hold of the second monkey's tail, and so each monkey grasps the tail of his predecessor, and one by one they hang suspended from the tree till the legs of the first monkey touch the ground. They then put themselves in motion, swinging in larger and larger sections of a circle, till the foremost monkey succeeds in catching hold of a twig of the opposite tree.

In a moment he is firmly seated on a strong branch, and pulling away, he drags the monkey after him to the branch, and then, liberated from his hold jumps from branch to branch, and chatters to his brother apes as they hang from tree to tree, forming a catenarian curve which would excite the admiration of a Brunel or a Stephenson. The last monkey then lets go his hold of the first tree, and in a moment is oscillating fearfully across the stream, till at length the whole tribe find themselves safely landed on the opposite side.

They appear to have a language of their own, and the chattering they keep up in their own colonies is very loud and continued. Indeed, the black people say monkeys could talk if they liked, but are afraid if they do so, man would make them work for him.

Some of the large species of monkeys are very fierce and dangerous, but the smaller ones are more gentle, though mischief is the great delight of all the race. They are great favorites with sailors, and if one is on board ship he is pretty sure of having many friends, even though his mischievous gambols annoy occasionally. A monkey kindly treated in a family can be made to do a great many little things, such as rocking the baby's cradle, or even assisting the maid to hang out the clothes to dry on a washing-day — as they are extremely imitative.

An Irish lady once told me that a large pet monkey they had at their place near Cork, who had seen the cook washing the potatoes and peeling them, and then putting them into the saucepan to boil, went to the kitchen one night, after all the servants had gone to bed, got out some potatoes, washed them, and prepared them, as he had seen his good friend the cook do; he then got some sticks, stirred up the embers of the fire, put on the pan with the potatoes, and left them there to boil, making, however, a considerable amount of dirt in his cooking endeavors, and much delighted with his own performance, which was evident by the signs and grimaces, and chattering which he kept up incessantly; but a part of his energy was of a less safe kind, for he drew up the large clothes-horse in front of the fire, and pulled out all of the articles he could find, hanging them up to dry, as he had frequently seen done when the bed-linen was aired by the housemaid, and thus might have set the house on fire.

There is a curious fact connected with monkeys at Gibraltar. At a certain season of the year great numbers of those creatures appear on the rocks, and as there are no colonies of them in Europe, and those particular ones abound in Africa, it was believed there must be subterranean passages under the Straits of Gibraltar known to the monkeys, by which they pass across — it is always amongst the rocks they make their appearance.

Some officers have had the boldness to be let down by ropes to a considerable depth, hoping to find out the existence of such a passage, but the authorities at Gibraltar forbid this rash attempt to be repeated, as it is attended with very considerable danger; so that all which at present is known regarding those pilgrim monkeys is, that they come and disappear at stated periods, but no one positively can say where is their real home.

The muscular strength of these creatures is very extraordinary, and the leaps they make from tree to tree, or rock to rock, enormous. They have great powers of memory, and remember acts of kindness surprisingly, but their appreciation of any injury is equally strong, and their memory so retentive, that they will revenge themselves on the unfortunate culprit long after he has forgotten the offence.

I recollect hearing a lady tell me of a large pet monkey she had, who was the terror of all her acquaintances, and one lady so much disliked the creature, that he was always banished from the room when she called. This lady frequently rode on horseback to see her friends, attended by her groom. On her visit one day, Jacko was, according to custom, ordered out of the way. It was a country place, with a long approach, and the entrance gate had stone pillars, but there was no lodge. On riding down to the gate, the monkey was observed sitting on one of the stone pillars; the groom rode on to open the gate for the lady to pass out, and just as she did so, the monkey jumped down on the back of her horse, and put his fore feet round the lady's waist, while the sudden accession of company frightened the horse, who set off full gallop, to the dismay of the terrified lady, and the faster the horse went, the tighter the monkey held on; they never stopped till they reached the lady's house; when the poor lady was so ill in consequence of her alarm and very hard ride, that she fainted, and Jacko's fate was sealed; he could not be tolerated any longer, and he was sent off to sea in one of the many ships which touched at the neighboring port. What became of him I know not, but when tricks and mischief such as this became amusement, he was too dangerous to be petted any more.

Sagacious Rats.

There are many well-attested facts of the sagacity of rats, one or two of which you might like to hear. I will mention one which happened in a large country house in Dumbartonshire, not very far from Loch Lomond.

The house was situated very near the water, consequently was infested with water-rats, and they had gained such ascendancy, and were in such vast numbers in the cellars, that they threatened serious injury to the foundations. It was therefore deemed advisable to endeavor to get rid of them by poison; and a quantity was laid in the cellars, to which no one had access but those who kept the keys, so there was no danger to the poor dogs or cats of the family; it is very unjustifiable, on any pretext, to lay poison in an exposed place, where either your own or your neighbors' domestic animals could be injured by it, and caused to die a painful and miserable death.

Morning after morning, when the poisoned messes were searched for — pieces of meat, etc., having been put in the traps — it was found that everything was cleared away. Good hopes, of course, were felt that the large quantities consumed must end in the destruction of the hordes of depredators; yet, no! they seemed as numerous and bold as ever; after a time the frightful smells from the cellar made this gentleman think many dead rats must be behind the casks and in the bins; men were procured, and examination made, when, what was their astonishment to discover that not one bit of the poisoned meat had been eaten, but that each night the rats had carried it away, and hidden it entirely.

To give an idea of their greediness, I may tell you of a gentleman (who inhabited the same part of Scotland, very many years ago, when the formidable idea of French invasion filled every one's mind with fear, and made people desire to secrete away as much as possible), who put up in leather bags a very large sum of money in guineas, which was placed in his cellar, the paving stones of which were taken up, and the bags of gold deposited under them.

Years passed, and the alarm disappeared also. When the old gentleman and his son went to his depository to disinter the hidden treasure, imagine their dismay when they found no traces either of bags or gold; and all their riches gone, which they looked forward to bringing again into use.

At first, it was feared some person must have got intimation of the large sum they had concealed, and had taken their own measures for carrying it off. They did not, however, give up their search, on account of their suspicions; but got proper people to bring picks and shovels, and a determined search was made; when, at length, they got a trace of who the real thieves were, by finding a loose guinea; after a time, another and another came to light, then a mass of gold, and they found themselves on the track of the evil-doers; and the fact was apparent. The rats, for the sake of the leathern bags, had undermined the place, and great numbers must have contributed their joint efforts to move such heavy weights; but they dragged the whole mass to a considerable distance, as a few scattered coins proved; they ate the leather, and the whole amount of money was traced out and found, with scarcely one piece missing. Now this fact proves that rats act in concert and by combination, and that they have immense muscular power.

I recollect a lady who lived in Queen Street, in Edinburgh, telling me of a curious sight she witnessed, which proves the extreme cleanliness of rats. One day after breakfast, I think on a Sunday, when the streets are unusually quiet, she was standing at her dining-room window, looking at the sublime view of the surrounding landscape, — the Grampians in the distance, the beautiful coasts of Fife and Stirlingshire, and the broad and silvery Frith of Forth glittering in the beams of a bright sun, when she was attracted by seeing a large rat come down her area wall, run along, and climb the opposite wall to the next house, followed by a considerable train of others — some dozens, she said. She wondered at the sight, but went away, and forgot it. Some days afterwards she was again doing the same thing, at about the same hour, and she saw the like train of long tails; they all followed their leader, and she watched for a long time. She was beginning to get tired, when, at length, the same procession re-appeared, down one area and up another. This second day's observation led her to close inquiry; her servant, who was set to watch them, followed them, unobserved, and it was discovered, that at an un-occupied house, a few doors off, there was a large reservoir of water in the yard, covered over, and this place the rats used regularly as their plunge and swimming bath, where they sported and amused themselves, cleaned all their coats thoroughly, and then returned to their respective homes; it was the observer of this curious fact who told me the story, so I believe it to be perfectly true.

A Dog with Two Homes.

A little Blenheim belonged to Mr. French, a London merchant, living in Cornhill, about the year 1800. His wife was very fond of animals, as they had no children. On a summer tour they visited Blenheim, and there purchased of the game-keeper one of the beautiful little  Blenheim spaniels, which became a great pet with both husband and wife, and for five years never was out of their sight, accompanying his mistress when she drove out, and following his master in his walks.

At the end of that time the dog was missing; every inquiry was made for it, the Bow Street officers applied to, and advertisements inserted in the papers, but in vain; nothing could be heard of it by any means, till about eighteen months afterwards, when suddenly it rushed in at the door, as the servant opened it to the milkman, and ran up to his mistress's room, but in a very dirty state, and covered with pitch and tar. It was, however, joyously received, and made much of, and wagged its tail, as if equally rejoiced to see its friends once more.

At the end of three months the dog again disappeared, and returned at the same interval, and thus it went on for about three or four years, without the Frenches being able to ascertain where the little Blenheim could possibly go.

At length the mystery was solved. Mr. French was walking in Hyde Park one day, accompanied by his little dog, when suddenly it ran up to a man with a weather-beaten face, skipping about, and seeming quite delighted to see him. Mr. French called him off, and when the newcomer claimed the dog as his property, an explanation followed.

It turned out that the gentleman was the captain of an East Indiaman, and the little dog had followed him on board at the very time the Frenches first missed him, sailed with him in the ship, and became a great favorite with himself and the whole ship's crew. When the ship returned to London, the captain fully intended to take the little dog to his country house, but suddenly missed him, and did not see him again till the day on which the ship sailed, and this happened each voyage; the captain therefore concluded that the dog must belong to one of the sailors, who probably took him home with him, but feared to claim him whilst at sea. The most astonishing part of the story is, how the dog could know when the ship was ready for sea.

About Bees.

Bees have great instinct, and learn, however strange it may seem, to know and be fond of those who are kind to them, in an incredibly short time. This may be proved by gently assisting such as require it; and remember, also, never to strike at them when they come near, for it naturally enough makes them angry to be so treated.

The queen bee lays her eggs at different times, according to the season; a swarm has been known in March, and also in August, but the usual time is May and June. The queen goes round the cells and lays her eggs, according as they are to be drones, workers, or queens. The egg is hatched into a grub in about four days, and the workers then feed it with a clear, colorless fluid; after a few days they are covered up, and in twenty-four days from laying they escape full-grown bees. A drone takes twenty-two days, and a queen eighteen.

Huber, the great naturalist, says, in his book upon bees, that if a stock has lost its queen in hatching time, and there are eggs or grubs not more than three days old at the time of the queen's death, they can take one, and, by giving it stronger food, bring it out a queen. A queen bee will lay two hundred eggs in a few hours, and in the year she will generally have laid twenty or thirty thousand.

When, owing to the continued increase of young bees, the hives are too full, and when one of the young

princesses is ready, a swarm ensues. Before swarming, the young princess may be heard calling to her
future subjects, and then the deep note of the queen
may be distinguished, forbidding her to come out yet,
for the queen is very bitter against her royal progeny,
and would kill them if she could (for that is the only
use she makes of her sting), were she not prevented by
the workers; for though the queen has immense
power, the government is decidedly a constitutional
monarchy. At length the permission is accorded, and
the colony starts.

When the swarm comes out, it consists of both old and
young bees, and, indeed, some say that the old queen
leads it, the young one taking the vacant throne. Care
should be taken to be near at swarming time, when
the indications of a far greater number of bees than
usual, and of their sometimes hanging out in a cluster,
are very observable. They should, as soon as settled,
be shaken into a hive rubbed with honey, with one
good shake, so as to be sure the queen is in, and then
set down, having the rim resting on a stone, to allow
the numbers of bees who are about to go in. The
future position should be a dry place, sheltered from
wind and rain, facing south, with, perhaps, an inclination to the east, if they could be protected from that
quarter during the easterly winds. The place should
be of an even temperature, and not too hot, as heat
greatly inconveniences the bees; indeed, a new swarm,
when in its hive, before it is set in its ultimate position,
should have a cloth round it, to shield it from the rays
of the sun if they are powerful, as the heat sometimes
causes them to rise and go off; but after they become

settled there is much less chance; and, even then, a
very hot sun greatly inconveniences the bees, and sometimes even melts the combs, and so destroys the hive.
If a new swarm do go off, follow them in the exact
direction of the wind, as they can fly in no other way.

The old straw hives answer the purpose, and are
both cheapest and simplest, but the cross sticks usually
seen in them are of no sort of use. The hives should
be near a small stream of water; a small pan or two

of water would do if they had stones in them for the
bees to rest on. I have heard it suggested that the
hives should be suspended, and if they were kept from
wind, it would be a good thing, as they might hang
from a dial-plate, and so the progress of the hive be
accurately weighed, and much useful information be
gained. Young swarms should be fed for the first few
days, whatever be the state of the honey-flowers. This
is done by lifting the hive, and putting the food inside.
At other seasons of the year, when the hives are full

of comb, it is done by taking out the bung at the top, and laying the honey there, and then covering it with a basin.

A full-sized bee weighs rather less than a grain and a half, and a pound has been calculated to contain about four thousand five hundred. Each bee will carry about half a grain of honey, and a strong swarm will make two pounds of honey in a day. They seldom fly more than half a mile, though, if it be a very fine day, and there be any sweet attraction, they will fly as far as two miles, being generally absent from five to fifteen minutes. They feed in the fields, and will not touch honey in summer, unless they are badly off for food. If the year be at all bad, they should be kept fed, and I have known the feeding go on till July in a very bad year. The drones are about three times the weight of the common bees; they are fed by the workers, and only come out for about a couple of hours in the middle of the day to take exercise, remaining at home the rest of their time to take care of the young bees. Wherever you see many drones you may be pretty sure that there are, or will be, plenty of young bees.

A bee lives about a year, and the births and deaths go on for the greater part of the year, though the great mass of young bees are brought to maturity in the spring, after which the drones, being of little or no use, are killed off by the workers. The queen very rarely goes out, but she does occasionally, for air, and she is attended by a body-guard of bees, large and strong, being picked men. They attend her with the greatest care, and serve also to communicate her wishes to the workers; they are, in fact, her household troops. It is also said that they may be seen commanding the other workers in the battles which sometimes occur.

Care should be taken not to disturb the hives, as it annoys the bees, and there is also a great chance of breaking the combs and smothering the bees beneath them. The bung at the top should, however, be occasionally taken off, to see whether any honey is made, for, if there be, it is sure to be near the top; if there be, and the honey season is plentiful, small combs, of the same shape as hives, only about five inches across, and the same in height, should be put on the top of such hives as are strong, and have not had too many swarms. A new swarm ought never, if possible, to be allowed to swarm again; nor ought an old hive to have more than two swarms. Swarming takes place from the heat of the hive, and if it be kept too cool, they cannot bring the grubs to perfection, and, of course, the more grubs the less honey, for nearly half the bees are sometimes obliged to be in attendance on the nursery. When the combs are thought to be full, take them off. They should hold about ten or twelve pounds, which will be of the very best; if it have, like mine, a common straw crown, it should be taken off only when the bees are asleep at night, but a glass bell, covered with a straw crown, would be better, for when the crown is taken off, the bees will leave the glass, as they cannot bear to work in the light. Bees should always have enough honey to last them out the winter, and a little feeding in October and November is not amiss in light hives.

A gentleman at Titchfield kept bees, and the hives were in a field behind the house; one of his favorite

riding horses was turned into this field every evening.
One night, however, this horse was heard galloping
round and round the field; but nobody thought there
was anything very extraordinary in his doing so, and
only supposed he was very frisky. At daylight, however, when the groom went to take him in, he found
the poor horse in a dreadful state, and discovered that
he had accidentally thrown down one of the hives, and
that, in revenge, the bees had stung him nearly to
death, and that his mad gallops had been caused by
his agonies; it was three months before he was sufficiently recovered to leave his stable. In the interim
the gentleman rode another horse, which was also
turned into this home-field every evening, precaution
having been taken to fence the hives, so that no
horse could again upset them. The bees did not in
the least interfere with the fresh horse, nor with
several others that were occasionally put into the field
for a night; when, therefore, the favorite was sufficiently well for the gentleman to mount him again, he
was, as before, turned into the field, and, strange to
say, was, the next morning, found dead from a second
assault of his enemies, the bees.

RAB AND HIS FRIENDS

By JOHN BROWN, M.D.

OUR–AND–THIRTY years ago, Bob Ainslie and I were coming up Infirmary Street from the Edinburgh High School, our heads together, and our arms intertwisted, as only lovers and boys know how, or why.

When we got to the top of the street, and turned north, we espied a crowd at the Tron Church. "A dog-fight!" shouted Bob, and was off; and so was I, both of us all but praying that it might not be over before we got up! And is not this boy-nature? and human nature too? and don't we all wish a house on fire not to be out before we see it? Dogs like fighting; old Isaac says they "delight" in it, and for the best of all reasons; and boys are not cruel because they like to see the fight. They see three of the great cardinal virtues of dog or man — courage, endurance, and skill — in intense action. This is very different from a love of making dogs fight, and enjoying, and aggravating, and making gain by their pluck. A boy, be he ever so fond himself of fighting, if he be a good boy, hates and despises all this, but he would have run off with Bob and me fast enough; it is a natural and a not wicked interest that all boys and men have in witnessing intense energy in action.

Does any curious and finely ignorant woman wish to know how Bob's eye at a glance announced a dog-fight to his brain? He did not, he could not, see the dogs fighting; it was a flash of an inference, a rapid induction. The crowd round a couple of dogs fighting is a crowd masculine mainly, with an occasional active, compassionate woman, fluttering wildly round the outside, and using her tongue and her hands freely upon the men, as so many " brutes "; it is a crowd annular, compact, and mobile; a crowd centripetal, having its eyes and its heads all bent downwards and inwards to one common focus.

Well, Bob and I are up, and find it is not over: a small, thoroughbred, white bull-terrier is busy throttling a large shepherd's dog, unaccustomed to war, but not to be trifled with. They are hard at it; the scientific little fellow doing his work in great style, his pastoral enemy fighting wildly, but with the sharpest of teeth and a great courage. Science and breeding, however, soon had their own; the Game Chicken, as the premature Bob called him, working his way up, took his final grip of poor Yarrow's throat, — and he lay gasping and done for. His master, a brown, handsome, big, young shepherd from Tweedsmuir, would have liked to have knocked down any man, would " drink up Esil, or eat a crocodile," for that part, if he had a chance : it was no use kicking the little dog; that would only make him hold the closer. Many were the means shouted out in mouthfuls, of the best possible ways of ending it. " Water ! " but there was none near, and many cried for it who might have got it from the well at Blackfriars Wynd. " Bite the tail ! " and a large, vague, benevolent, middle-aged man, more desirous than wise, with some struggle got the bushy end of Yarrow's tail into his ample mouth, and bit it with all his might. This was more than enough for the much-enduring, much-perspiring shepherd, who, with a gleam of joy over his broad visage, delivered a terrific facer upon our large, vague, benevolent, middle-aged friend, — who went down like a shot.

Still the Chicken holds ; death not far off. " Snuff ! a pinch of snuff ! " observed a calm, highly dressed young buck, with an eye-glass in his eye. " Snuff, indeed ! " growled the angry crowd, affronted and glaring. " Snuff ! a pinch of snuff ! " again observes the buck, but with more urgency ; whereon were produced several open boxes, and from a mull which may have been at Culloden he took a pinch, knelt down, and presented it to the nose of the Chicken. The laws of physiology and of snuff take their course ; the Chicken sneezes, and Yarrow is free !

The young pastoral giant stalks off with Yarrow in his arms, — comforting him.

But the bull-terrier's blood is up, and his soul unsatisfied ; he grips the first dog he meets, and, discovering she is not a dog, in Homeric phrase, he makes a brief sort of *amende*, and is off. The boys, with Bob and

me at their head, are after him; down Niddry Street
he goes, bent on mischief; up the Cowgate like an
arrow, — Bob and I, and our small men, panting
behind.

There, under the single arch of the South Bridge, is
a huge mastiff, sauntering down the middle of the
causeway, as if with his hands in his pockets; he is
old, gray, brindled, as big as a little Highland bull, and
has the Shakespearian dewlaps shaking as he goes.

The Chicken makes straight at him, and fastens on
his throat. To our astonishment, the great creature
does nothing but stand
still, hold himself up,
and roar, — yes, roar;
a long, serious remon-
strative roar. How is
this? Bob and I are
up to them. *He is muz-
zled!* The baillies had
proclaimed a general
m u z z l i n g,
and his mas-
ter, study-
ing strength and economy mainly, had encompassed
his huge jaws in a home-made apparatus, constructed
out of the leather of some ancient *breechin*. His mouth
was open as far as it could; his lips curled in a rage, —
a sort of terrible grin; his teeth gleaming, ready,
from out the darkness; the strap across his mouth
tense as a bowstring; his whole frame stiff with indignation and surprise; his roar asking us all round,
" Did you ever see the like of this?" He looked a

statue of anger and astonishment, done in Aberdeen
granite.

We soon had a crowd; the Chicken held on. "A
knife!" cried Bob; and a cobbler gave him his knife:
you know the kind of knife, worn away obliquely to a
point, and always keen. I put its edge to the tense
leather; it ran before it; and then! — one sudden jerk
of that enormous head, a sort of dirty mist about his
mouth, no noise, and the bright and fierce little fellow
is dropped, limp and dead. A solemn pause: this was
more than any of us had bargained for. I turned the
little fellow over, and saw he was quite dead; the
mastiff had taken him by the small of the back like a
rat, and broken it.

He looked down at his victim appeased, ashamed,
and amazed; snuffed him all over, stared at him, and,
taking a sudden thought, turned round and trotted off.
Bob took the dead dog up, and said: "John, we'll
bury him after tea." — "Yes," said I, and was off after
the mastiff. He made up the Cowgate at a rapid
swing; he had forgotten some engagement. He turned
up the Candlemaker Row, and stopped at the Harrow
Inn.

There was a carrier's cart ready to start, and a keen,
thin, impatient, black-a-vised little man, his hand at his
gray horse's head, looking about angrily for something.

"Rab, ye thief!" said he, aiming a kick at my great
friend, who drew cringing up, and avoiding the heavy
shoe with more agility than dignity, and watching his
master's eye, slunk dismayed under the cart, his ears
down, and as much as he had of tail down too.

What a man this must be, thought I, to whom my

tremendous hero turns tail! The carrier saw the
muzzle hanging, cut and useless, from his neck, and I
eagerly told him the story, which Bob and I always
thought, and still think, Homer, or King David, or Sir
Walter alone were
worthy to rehearse.
The severe little man
was miti-
gated,
and con-
descended
to say,
"Rab, my
man, puir
Rabbie,"
— where-
upon the
stump of
a tail rose
up, the
ears were
cocked,
the eyes
filled, and were
comforted; the
two friends were recon-
ciled. "Hupp!" and a
stroke of the whip were given to Jess; and off went
the three.

Bob and I buried the Game Chicken that night (we
had not much of a tea) in the back-green of his house

in Melville Street, No. 17, with considerable gravity and silence; and being at the time in the Iliad, and, like all boys, Trojans, we called him Hector, of course.

Six years have passed, — a long time for a boy and a dog: Bob Ainslie is off to the wars; I am a medical student, and clerk at Minto House Hospital.

Rab I saw almost every week on the Wednesday; and we had much pleasant intimacy. I found the way to his heart by frequent scratching of his huge head, and an occasional bone. When I did not notice him he would plant himself straight before me, and stand wagging that bud of a tail, and looking up, with his head a little to the one side. His master I occasionally saw; he used to call me "Maister John," but was laconic as any Spartan.

One fine October afternoon, I was leaving the hospital, when I saw the large gate open, and in walked Rab, with that great and easy saunter of his. He looked as if taking general possession of the place; like the Duke of Wellington entering a subdued city, satiated with victory and peace. After him came Jess, now white from age, with her cart; and in it a woman carefully wrapped up, — the carrier leading the horse anxiously and looking back. When he saw me, James (for his name was James Noble) made a curt and grotesque "boo," and said, "Maister John, this is the mistress; she's got trouble in her breest, — some kind o' an income, we're thinkin'."

By this time I saw the woman's face; she was sitting on a sack filled with straw, her husband's plaid round her, and his big coat, with its large white metal buttons, over her feet.

I never saw a more unforgetable face, pale, serious, *lonely*,[1] delicate, sweet, without being at all what we call fine. She looked sixty, and had on a mutch, white as snow, with its black ribbon; her silvery, smooth hair setting off her dark-gray eyes, — eyes such as one sees only twice or thrice in a life-time, full of suffering, full also of the overcoming of it; her eyebrows[2] black and delicate, and her mouth firm, patient and contented, which few mouths ever are.

As I have said, I never saw a more beautiful countenance, or one more subdued to settled quiet. " Ailie," said James, " this is Maister John, the young doctor; Rab's freend, ye ken. We often speak aboot you, doctor." She smiled, and made a movement, but said nothing; and prepared to come down, putting her plaid aside and rising. Had Solomon, in all his glory, been handing down the Queen of Sheba at his palace gate, he could not have done it more daintily, more tenderly, more like a gentleman, than did James, the Howgate carrier, when he lifted down Ailie his wife. The contrast of his small, swarthy, weather-beaten, keen, worldly face to hers — pale, subdued, and beautiful — was something wonderful. Rab looked on, concerned and puzzled, but ready for anything that might turn up, — were it to strangle the nurse, the porter, or even me. Ailie and he seemed great friends.

[1] It is not easy giving this look by one word; it was expressive of her being so much of her life alone.

[2] Black brows, they say,
Become some women best; so that there be not
Too much hair there, *but in a semicircle*,
Or a half-moon made with a pen. — A WINTER'S TALE.

" As I was sayin', she's got a kind o' trouble in her
breest, doctor; wull ye tak' a look at it?" We
walked into the consulting-room, all four; Rab grim
and comic, willing to be happy and confidential if
cause could be shown, willing also to be the reverse, on
the same terms. . . . Why was that gentle, modest,
sweet woman, clean and lovable, condemned by God to
bear such a burden?

I got her away to bed. " May Rab and me bide?"
said James. " *You* may; and Rab, if he will behave
himself." " I'se warrant he's do that, doctor;" and in
slunk the faithful beast. I wish you could have seen
him. There are no such dogs now. He belonged to a
lost tribe. As I have said, he was brindled and gray
like Rubislaw granite: his hair short, hard and close,
like a lion's; his body thick-set, like a little bull, — a
sort of compressed Hercules of a dog. He must have
been ninety pounds weight at the least; he had a large,
blunt head; his muzzle black as night, his mouth
blacker than any night, a tooth or two — being all he
had — gleaming out of his jaws of darkness. His
head was scarred with the records of old wounds, a
sort of series of fields of battle all over it; one eye out,
one ear cropped as close as was Archbishop Leighton's
father's; the remaining eye had the power of two; and
above it, and in constant communication with it, was
a tattered rag of an ear, which was forever unfurling
itself, like an old flag; and then that bud of a tail,
about one inch long, if it could in any sense be said to
be long, being as broad as long — the mobility, the in-
stantaneousness of that bud were very funny and surprising, and its expressive twinklings and winkings,

the intercommunications between the eye, the ear, and it, were of the oddest and swiftest.

Rab had the dignity and simplicity of great size ; and, having fought his way all along the road to absolute supremacy, he was as mighty in his own line as Julius Cæsar or the Duke of Wellington, and had the gravity [1] of all great fighters.

You must have often observed the likeness of certain men to certain animals, and of certain dogs to men. Now, I never looked at Rab without thinking of the great Baptist preacher, Andrew Fuller.[2] The same large, heavy, menacing, combative, sombre, honest countenance, the same deep, inevitable eye, the same look — as of thunder asleep, but ready, — neither a dog nor a man to be trifled with.

Next day, my master, the surgeon, examined Ailie. There was no doubt it must kill her, and soon. It could be removed — it might never return — it would give her speedy relief — she should have it done. She curtesied, looked at James, and said, " When ? " — " To-morrow," said the kind surgeon, a man of few

[1] A Highland gamekeeper, when asked why a certain terrier of singular pluck was so much more solemn than the other dogs, said, " O, sir, life's full o' sairiousness to him, —he just never can get enuff o' fechtin'."

[2] Fuller was, in early life, when a farmer lad at Soham, famous as a boxer; not quarrelsome, but not without " the stern delight " a man of strength and courage feels in their exercise.   Dr. Charles Stewart of Dunearn, whose rare gifts and graces as a physician, a divine, a scholar, and a gentleman, live only in the memory of those few who knew and survive him, liked to tell how Mr. Fuller used to say, that when he was in the pulpit and saw a *buirdly* man come along the passage he would instinctively draw himself up, measure his imaginary antagonist, and forecast how he would deal with him, his hands meanwhile condensing into fists, and tending to " square."   He must have been a hard hitter if he boxed as he preached, — what " The Fancy " would call " an ugly customer."

words.   She and James and Rab and I retired.   I noticed that he and she spoke little, but seemed to antici-
pate everything in each other.   The following day at
noon, the students came in, hurrying up the great stair.
At the first landing-place, on a small, well-known black-
board, was a bit of paper fastened by wafers, and many
remains of old wafers beside it.   On the paper were
the words : " An operation to-day.   J. B., *Clerk*."

Up ran the youths, eager to secure good places ; in
they crowded, full of interest and talk.   " What's the
case ? "   " Which side is it ? "

Don't think them heartless ; they are neither better
nor worse than you or I ; they get over their pro-
fessional horrors, and into their proper work, — and in
them pity, as an *emotion*, ending in itself or at best in
tears and a long-drawn breath, lessens, while pity as a
motive is quickened, and gains power and purpose.   It
is well for poor human nature that it is so.

The operating theatre is crowded ; much talk and
fun, and all the cordiality and stir of youth.   The surgeon with his staff of assistants is there.   In comes
Ailie : one look at her quiets and abates the eager
students.   That beautiful old woman is too much for
them ; they sit down, and are dumb, and gaze at her.
These rough boys feel the power of her presence.   She
walks in quickly, but without haste ; dressed in her
mutch, her neckerchief, her white dimity short-gown,
her black bombazine petticoat, showing her white
worsted stockings and her carpet-shoes.   Behind her
was James and Rab.   James sat down in the distance, and took that huge and noble head between his
knees.

Rab looked perplexed and dangerous; forever cocking his ear and dropping it as fast. . . .

It is over: she is dressed, steps gently and decently down from the table, looks for James; then turning to the surgeon and the students she courtesies, and in a low, clear voice begs their pardon if she has behaved ill. The students — all of us — wept like children; the surgeon happed her up carefully, and, resting on James and me, Ailie went to her room, Rab following. We put her to bed. James took off his heavy shoes, crammed with tackets, heel-capt and toe-capt, and put them carefully under the table, saying, "Maister John, I'm for nane o' yer strynge nurse bodies for Ailie. I'll be her nurse, and I'll gang aboot on my stockin' soles as canny as pussy." And so he did; and handy and clever, and swift and tender as any woman, was that horny-handed, snell, peremptory little man. Everything she got he gave her; he seldom slept; and often I saw his small, shrewd eyes, out of the darkness, fixed on her. As before, they spoke little.

Rab behaved well, never moving, showing us how meek and gentle he could be, and occasionally, in his sleep, letting us know that he was demolishing some adversary. He took a walk with me every day, generally to the Candlemaker Row; but he was sombre and mild; declined doing battle, though some fit cases offered, and, indeed, submitted to sundry indignities; and was always very ready to turn, and came faster back, and trotted up the stair with much lightness, and went straight to that door.

Jess, the mare, had been sent, with her weather-worn cart, to Howgate, and had, doubtless, her own dim and placid meditations and confusions, on the absence of her master and Rab, and her unnatural freedom from the road and her cart.

For some days Ailie did well. The wound healed "by the first intention;" for, as James said, "Oor Ailie's skin's ower clean to heil." The students came in quiet and anxious, and surrounded her bed. She said she liked to see their young, honest faces. The surgeon dressed her, and spoke to her in his own short, kind way, pitying her through his eyes, Rab and James outside the circle, — Rab being now reconciled, and even cordial, and having made up his mind that as yet nobody required worrying, but, as you may suppose, *semper paratus*.

So far well: but, four days after the operation, my patient had a sudden and long shivering, a "groosin'," as she called it. I saw her soon after; her eyes were too bright, her cheek colored; she was restless, and ashamed of being so; the balance was lost; mischief had begun. On looking at the wound a blush of red told the secret: her pulse was rapid, her breathing anxious and quick; she wasn't herself, as she said, and was vexed at her restlessness. We tried what we could. James did everything, was everywhere; never in the way, never out of it; Rab subsided under the table into a dark place, and was motionless, all but his eye, which followed every one. Ailie got worse; began to wander in her mind, gently; was more demonstrative in her ways to James, rapid in her questions, and sharp at times. He was vexed, and said, "She was never that way afore; no, never." For a time she knew her head was wrong, and was always asking our pardon, — the dear, gentle old woman; then delirium set in strong, without pause. Her brain gave way, and then came that terrible spectacle, —

"The intellectual power, through words and things,
 Went sounding on its dim and perilous way;"

she sang bits of old songs and Psalms, stopping suddenly, mingling the Psalms of David and the diviner words of his Son and Lord with homely odds and ends and scraps of ballads.

Nothing more touching, or in a sense more strangely beautiful, did I ever witness. Her tremulous, rapid, affectionate, eager Scotch voice, the swift, aimless, bewildered mind, the baffled utterance, the bright and perilous eye; some wild words, some household cares, something for James, the names of the dead, Rab called rapidly and in a "fremyt" voice, and he starting up surprised, and slinking off as if he were to blame somehow, or had been dreaming he heard; many eager questions and beseechings which James and I could make nothing of, and on which she seemed to set her all, and then sink back ununderstood. It was very sad, but better than many things that are not called sad. James hovered about, put out and miserable, but active and exact as ever; read to her, when there was a lull, short bits from the Psalms, prose and metre, chanting the latter in his own rude and serious way, showing great knowledge of the fit words, bearing up like a man, and doting over her as his "ain Ailie." "Ailie, ma woman!" "Ma ain bonnie wee dawtie!"

The end was drawing on: the golden bowl was breaking; the silver cord was fast being loosed; that *animula blandula, vagula, hospes, comesque*, was about to flee. The body and the soul, companions for sixty years, were being sundered, and taking leave. She was walking alone through the valley of that shadow into which one day we must all enter; and yet she was not alone, for we know whose rod and staff were comforting her.

One night she had fallen quiet, and, as we hoped, asleep; her eyes were shut. We put down the gas, and sat watching her. Suddenly she sat up in bed, and taking a bed gown which was lying on it, rolled up, she held it eagerly to her breast — to the right side. We could see her eyes bright with a surprising tenderness and joy, bending over this bundle of clothes. She held it as a woman holds her sucking child; opening out her nightgown impatiently, and holding it close, and brooding over it, and murmuring foolish little words, as over one whom his mother comforteth, and who sucks and is satisfied. It was pitiful and strange

to see her wasted dying look, keen and yet vague, —
her immense love.

"Preserve me!" groaned James, giving way. And
then she rocked back and forward, as if to make it
sleep, hushing it, and wasting on it her infinite fond-
ness. "Wae's me, doctor; I declare she's thinkin' it's
that bairn." —"What bairn?" — "The only bairn we
ever had; our wee Mysie, and she's in the Kingdom,
forty years and mair." It was plainly true; . . . again
once more they were together, and she had her ain
wee Mysie in her bosom.

This was the close. She sank rapidly; the delirium
left her; but, as she whispered, she was "clean silly";
it was the lightening before the final darkness. After
having for some time lain still, her eyes shut, she said,
"James!" He came close to her, and, lifting up her
calm, clear, beautiful eyes, she gave him a long look,
turned to me kindly but shortly, looked for Rab but
could not see him, then turned to her husband again,
as if she would never leave off looking, shut her eyes,
and composed herself. She lay for some time breathing quick, and passed away so gently that, when we
thought she was gone, James, in his old-fashioned way,
held the mirror to her face. After a long pause, one
small spot of dimness was breathed out; it vanished
away, and never returned, leaving the blank, clear
darkness of the mirror without a stain. "What is our
life? it is even a vapor, which appeareth for a little
time, and then vanisheth away."

Rab all this time had been full awake and motionless; he came forward beside us: Ailie's hand, which
James had held, was hanging down; it was soaked with

his tears; Rab licked it all over carefully, looked at her, and returned to his place under the table.

James and I sat, I don't know how long, but for some time, — saying nothing. He started up abruptly, and with some noise went to the table, and, putting his right fore and middle fingers each into a shoe,  pulled them out, and put them on, breaking one of the leather latchets, and muttering in anger, "I never did the like o' that afore!"

I believe he never did; nor after either. "Rab!"

he said roughly, and pointing with his thumb to the bottom of the bed. Rab leapt up, and settled himself, his head and eye to the dead face. "Maister John, ye'll wait for me," said the carrier, and disappeared in the darkness, thundering down-stairs in his heavy shoes. I ran to a front window; there he was, already round the house, and out at the gate, fleeing like a shadow.

I was afraid about him, and yet not afraid; so I sat down beside Rab, and, being wearied, fell asleep. I awoke from a sudden noise outside. It was November, and there had been a heavy fall of snow. Rab was *in statu quo;* he heard the noise too, and plainly knew it, but never moved. I looked out, and there, at the gate, in the dim morning — for the sun was not up —

was Jess and the cart, a cloud of steam rising from the old mare. I did not see James; he was already at the door, and came up the stairs and met me. It was less than three hours since he left and he must have posted out — who knows how? — to Howgate, full nine miles off, yoked Jess, and driven her astonished into town. He had an armful of blankets, and was streaming with perspiration. He nodded to me, spread out on the floor two pairs of clean old blankets having at their corners, " A. G., 1794," in large letters in red worsted. These were the initials of Alison Græme, and James may have looked in at her from without, — himself unseen but not unthought of, — when he was " wat, wat, and weary," and, after having walked many a mile over the hills, may have seen her sitting, while " a' the lave were sleepin'," and by the firelight working her name on the blankets for her ain James's bed.

He motioned Rab down, and, taking his wife in his arms, laid her in the blankets, and happed her carefully and firmly up, leaving the face uncovered; and then, lifting her, he nodded again sharply to me, and with a resolved but utterly miserable face strode along the passage and down-stairs, followed by Rab. I followed with a light, but he didn't need it. I went out, holding stupidly the candle in my hand, in the calm, frosty, air; we were soon at the gate. I could have helped him, but I saw he was not to be meddled with, and he was strong and did not need it. He laid her down as tenderly, as safely, as he had lifted her out ten days before, — as tenderly as when he had her first in his arms when she was only " A. G.," — sorted

her, leaving that beautiful sealed face open to the
heavens; and then, taking Jess by the head, he moved
away. He did not notice me, neither did Rab, who
presided behind the cart. I stood till they passed
through the long shadow of the College, and turned
up Nicolson Street. I heard the solitary cart sound
through the streets, and die away and come again;
and I returned, thinking of that company going up
Libberton Brae, then along Roslin Muir, the morning
light touching the Pentlands and making them like

on-looking ghosts; then down the hill through Auch-
indinny woods, past "haunted Woodhouselee"; and,
as daybreak came sweeping up the bleak Lammer-
muirs, and fell on his own door, the company would
stop, and James would take the key, and lift Ailie up
again, laying her on her own bed, and, having put Jess
up, would return with Rab and shut the door.

James buried his wife, with his neighbors mourning,
Rab inspecting the solemnity from a distance. It was
snow, and that black, ragged hole would look strange in

the midst of the swelling, spotless cushion of white.
James looked after everything; then rather suddenly
fell ill, and took to bed; was insensible when the
doctor came,
and soon
died. A sort
of low fever
was prevail-
ing in the
village, and
his want of
sleep, his
exhaustion,
and his mis-
ery made
him apt to
take it. The
grave was

not difficult to reopen.   A fresh fall of snow had again
made all things white and smooth; Rab once more
looked on, and slunk home to the stable.

And what of Rab? I asked for him next week at
the new carrier who got the good-will of James's
business, and was now master of Jess and her cart.
"How's Rab?" He put me off, and said rather
rudely, "What's *your* business wi' the dowg?" I
was not to be so put off. "Where's Rab?" He,
getting confused and red, and intermeddling with his
hair, said, "'Deed, sir, Rab's deid." — "Dead! what
did he die of?" — "Weel, sir," said he, getting redder,
"he didna exactly dee; he was killed. I had to brain

him wi' a rack-pin; there was nae doin' wi' him. He
lay in the treviss wi' the mear, and wadna come oot.
I tempit him wi' kail and meat, but he wad tak naething, and keepit me frae feedin' the beast, and he
was aye gur gurrin', and grup gruppin' me by the
legs. I was laith to make awa wi' the auld dowg, his
like wasna atween this and Thornhill, — but, 'deed,
sir, I could do naething else." I believed him. Fit
end for Rab, quick and complete. His teeth and his
friends gone, why should he keep the peace, and be
civil?

OUR NEW NEIGHBORS AT PONKAPOG

By THOMAS BAILEY ALDRICH.

WHEN I saw the little house building, an eighth of a mile beyond my own, on the Old Bay Road, I wondered who were to be the tenants. The modest structure was set well back from the road, among the trees, as if the inmates were to care nothing whatever for a view of the stylish equipages which sweep by during the summer season. For my part, I like to see the passing, in town or country ; but each has his own unaccountable taste. The proprietor, who seemed to be also the architect of the new house, superintended the various details of the work with an assiduity that gave me a high opinion of his intelligence and executive ability, and I congratulated myself on the prospect of having some very agreeable neighbors.

It was quite early in the spring, if I remember, when they moved into the cottage — a newly married couple, evidently : the wife very young, pretty, and with the air of a lady ; the husband somewhat older, but still in

the first flush of manhood. It was understood in the
village that they came from Baltimore; but no one knew
them personally, and they brought no letters of introduction. (For obvious reasons I refrain from mention-
ing names.) It was clear that, for the present at least,
their own company was entirely sufficient for them.
They made no advances toward the acquaintance of any
of the families in the neighborhood, and consequently
were left to themselves. That, apparently, was what
they desired, and why they came to Ponkapog. For
after its black bass and wild duck and teal, solitude is
the chief staple of Ponkapog. Perhaps its perfect rural
loveliness should be included. Lying high up under
the wing of the Blue Hills, and in the odorous breath
of pines and cedars, it chances to be the most enchant-
ing bit of unlaced dishevelled country within fifty miles
of Boston, which, moreover, can be reached in half an
hour's ride by railroad. But the nearest railroad station (Heaven be praised!) is two miles distant, and the
seclusion is without a flaw. Ponkapog has one mail a
day; two mails a day would break the charm.

The village — it looks like a compact village at a
distance, but unravels and disappears the moment you
drive into it — has quite a large floating population.
I do not allude to the perch and pickerel in Ponkapog
Pond. Along the Old Bay Road, a highway even in
the colonial days, there are a number of attractive
villas and cottages straggling off towards Milton,
which are occupied for the summer by persons from
the city. These birds of passage are a distinct class
from the permanent inhabitants, and the two seldom
closely assimilate unless there has been some previous

connection. It seemed to me that our new neighbors were to come under the head of permanent inhabitants; they had built their own house, and had the air of intending to live in it all the year round.

"Are you not going to call on them?" I asked my wife one morning.

"When they call on *us*," she replied lightly.

"But it is our place to call first, they being strangers."

This was said as seriously as the circumstance demanded; but my wife turned it off with a laugh, and I said no more, always trusting to her intuitions in these matters.

She was right. She would not have been received, and a cool "Not at home" would have been a bitter social pill to us if we had gone out of our way to be courteous.

I saw a great deal of our neighbors, nevertheless. Their cottage lay between us and the post-office — where *he* was never to be met with by any chance — and I caught frequent glimpses of the two working in the garden. Floriculture did not appear so much an object as exercise. Possibly it was neither; may be they were engaged in digging for specimens of those arrowheads and flint hatchets which are continually coming to the surface hereabouts. These is scarcely an acre in which the ploughshare has not turned up some primitive stone weapon or domestic utensil, disdainfully left to us by the red men who once held this domain — an ancient tribe called the Punkypoags, a forlorn descendant of which, one Polly Crowd, figures in the annual Blue Book, down to the close of the

Southern war, as a state pensioner. At that period she appears to have struck a trail to the Happy Hunting Grounds. I quote from the local historiographer.

Whether they were developing a kitchen-garden, or emulating Professor Schliemann[1] at Mycenæ, the new-comers were evidently persons of refined musical taste: the lady had a contralto voice of remarkable sweetness, although of no great compass, and I used often to linger of a morning by the high gate and listen to her executing an arietta, conjecturally at some window up-stairs, for the house was not visible from the turnpike. The husband, somewhere about the grounds, would occasionally respond with two or three bars. It was all quite an ideal, Arcadian business. They seemed very happy together, these two persons, who asked no odds whatever of the community in which they had settled themselves.

There was a queerness, a sort of mystery, about this couple which I admit piqued my curiosity, though as a rule I have no morbid interest in the affairs of my neighbors. They behaved like a pair of lovers who had run off and got married clandestinely. I willingly acquitted them, however, of having done anything unlawful; for, to change a word in the lines of the poet —

> "It is a joy to *think* the best
> We may of human kind."

Admitting the hypothesis of elopement, there was no mystery in their neither sending nor receiving letters.

[1] Heinrich Schliemann (1822–1890), a distinguished archæologist, who explored and excavated the site of ancient Troy, and later made similar researches at Mycenæ, his discoveries being of great interest and importance.

But where did they get their groceries? I do not mean the money to pay for them — that is an enigma apart — but the groceries themselves. No express wagon, no butcher's cart, no vehicle of any description, was ever observed to stop at their domicile. Yet they did not order family stores at the sole establishment in the village — an inexhaustible little bottle of a shop which, I advertise it gratis, can turn out anything in the way of groceries, from a handsaw to a pocket-handkerchief. I confess that I allowed this unimportant detail of their *ménage* to occupy more of my speculation than was creditable to me.

In several respects our neighbors reminded me of those inexplicable persons we sometimes come across in great cities, though seldom or never in suburban places, where the field may be supposed too restricted for their operations — persons who have no perceptible means of subsistence, and manage to live royally on nothing a year. They hold no government bonds, they possess no real estate (our neighbors did own their house), they toil not, neither do they spin; yet they reap all the numerous soft advantages that usually result from honest toil and skilful spinning. How do they do it? But this is a digression, and I am quite of the opinion of the old lady in "David Copperfield," [1] who says, "Let us have no meandering!"

Though my wife declined to risk a ceremonious call on our neighbors as a family, I saw no reason why I should not speak to the husband as an individual, when I happened to encounter him by the wayside. I made several approaches to do so, when it occurred to my pene-

[1] One of the best, if not the best, of the novels of Dickens.

tration that my neighbor had the air of trying to avoid
me.   I resolved to put the suspicion to the test, and one
forenoon, when he was sauntering along on the opposite
side of the road, in the vicinity of Fisher's sawmill, I
deliberately crossed over to address him.   The brusque
manner in which he hurried away was not to be misunderstood.   Of course I was not going to force myself
upon him.

It was at this time that I began to formulate unchari-
table suppositions touching our neighbors, and would
have been as well pleased if some of my choicest fruit-
trees had not overhung their wall.   I determined to
keep my eyes open later in the season, when the fruit
should be ripe to pluck.   In some folks, a sense of the
delicate shades of difference between *meum* and *tuum* does
not seem to be very strongly developed in the Moon of
Cherries, to use the old Indian phrase.

I was sufficiently magnanimous not to impart any
of these sinister impressions to the families with whom
we were on visiting terms; for I despise a gossip.   I
would say nothing against the persons up the road until
I had something definite to say.   My interest in them
was — well, not exactly extinguished, but burning low.
I met the gentleman at intervals, and passed him without recognition; at rare intervals I saw the lady.

After a while I not only missed my occasional glimpses
of her pretty, slim figure, always draped in some soft
black stuff with a bit of something bright at the throat,
but I inferred that she did not go about the house singing in her light-hearted manner, as formerly.   What
had happened?   Had the honeymoon suffered eclipse
already?   Was she ill?   I fancied she was ill, and that

I detected a certain anxiety in the husband, who spent the mornings digging solitarily in the garden, and seemed to have re-linquished those long jaunts to the brow of Blue Hill, where there is a superb view of all Norfolk County combined with sundry vener-able rattlesnakes with twelve rattles.

As the days went by it be-came certain that the lady was confined to the house, per-haps seriously ill, possibly a confirmed invalid. Whether she was attended by a physician from Canton or from Milton, I was un-able to say; but neither the gig with the large allopathic sorrel horse, nor the gig with the homœopathic white mare, was ever seen hitched at the gate during the day. If a physician had charge of the case, he visited his patient only at night. All this moved my sympathy, and I reproached my-self with having had hard thoughts of our neighbors.

Trouble had come to them early. I would have liked
to offer them such small, friendly services as lay in my
power, but the memory of the repulse I had sustained
still rankled in me. So I hesitated.

One morning my two boys burst into the library with
their eyes sparkling.

" You know the old elm down the road ? " cried one.

" Yes."

" The elm with the hang-bird's nest ? " shrieked the
other.

" Yes, yes — the Baltimore oriole."

" Well, we both just climbed up, and there's three
young ones in it ! "

Then I smiled to think that our neighbors had got
such a promising little family.

MOUFFLOU

By OUIDA.

M OUFFLOU'S masters were
some boys and girls. They
were very poor, but they
were very merry. They
lived in an old, dark, tumble-
down place, and their father
had been dead five years; their
mother's care was all they
knew; and Tasso was the eldest
of them all, a lad of nearly twenty, and he was so kind,
so good, so laborious, so cheerful, and so gentle, that
the children all younger than he adored him. Tasso
was a gardener. Tasso, however, though the eldest and
mainly the bread-winner, was not so much Moufflou's
master as was little Romolo, who was only ten, and a
cripple. Romolo, called generally Lolo, had taught
Moufflou all he knew; and that all was a very great
deal, for nothing cleverer than was Moufflou had ever
walked upon four legs.

Why Moufflou?

Well, when the poodle had been given to them by a
soldier who was going back to his home in Piedmont,
he had been a white woolly creature of a year old, and

the children's mother, who was a Corsican by birth, had said that he was just like a *moufflon,* as they call sheep in Corsica. White and woolly this dog remained, and he became the handsomest and biggest poodle in all the city, and the corruption of Moufflou from Moufflon remained the name by which he was known; it was silly, perhaps, but it suited him and the children, and Moufflou he was.

They lived in an old quarter of Florence, in that picturesque zigzag which goes round the grand church of Or San Michele, and which is almost more Venetian than Tuscan in its mingling of color, charm, stateliness, popular confusion, and architectural majesty. The tall old houses are weather-beaten into the most delicious hues; the pavement is enchantingly encumbered with peddlers and stalls and all kinds of trades going on in the open air, in that bright, merry, beautiful Italian custom which, alas, alas! is being driven away by new-fangled laws which deem it better for the people to be stuffed up in close, stewing rooms without air, and would fain do away with all the good-tempered politics and the sensible philosophies and the wholesome chatter which the open-street trades and street gossipry encourage, for it is good for the populace to *sfogare,* and in no other way can it do so one-half so innocently. Drive it back into musty shops, and it is driven at once to mutter sedition. . . . But you want to hear about Moufflou.

Well, Moufflou lived here in that high house with the sign of the lamb in wrought iron, which shows it was once a warehouse of the old guild of the Arte della Lana. They are all old houses here, drawn round about that grand church which I called once, and will call again, like a mighty casket of oxidized silver. A mighty casket, indeed, holding the Holy Spirit within it; and with the vermilion and the blue and the orange glowing in its niches and its lunettes like enamels, and its statues of the apostles strong and noble, like the times in which they were created, — St. Peter with his keys, and St. Mark with his open book, and St. George leaning on his sword, and others also, solemn and austere as they, austere though benign, for do they not guard the White Tabernacle of Orcagna within?

The church stands firm as a rock, square as a fortress of stone, and the winds and the waters of the skies may beat about it as they will, they have no power to disturb its sublime repose. Sometimes I think of all the noble things in all our Italy Or San Michele is the noblest, standing there in its stern magnificence, amidst people's hurrying feet and noisy laughter, a memory of God.

The little masters of Moufflou lived right in its shadow, where the bridge of stone spans the space between the houses and the church high in mid-air: and little Lolo loved the church with a great love. He loved it in the morning-time, when the sunbeams turned it into dusky gold and jasper; he loved it in the evening-time, when the lights of its altars glimmered in the dark, and the scent of its incense came out into the street; he loved it in the great feasts, when the huge clusters of lilies were borne inside it; he loved it in the solemn nights of winter; the flickering gleam of the dull lamps shone on the robes of an apostle, or the sculpture of a shield, or the glow of a casement-moulding in majolica. He loved it always, and without knowing why, he called it *la mia chiesa.*

Lolo, being lame and of delicate health, was not enabled to go to school or to work, though he wove the straw covering of wine-flasks and plaited the cane matting with busy fingers. But for the most part he did as he liked, and spent most of his time sitting on the parapet of Or San Michele, watching the vendors of earthenware at their trucks, or trotting with his crutch (and he could trot a good many miles when he chose) out with Moufflou down a bit of the Stocking-makers' Street, along under the arcades of the Uffizi, and so over the Jewelers' Bridge, and out by byways that he knew into the fields on the hill-side upon the other bank of Arno. Moufflou and he would spend half the day — all the day — out there in daffodil-time ; and Lolo would come home with great bundles and sheaves of golden flowers, and he and Moufflou were happy.

His mother never liked to say a harsh word to Lolo, for he was lame through her fault : she had let him fall in his babyhood, and the mischief had been done to his hip never again to be undone. So she never raised her voice to him, though she did often to the others, — to curly-pated Cecco, and pretty black-eyed Dina, and saucy Bice, and sturdy Beppo, and even to the good, manly, hard-working Tasso. Tasso was the mainstay of the whole, though he was but a gardener's lad, working in the green Cascine at small wages. But all he earned he brought home to his mother ; and he alone kept in order the lazy, high-tempered Sandro, and he alone kept in check Bice's love of finery, and

he alone could with shrewdness and care make both
ends meet and put *minestra* always in the pot and
bread always in the cupboard.

When his mother thought, as she thought indeed
almost ceaselessly, that with a few months he would
be of the age to draw his number, and might draw a
high one and be taken from her for three years, the
poor soul believed her
very heart would burst
and break; and many
a day at twilight she
would start out un-
perceived and
creep into the
great church
and pour her
soul forth in
supplication
before the
White Taber-
nacle.

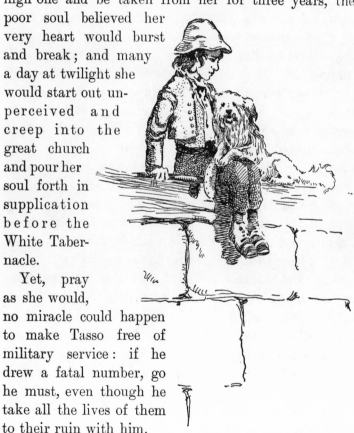

Yet, pray
as she would,
no miracle could happen
to make Tasso free of
military service: if he
drew a fatal number, go
he must, even though he
take all the lives of them
to their ruin with him.

One morning Lolo sat as usual on the parapet of the
church, Moufflou beside him. It was a brilliant morn-

ing in September. The men at the hand-barrows and
at the stalls were selling the crockery, the silk hand-
kerchiefs, and the straw hats which form the staple of
the commerce that goes on round about Or San Michele,
— very blithe, good-natured, gay commerce, for the
most part, not got through, however, of course, without
bawling and screaming, and shouting and gesticulating,
as if the sale of a penny pipkin or a twopenny pie-pan
were the occasion for the exchange of many thousands
of pounds sterling and cause for the whole world's
commotion. It was about eleven o'clock; the poor
petitioners were going in for alms to the house of the
fraternity of San Giovanni Battista; the barber at the
corner was shaving a big man with a cloth tucked
about his chin, and his chair set well out on the pavement; the sellers of the pipkins and pie-pans were
screaming till they were hoarse, " *Un soldo l'uno, due
soldi tre!* " big bronze bells were booming till they
seemed to clang right up to the deep-blue sky; some
brethren of the Misericordia went by bearing a black
bier; a large sheaf of glowing flowers — dahlias, zinnias,
asters, and daturas — was borne through the huge
arched door of the church near St. Mark and his open
book. Lolo looked on at it all, and so did Moufflou,
and a stranger looked at them as he left the church.

" You have a handsome poodle there, my little man,"
he said to Lolo, in a foreigner's too distinct and careful
Italian.

" Moufflou is beautiful," said Lolo, with pride.
" You should see him when he is just washed; but we
can only wash him on Sundays, because then Tasso is
at home."

"How old is your dog?"

"Three years old."

"Does he do any tricks?"

"Does he!" said Lolo, with a very derisive laugh: "why, Moufflou can do anything! He can walk on two legs ever so long; make ready, present, and fire; die; waltz; beg, of course; shut a door; make a wheelbarrow of himself: there is nothing he will not do. Would you like to see him do something?"

"Very much," said the foreigner.

To Moufflou and to Lolo the street was the same thing as home; this cheery *piazzetta* by the church, so utterly empty sometimes, and sometimes so noisy and crowded, was but the wider threshold of their home to both the poodle and the child.

So there, under the lofty and stately walls of the old church, Lolo put Moufflou through his exercises. They were second nature to Moufflou, as to most poodles. He had inherited his address at them from clever parents, and, as he had never been frightened or coerced, all his lessons and acquirements were but play to him. He acquitted himself admirably, and the crockery-vendors came and looked on, and a sacristan came out of the church and smiled, and the barber left his customer's chin all in a lather while he laughed, for the good folk of the quarter were all proud of Moufflou and never tired of him, and the pleasant, easy-going, good-humored disposition of the Tuscan populace is so far removed from the stupid buckram and whalebone in which the new-fangled democracy wants to imprison it.

The stranger also was much diverted by Moufflou's

talents, and said, half aloud, "How this clever dog would amuse poor Victor! Would you bring your poodle to please a sick child I have at home?" he said, quite aloud, to Lolo, who smiled and answered that he would.   Where was the sick child?

"At the Gran Bretagna; not far off," said the gentleman.   "Come this afternoon, and ask for me by this name."

He dropped his card and a couple of francs into Lolo's hand, and went his way.   Lolo, with Moufflou scampering after him, dashed into his own house, and stumped up the stairs, his crutch making a terrible noise on the stone.

"Mother, mother! see what I have got because Moufflou did his tricks," he shouted.   "And now you can buy those shoes you want so much, and the coffee that you miss so of a morning, and the new linen for Tasso, and the shirts for Sandro."

For to the mind of Lolo two francs was as two millions, — source unfathomable of riches inexhaustible!

With the afternoon he and Moufflou trotted down the arcades of the Uffizi and down the Lung' Arno to the hotel of the stranger, and, showing the stranger's card, which Lolo could not read, they were shown at once into a great chamber, all gilding and fresco and velvet furniture.

But Lolo, being a little Florentine, was never troubled by externals, or daunted by mere sofas and chairs: he stood and looked around him with perfect composure; and Moufflou, whose attitude, when he was not romping, was always one of magisterial gravity, sat on his haunches and did the same.

Soon the foreigner he had seen in the forenoon
entered and spoke to him, and led him into another
chamber, where stretched on a couch was a little wan-
faced boy about seven years old; a pretty boy, but so
palid, so wasted, so helpless. This poor little boy was
heir to a great name and a great fortune, but all the
science in the world could not make him strong enough
to run among the daisies, or able to draw a single
breath without pain. A feeble smile lit up his face as
he saw Moufflou and Lolo; then a shadow chased
it away.

"Little boy is lame like me," he said, in a tongue
Lolo did not understand.

"Yes, but he is a strong little boy, and can move
about, as perhaps the suns of his country will make
you do," said the gentleman, who was the poor little
boy's father. "He has brought you his poodle to
amuse you. What a handsome dog! is it not?"

"Oh, *bufflins!*" said the poor little fellow, stretching out his wasted hands to Moufflou, who submitted
his leonine crest to the caress.

Then Lolo went through the performance, and
Moufflou acquitted himself ably as ever; and the little
invalid laughed and shouted with his tiny thin voice,
and enjoyed it all immensely, and rained cakes and
biscuits on both the poodle and its master. Lolo
crumped the pastries with willing white teeth, and
Moufflou did no less. Then they got up to go, and the
sick child on the couch burst into fretful lamentations
and outcries.

"I want the dog! I will have the dog!" was all
he kept repeating.

But Lolo did not know what he said, and was only sorry to see him so unhappy.

"You shall have the dog to-morrow," said the gentleman, to pacify his little son ; and he hurried Lolo and Moufflou out of the room, and consigned them to a servant, having given Lolo five francs this time.

"Why, Moufflou," said Lolo, with a chuckle of delight, "if we could find a foreigner every day, we could eat meat at supper, Moufflou, and go to the theatre every evening ! "

And he and his crutch clattered home with great eagerness and excitement, and Moufflou trotted on his four frilled feet, the blue bow with which Bice had tied up his curls on the top of his head, fluttering in the wind. But, alas ! even his five francs could bring no comfort at home. He found his whole family wailing and mourning in utterly inconsolable distress.

Tasso had drawn his number that morning, and the number was seven, and he must go and be a conscript for three years.

The poor young man stood in the midst of his weeping brothers and sisters, with his mother leaning against his shoulder, and down his own brown cheeks the tears were falling. He must go, and lose his place in the public gardens, and leave his people to starve as they might, and be put in a tomfool's jacket, and drafted off among cursing and swearing and strange faces, friendless, homeless, miserable ! And the mother, — what would become of the mother ?

Tasso was the best of lads and the mildest. He was quite happy sweeping up the leaves in the long alleys of the Cascine, or mowing the green lawns under the ilex avenues, and coming home at supper-time among the merry little people and the good woman that he loved. He was quite contented; he wanted nothing, only to be let alone; and they would not let him alone. They would haul him away to put a heavy musket in his hand and a heavy knapsack on his back, and drill him, and curse him, and make him into a human target, a live popinjay.

No one had any heed for Lolo and his five francs, and Moufflou, understanding that some great sorrow had fallen on his friends, sat down and lifted up his voice and howled.

Tasso must go away!—that was all they understood. For three long years they must go without the sight of his face, the aid of his strength, the pleasure of his smile: Tasso must go! When Lolo understood the calamity that had befallen them, he gathered Moufflou up against his breast, and sat down too on the floor beside him and cried as if he would never stop crying.

There was no help for it: it was one of those misfortunes which are, as we say in Italian, like a tile tumbled on the head. The tile drops from a height, and the poor head bows under the unseen blow. That is all.

" What is the use of that ? " said the mother, passionately, when Lolo showed her his five francs. " It will not buy Tasso's discharge."

Lolo felt that his mother was cruel and unjust, and crept to bed with Moufflou. Moufflou always slept on Lolo's feet.

The next morning Lolo got up before sunrise, and he

and Moufflou accompanied Tasso to his work in the Cascine.

Lolo loved his brother, and clung to every moment whilst they could still be together.

"Can nothing keep you, Tasso?" he said, despairingly, as they went down the leafy aisles, whilst the Arno water was growing golden as the sun rose.

Tasso sighed.

"Nothing, dear. Unless Gesù would send me a thousand francs to buy a substitute."

And he knew he might as well have said, "If one could coin gold ducats out of the sunbeams on Arno water."

Lolo was very sorrowful as he lay on the grass in the meadow where Tasso was at work, and the poodle lay stretched beside him.

When Lolo went home to dinner (Tasso took his wrapped in a handkerchief) he found his mother very agitated and excited. She was laughing one moment, crying the next. She was passionate and peevish, tender and jocose by turns; there was something forced and feverish about her which the children felt but did not comprehend. She was a woman of not very much intelligence, and she had a secret, and she carried it ill, and knew not what to do with it; but they could not tell that. They only felt a vague sense of disturbance and timidity at her unwonted manner.

The meal over (it was only bean-soup, and that is soon eaten), the mother said sharply to Lolo, "Your Aunt Anita wants you this afternoon. She has to go out, and you are needed to stay with the children: be off with you."

Lolo was an obedient child; he took his hat and jumped up as quickly as his halting hip would let him. He called Moufflou, who was asleep.

"Leave the dog," said his mother, sharply. "'Nita will not have him messing and carrying mud about her nice clean rooms. She told me so. Leave him, I say."

"Leave Moufflou!" echoed Lolo, for never in all Moufflou's life had Lolo parted from him. Leave Moufflou! He stared open-eyed and open-mouthed at his mother. What could have come to her?

"Leave him, I say," she repeated, more sharply than ever. "Must I speak twice to my own children? Be off with you, and leave the dog, I say."

And she clutched Moufflou by his long silky mane and dragged him backward, whilst with the other hand she thrust out of the door Lolo and Bice.

Lolo began to hammer with his crutch at the door thus closed on him; but Bice coaxed and entreated him.

"Poor mother has been so worried about Tasso," she pleaded. "And what harm can come to Moufflou? And I do think he was tired, Lolo; the Cascine is a long way; and it is quite true that Aunt 'Nita never liked him."

So by one means and another she coaxed her brother away; and they went almost in silence to where their Aunt Anita dwelt, which was across the river, near the dark-red bell-shaped dome of Santo-Spirito.

It was true that her aunt had wanted them to mind her room and her babies whilst she was away carrying home some lace to a villa outside the Roman gate, for she was a lace-washer and clear-starcher by trade.

There they had to stay in the little dark room with the two babies, with nothing to amuse the time except the clang of the bells of the church of the Holy Spirit, and the voices of the lemonade-sellers shouting in the street below. Aunt Anita did not get back till it was more than dusk, and the two children trotted homeward hand in hand, Lolo's leg dragging itself painfully along, for without Moufflou's white figure dancing on before him

he felt very tired indeed.   It was pitch dark when they got to Or San Michele, and the lamps burned dully.

Lolo stumped up the stairs wearily, with a vague, dull fear at his small heart.

"Moufflou, Moufflou!" he called. Where was Moufflou? Always at the first sound of his crutch the poodle came flying toward him. "Moufflou, Moufflou!" he called all the way up the long, dark, twisting stone stair. He pushed open the door, and he called again, "Moufflou, Moufflou!"

But no dog answered to his call.

"Mother, where is Moufflou?" he asked, staring with blinking, dazzled eyes into the oil-lit room where his mother sat knitting. Tasso was not then home from work. His mother went on with her knitting; there was an uneasy look on her face.

"Mother, what have you done with Moufflou, *my* Moufflou?" said Lolo, with a look that was almost stern on his ten-year-old face.

Then his mother, without looking up and moving her knitting-needles very rapidly, said, —

"Moufflou is sold!"

And little Dina, who was a quick, pert child, cried, with a shrill voice, —

"Mother has sold him for a thousand francs to the foreign gentleman."

"Sold him!"

Lolo grew white and grew cold as ice: he stammered, threw up his hands over his head, gasped a little for breath, then fell down in a dead swoon, his poor useless limb doubled under him.

When Tasso came home that sad night and found his little brother shivering, moaning, and half delirious, and when he heard what had been done, he was sorely grieved.

"Oh, mother, how could you do it?" he cried. "Poor, poor Moufflou! and Lolo loves him so!"

"I have got the money," said his mother, feverishly, "and you will not need to go for a soldier; we can buy your substitute. What is a poodle, that you mourn about it? We can get another poodle for Lolo."

"Another will not be Moufflou," said Tasso, and yet

was seized with such a frantic happiness himself at the
knowledge that he would not need to go to the army,
that he too felt as if he were drunk on new wine, and
had not the heart to rebuke his mother.

"A thousand francs!" he muttered; "a thousand
francs! *Dio mio!* Who could ever have fancied anybody would have given such a price for a common
white poodle? One would think the gentleman had
bought the church and the tabernacle!"

"Fools and their money are soon parted," said his
mother, with cross contempt.

It was true: she had sold Moufflou.

The English gentleman had called on her while Lolo
and the dog had been in the Cascine, and had said that
he was desirous of buying the poodle, which had so
diverted his sick child that the little invalid would not
be comforted unless he possessed it. Now, at any other
time the good woman would have sturdily refused any
idea of selling Moufflou; but that morning the thousand
francs which would buy Tasso's substitute were forever
in her mind and before her eyes. When she heard the
foreigner her heart gave a great leap, and her head
swam giddily, and she thought, in a spasm of longing
— if she could get those thousand francs! But though
she was so dizzy and so upset she retained her grip on
her native Florentine shrewdness. She said nothing of
her need of the money; not a syllable of her sore distress. On the contrary, she was coy and wary, affected
great reluctance to part with her pet, invented a great
offer made for him by a director of a circus, and finally
let fall a hint that less than a thousand francs she could
never take for poor Moufflou.

The gentleman assented with so much willingness to the price that she instantly regretted not having asked double. He told her that if she would take the poodle that afternoon to his hotel the money should be paid to her; so she dispatched her children after their noonday meal in various directions, and herself took Moufflou to his doom. She could not believe her senses when ten hundred-franc notes were put into her hand. She scrawled her signature, Rosina Calabucci, to a formal receipt, and went away, leaving Moufflou in his new owner's rooms, and hearing his howls and moans pursue her all the way down the staircase and out into the air.

She was not easy at what she had done.

"It seemed," she said to herself, "like selling a Christian."

But then to keep her eldest son at home, — what a joy that was! On the whole, she cried so and laughed so as she went down the Lung' Arno that once or twice people looked at her, thinking her out of her senses, and a guard spoke to her angrily.

Meanwhile, Lolo was sick and delirious with grief. Twenty times he got out of his bed and screamed to be allowed to go with Moufflou, and twenty times his mother and his brothers put him back again and held him down and tried in vain to quiet him.

The child was beside himself with misery. "Moufflou! Moufflou!" he sobbed at every moment; and by night he was in a raging fever, and when his mother, frightened, ran and called in the doctor of the quarter, that worthy shook his head and said something as to a shock of the nervous system, and muttered a long word, — meningitis."

Lolo took a hatred to the sight of Tasso, and thrust him away, and his mother, too.

"It is for you Moufflou is sold," he said, with his little teeth and hands tight clinched.

After a day or two Tasso felt as if he could not bear his life, and went down to the hotel to see if the foreign gentleman would allow him to have Moufflou back for half an hour to quiet his little brother by a sight of him. But at the hotel he was told that the *Milord Inglese* who had bought the dog of Rosina Calabucci had gone that same night of the purchase to Rome, to Naples, to Palermo, *chi sa?*

"And Moufflou with him?" asked Tasso.

"The *barbone* he had bought with him," said the porter of the hotel. "Such a beast! Howling, shrieking, raging all the day, and all the paint scratched off the *salon* door."

Poor Moufflou! Tasso's heart was heavy as he heard of that sad helpless misery of their bartered favorite and friend.

"What matter?" said his mother, fiercely, when he told her. "A dog is a dog. They will feed him better than we could. In a week he will have forgotten — *chè!*"

But Tasso feared that Moufflou would not forget. Lolo certainly would not. The doctor came to the bedside twice a day, and ice and water were kept on the aching hot little head that had got the malady with the long name, and for the chief part of the time Lolo lay quiet, dull, and stupid, breathing heavily, and then at intervals cried and sobbed and shrieked hysterically for Moufflou.

"Can you not get what he calls for to quiet him with the sight of it?" said the doctor. But that was not possible, and poor Rosina covered her head with her apron and felt a guilty creature.

"Still, you will not go to the army," she said to Tasso, clinging to that immense joy for her consolation. "Only think! we can pay Guido Squarcione to go for you. He always said he would go if anybody would pay him. Oh, my Tasso, surely to keep you is worth a dog's life!"

"And Lolo's?" said Tasso, gloomily. "Nay, mother, it works ill to meddle too much with fate. I drew my number; I was bound to go. Heaven would have made it up to you somehow."

"Heaven sent me the foreigner; the Madonna's own self sent him to ease a mother's pain," said Rosina, rapidly and angrily. "There are the thousand francs safe to hand in the *cassone*, and what, pray, is it we miss? Only a dog like a sheep, that brought gallons of mud in with him every time it rained, and ate as much as any one of you."

"But Lolo?" said Tasso, under his breath.

His mother was so irritated and so tormented by her own conscience that she upset all the cabbage broth into the burning charcoal.

"Lolo was always a little fool, thinking of nothing but the church and the dog, and nasty field-flowers," she said angrily. "I humored him ever too much because of the hurt to his hip, and so — and so — "

Then the poor soul made matters worse by dropping her tears into the saucepan, and fanning the charcoal so furiously that the flame caught her fan of cane-

leaves, and would have burned her arm had not Tasso
been there.

"You are my prop and safety always. Who would
not have done what I did? Not Santa Felicità herself," she said, with a great sob.

But all this did not cure poor Lolo.

The days and the weeks of the golden autumn
weather passed away, and he was always in danger,
and the small close room where he slept with Sandro
and Beppo and Tasso was not one to cure such an
illness as had now beset him. Tasso went to his work
with a sick heart in the Cascine, where the colchicum
was all lilac among the meadow grass, and the ashes
and elms were taking their first flush of the coming
autumnal change. He did not think Lolo would ever
get well, and the good lad felt as if he had been the
murderer of his little brother.

True, he had had no hand or voice in the sale of
Moufflou, but Moufflou had been sold for his sake. It
made him feel half guilty, very unhappy, quite unworthy all the sacrifice that had been made for him.
"Nobody should meddle with fate," thought Tasso,
who knew his grandfather had died in San Bonifazio
because he had driven himself mad over the dream-
book trying to get lucky numbers for the lottery and
become a rich man at a stroke.

It was rapture, indeed, to know that he was free of
the army for a time at least, that he might go on
undisturbed at his healthful labor, and get a rise in
wages as time went on, and dwell in peace with his
family, and perhaps — perhaps in time earn enough to
marry pretty flaxen-haired Biondina, the daughter of

the barber in the piazzetta. It was rapture indeed; but then poor Moufflou!—and poor, poor Lolo! Tasso felt as if he had bought his own exemption by seeing his little brother and the good dog torn in pieces and buried alive for his service.

And where was poor Moufflou?

Gone far away somewhere south in the hurrying, screeching, vomiting, braying train that it made Tasso giddy only to look at as it rushed by the green meadows beyond the Cascine on its way to the sea.

"If he could see the dog he cries so for, it might save him," said the doctor, who stood with a grave face watching Lolo.

But that was beyond any one's power. No one could tell where Moufflou was. He might be carried away to England, to France, to Russia, to America,—who could say? They did not know where his purchaser had gone. Moufflou even might be dead.

The poor mother, when the doctor said that, went and looked at the ten hundred-franc notes that were once like angels' faces to her, and said to them,—

"Oh, you children of Satan, why did you tempt me? I sold the poor, innocent, trustful beast to get you, and now my child is dying!"

Her eldest son would stay at home, indeed; but if this little lame one died! Rosina Calabucci would have given up the notes and consented never to own five francs in her life if only she could have gone back over the time and kept Moufflou, and seen his little master running out with him into the sunshine.

More than a month went by, and Lolo lay in the same state, his yellow hair shorn, his eyes dilated and

yet stupid, life kept in him by a spoonful of milk, a
lump of ice, a drink of lemon-water; always muttering,
when he spoke at all, "Moufflou, Moufflou, *dov' è*
Moufflou?" and lying for days together in somnolence
and unconsciousness, with the fire eating at his brain
and the weight lying on it like a stone.

The neighbors were kind, and brought fruit and the
like, and sat up with him, and chattered so all at once
in one continuous brawl that they were enough in themselves to kill him, for such is ever the Italian fashion
of sympathy in all illness.

But Lolo did not get well, did not even seem to see
the light at all, or to distinguish any sounds around
him; and the doctor in plain words told Rosina Calabucci that her little boy must die. Die, and the church
so near? She could not believe it. Could St. Mark,
and St. George, and the rest that he had loved so do
nothing for him? No, said the doctor, they could do
nothing; the dog might do something, since the brain
had so fastened on that one idea; but then they had
sold the dog.

"Yes; I sold him!" said the poor mother, breaking
into floods of remorseful tears.

So at last the end drew so nigh that one twilight
time the priest came out of the great arched door that
is next St. Mark, with the Host uplifted, and a little
acolyte ringing the bell before it, and passed across the
piazzetta, and went up the dark staircase of Rosina's
dwelling, and passed through the weeping, terrified
children, and went to the bedside of Lolo.

Lolo was unconscious, but the holy man touched
his little body and limbs with the sacred oil, and

prayed over him, and then stood sorrowful with bowed head.

Lolo had had his first communion in the summer, and in his preparation for it had shown an intelligence and devoutness that had won the priest's gentle heart.

Standing there, the holy man commended the innocent soul to God. It was the last service to be rendered to him save that very last of all when the funeral office should be read above his little grave among the millions of nameless dead at the sepulchres of the poor at Trebbiano.

All was still as the priest's voice ceased; only the sobs of the mother and of the children broke the stillness as they kneeled; the hand of Biondina had stolen into Tasso's.

Suddenly there was a loud, scuffling noise; hurrying feet came patter, patter, patter up the stairs, a ball of mud and dust flew over the heads of the kneeling figures, fleet as the wind Moufflou dashed through the room and leaped upon the bed.

Lolo opened his heavy eyes, and a sudden light of consciousness gleamed in them like a sunbeam. "Moufflou!" he murmured, in his little thin faint voice. The dog pressed close to his breast and kissed his wasted face.

Moufflou was come home!

And Lolo came home too, for death let go its hold upon him. Little by little, very faintly and flickeringly and very uncertainly at the first, life returned to the poor little body, and reason to the tormented, heated little brain. Moufflou was his physician; Moufflou, who, himself a skeleton under his matted curls, would not stir from his side and looked at him all day long with two beaming brown eyes full of unutterable love.

Lolo was happy; he asked no questions, — was too weak, indeed, even to wonder. He had Moufflou; that was enough.

Alas! though they dared not say so in his hearing, it was not enough for his elders. His mother and Tasso knew that the poodle had been sold and paid for; that they could lay no claim to keep him; and that almost certainly his purchaser would seek him out and assert his indisputable right to him. And then how would Lolo ever bear that second parting? — Lolo, so weak that he weighed no more than if he had been a little bird.

Moufflou had, no doubt, travelled a long distance and suffered much. He was but skin and bone; he bore the marks of blows and kicks; his once silken hair was all discolored and matted; he had, no doubt, travelled far. But then his purchaser would be sure to ask for him, soon or late, at his old home; and then? Well, then if they did not give him up themselves, the law would make them.

Rosina Calabucci and Tasso, though they dared say nothing before any of the children, felt their hearts in their mouths at every step on the stair, and the first interrogation of Tasso every evening when he came from his work was, "Has any one come for Moufflou?" For ten days no one came, and their first terrors lulled a little.

On the eleventh morning, a feast-day, on which Tasso was not going to his labors in the Cascine, there came a person, with a foreign look, who said the words they so much dreaded to hear : " Has the poodle that you sold to an English gentleman come back to you ? "

Yes : his English master claimed him !

The servant said that they had missed the dog in Rome a few days after buying and taking him there ; that he had been searched for in vain, and that his master had thought it possible the animal might have found his way back to his old home : there had been stories of such wonderful sagacity in dogs : anyhow, he had sent for him on the chance ; he was himself back on the Lung' Arno. The servant pulled from his pocket a chain, and said his orders were to take the poodle away at once : the little sick gentleman had fretted very much about his loss.

Tasso heard in a very agony of despair. To take Moufflou away now would be to kill Lolo — Lolo so feeble still, so unable to understand, so passionately alive to every sight and sound of Moufflou, lying for hours together motionless with his hand buried in the poodle's curls, saying nothing, only smiling now and then, and murmuring a word or two in Moufflou's ear.

" The dog did come home," said Tasso, at length, in a low voice : " angels must have shown him the road, poor beast ! From Rome ! Only to think of it, from Rome ! And he a dumb thing ! I tell you he is here, honestly : so will you not trust me just so far as this ? Will you let me go with you and speak to the English lord before you take the dog away ? I have a little brother sorely ill — "

He could not speak more, for tears that choked his voice.

At last the messenger agreed so far as this. Tasso might go first and see the master, but he would stay here and have a care they did not spirit the dog away, — "for a thousand francs were paid for him," added the man, "and a dog that can come all the way from Rome by itself must be an uncanny creature."

Tasso thanked him, went up-stairs, was thankful that his mother was at mass and could not dispute with him, took the ten hundred-franc notes from the old oak *cassone*, and with them in his breast-pocket walked out into the air. He was but a poor working lad, but he had made up his mind to do an heroic deed, for self-sacrifice is always heroic. He went straightway to the hotel where the English *milord* was, and when he had got there remembered that still he did not know the name of Moufflou's owner; but the people of the hotel knew him as Rosina Calabucci's son and guessed what he wanted, and said the gentleman who had lost the poodle was within up-stairs and they would tell him.

Tasso waited some half-hour with his heart beating sorely against the packet of hundred-franc notes. At last he was beckoned up-stairs, and there he saw a foreigner with a mild fair face, and a very lovely lady, and a delicate child who was lying on a couch. "Moufflou! Where is Moufflou?" cried the little child, impatiently, as he saw the youth enter.

Tasso took his hat off, and stood in the doorway, an embrowned, healthy, not ungraceful figure, in his working-clothes of rough blue stuff.

"If you please, most illustrious," he stammered, "poor Moufflou has come home."

The child gave a cry of delight: the gentleman and lady one of wonder. Come home! All the way from Rome!

"Yes, he has, most illustrious," said Tasso, gaining courage and eloquence: "and now I want to beg something of you. We are poor, and I drew a bad number, and it was for that my mother sold Moufflou. For myself, I did not know anything of it; but she thought she would buy my substitute, and of course she could; but Moufflou is come home, and my little brother Lolo, the little boy your most illustrious first saw playing with the poodle, fell ill of grief of losing Moufflou, and for a month has lain saying nothing sensible, but only calling for the dog, and my old grandfather died of worrying himself mad over the lottery numbers, and Lolo was so near dying that the Blessed Host had been brought, and the holy oil had been put on him, when all at once there rushes in Moufflou, skin and bone, and covered with mud, and at the sight of him Lolo comes back to his senses, and that is now ten days ago, and though Lolo is still as weak as a new-born thing, he is always sensible, and takes what we give him to eat, and lies always looking at Moufflou, and smiling, and saying, 'Moufflou! Moufflou!' and, most illustrious, I know well you have bought the dog, and the law is with you, and by the law you claim it; but I thought perhaps, as Lolo loves him so, you would let us keep the dog, and would take back the thousand francs, and myself I will go and be a soldier, and heaven will take care of them all somehow."

Then Tasso, having said all this in one breathless, monotonous recitative, took the thousand francs out of his breast-pocket and held them out timidly toward the foreign gentleman, who motioned them aside and stood silent.

"Did you understand, Victor?" he said, at last, to his little son.

The child hid his face in his cushions.

"Yes, I did understand something: let Lolo keep him; Moufflou was not happy with me."

But he burst out crying as he said it.

Moufflou had run away from him.

Moufflou had never loved him, for all his sweet cakes and fond caresses and platefuls of delicate savory meats. Moufflou had run away and found his own road over two hundred miles and more to go back to some little hungry children, who never had enough to eat themselves, and so, certainly, could never give enough to eat to the dog. Poor little boy! He was so rich and so pampered and so powerful, and yet he could never make Moufflou love him!

Tasso, who understood nothing that was said, laid the ten hundred-franc notes down on a table near him.

"If you would take them, most illustrious, and give me back what my mother wrote when she sold Moufflou," he said, timidly, "I would pray for you night and day, and Lolo would too; and as for the dog, we will get a puppy and train him for your little *signorino*; they can all do tricks, more or less, it comes by nature; and as for me, I will go to the army willingly; it is not right to interfere with fate; my old grandfather died mad because he would try to be a rich man, by dreaming about it and pulling destiny by the ears, as if she were a kicking mule; only, I do pray of you, do not take away Moufflou. And to think he trotted all those miles and miles, and you carried him by train too, and he never could have seen the road, and he has no power of speech to ask — "

Tasso broke down again in his eloquence, and drew the back of his hand across his wet eyelashes.

The English gentleman was not altogether unmoved.

" Poor faithful dog! " he said, with a sigh. " I am afraid we were very cruel to him, meaning to be kind. No; we will not claim him, and I do not think you should go for a soldier you seem so good a lad, and your mother must need you. Keep the money, my boy, and in payment you shall train up the puppy you talk of, and bring him to my little boy. I will come and see your mother and Lolo to-morrow. All the way from Rome! What wonderful sagacity! what matchless fidelity! "

You can imagine, without any telling of mine, the joy that reigned in Moufflou's home when Tasso returned thither with the money and the good tidings both. His substitute was bought without a day's delay, and Lolo rapidly recovered. As for Moufflou, he could never tell them his troubles, his wanderings, his difficulties, his perils; he could never tell them by what miraculous knowledge he had found his way across Italy, from the gates of Rome to the gates of Florence. But he soon grew plump again, and merry, and his love for Lolo was yet greater than before.

By the winter all the family went to live on an estate near Spezia that the English gentleman had purchased, and there Moufflou was happier than ever. The little English boy is gaining strength in the soft air, and he and Lolo are great friends, and play with Moufflou and the poodle puppy half the day upon the sunny terraces and under the green orange boughs. Tasso is one of the gardeners there; he will have to serve as a soldier probably in some category or another, but he is safe for the time, and is happy. Lolo, whose lameness will always exempt him from military service, when he grows to be a man means to be a florist, and a great one. He has learned to read, as the first step on the road of his ambition.

"But oh, Moufflou, how *did* you find your way home?" he asks the dog a hundred times a week.

How indeed!

No one ever knew how Moufflou had made that long journey on foot so many weary miles; but beyond a doubt he had done it alone and unaided, for if any one had helped him they would have come home with him to claim the reward.

And that you may not wonder too greatly at Moufflou's miraculous journey on his four bare feet, I will add here two facts known to friends of mine, of whose truthfulness there can be no doubt.

One concerns a French poodle who was purchased in Paris by the friend of my friend, and brought all the way from Paris to Milan by train. In a few days after his arrival in Milan the poodle was missing; and nothing

more was heard or known of him until many weeks later
his quondam owner in Paris, on opening his door one
morning, found the dog stretched dying on the threshold of his old home.

That is one fact; not a story, mind you, *a fact.*

The other is related to me by an Italian nobleman,
who in his youth belonged to the Guarda Nobile of
Tuscany. That brilliant corps of elegant gentlemen
owned a regimental pet, a poodle also, a fine merry and
handsome dog of its kind; and the officers all loved
and made much of him, except, alas! the commandant
of the regiment, who hated him, because when the
officers were on parade or riding in escort the poodle
was sure to be jumping and frisking about in front of
them. It is difficult to see where the harm of this was,
but this odious old martinet vowed vengeance against
the dog, and, being of course all powerful in his own
corps, ordered the exile from Florence of the poor
fellow. He was sent to a farm at Prato, twenty miles
off, along the hill; but very soon he found his way
back to Florence. He was then sent to Leghorn, forty
miles off, but in a week's time had returned to his old
comrades. He was then, by order of his unrelenting
foe, shipped to the island of Sardinia. How he did it no
one ever could tell, for he was carried safely to Sardinia
and placed inland there in kind custody, but in some
wonderful way the poor dog must have found out the
sea and hidden himself on board a returning vessel, for
in a month's time from his exile to the island he was
back again among his comrades in Florence. Now,
what I have to tell you almost breaks my heart to say,
and will, I think, quite break yours to hear; alas!

the brute of a commandant, untouched by such marvellous cleverness and faithfulness, was his enemy to the bitter end, and, in inexorable hatred, *had him shot!* Oh, when you grow to manhood and have power, use it with tenderness!

A STORY OF A CHIPMUNK

(FROM SQUIRRELS AND OTHER FUR BEARERS.)

BY JOHN BURROUGHS.

I WAS much amused one October in watching a chipmunk carry nuts and other food into his den. He had made a well-defined path from his door out through the weeds and dry leaves into the territory where his feeding-ground lay. The path was a crooked one; it dipped under weeds, under some large, loosely piled stones, under a pile of chestnut posts, and then followed the remains of an old wall. Going and coming, his motions were like clock-work. He always went by spurts and sudden sallies. He was never for one moment off his guard. He would appear at the mouth of his den, look quickly about, take a few leaps to a tussock of grass, pause a breath with one foot raised, slip quickly a few yards over some dry leaves, pause again by a stump beside a path, rush across the path to the pile of loose stones, go under the first and over the second, gain the pile of posts, make his way through that, survey his course a half moment from the other side of it, and then dart on to some other cover, and presently beyond my range, where I think he gathered acorns, as there were no other nut-bearing trees than oaks near. In four or five minutes I would see him coming back, always keeping rigidly to the course he took going out, pausing at the same spots, darting over or under the same objects, clearing at a bound the same pile of leaves. There was no variation in his manner of proceeding all the time I observed him.

He was alert, cautious, and exceedingly methodical. He had found safety in a certain course, and he did not at any time deviate a hair's breadth from it. Something seemed to say to him all the time, "Beware, beware!" The nervous, impetuous ways of these creatures are no doubt the result of the life of fear which they lead.

My chipmunk had no companion. He lived all by himself in true hermit fashion, as is usually the case with this squirrel. Provident creature that he is, one would think that he would long ago have discovered that heat, and therefore food, is economized by two or three nesting together.

One day in early spring, a chipmunk that lived near me met with a terrible adventure, the memory of which

will probably be handed down through many generations of its family. I was sitting in the summer-house
with Nig the cat upon my knee, when the chipmunk
came out of its den a few feet away, and ran quickly
to a pile of chestnut posts about twenty yards from
where I sat. Nig saw it, and was off my lap upon the
floor in an instant. I spoke sharply to the cat, when
she sat down and folded her paws under her, and
regarded the squirrel, as I thought, with only a dreamy
kind of interest. I fancied she thought it a hopeless
case there amid that pile of posts. "That is not your
game, Nig," I said, "so spare yourself any anxiety."
Just then I was called to the house, where I was
detained about five minutes. As I returned I met
Nig coming to the house with the chipmunk in her
mouth. She had the air of one who had won a wager.
She carried the chipmunk by the throat, and its body
hung limp from her mouth. I quickly took the squirrel
from her, and reproved her sharply. It lay in my hand
as if dead, though I saw no marks of the cat's teeth
upon it. Presently it gasped for its breath, then again
and again. I saw that the cat had simply choked it.
Quickly the film passed off its eyes, its heart began
visibly to beat, and slowly the breathing became regular.
I carried it back, and laid it down in the door of its den.
In a moment it crawled or kicked itself in. In the
afternoon I placed a handful of corn there, to express
my sympathy, and as far as possible make amends for
Nig's cruel treatment.

Not till four or five days had passed did my little
neighbor emerge again from its den, and then only for
a moment. That terrible black monster with the large

green-yellow eyes, — it might be still lurking near. How the black monster had captured the alert and restless squirrel so quickly, under the circumstances, was a great mystery to me. Was not its eye as sharp as the cat's, and its movements as quick? Yet cats do have the secret of catching squirrels, and birds, and mice, but I have never yet had the luck to see it done.

It was not very long before the chipmunk was going to and from her den as usual, though the dread of the black monster seemed ever before her, and gave speed and extra alertness to all her movements. In early summer four young chipmunks emerged from the den, and ran freely about. There was nothing to disturb them, for, alas! Nig herself was now dead.

THE HOMESICKNESS OF KEHONKA

By CHARLES G. D. ROBERTS.

THE April night, softly chill and full of the sense of thaw, was closing down over the wide salt marshes. Near at hand the waters of the Tantramar, resting at full tide, glimmered through the dusk and lapped faintly among the winter-ruined remnants of the sedge. Far off — infinitely far it seemed in that illusive atmosphere, which was clear yet full of the ghosts of rain — the last of daylight lay in a thin streak, pale and sharp, along a vast arc of the horizon. Overhead it was quite dark; for there was no moon, and the tenuous spring clouds were sufficient to shut out the stars. They clung in mid-heaven, but kept to their shadowy ranks without descending to obscure the lower air. Space and mystery, mystery and space, lay abroad upon the vague levels of marsh and tide.

Presently, from far along the dark heights of the sky, came voices, hollow, musical, confused. Swiftly they journeyed nearer; they grew louder. The sound — not vibrant, yet strangely far-carrying — was a clamorous monotony of honk-a-honk, honk-a-honk, honka, honka,

honk, honk. It hinted of wide distance voyaged over
on tireless wings, of a tropic winter passed in feeding
amid remote, high-watered meadows of Mexico and
Texas, of long flights yet to go, toward the rocky tarns
of Labrador and the reed beds of Ungava. As the
sound passed straight overhead the listener on the marsh
below imagined, though he could not see, the strongly
beating wings, the outstretched necks and heads, the
round, unswerving eyes of the wild goose flock in its V-
shaped array, winnowing steadily northward through the
night. But this particular flock was not set, as it
chanced, upon an all-night journey. The wise old
gander winging at the head of the V knew of good
feeding grounds near by, which he was ready to revisit.
He led the flock straight on, above the many windings
of the Tantramar, till its full-flooded sheen far below
him narrowed and narrowed to a mere brook. Here, in
the neighborhood of the uplands, were a number of
shallow, weedy, fresh water lakes, with shores so
choked with thickets, and fenced apart with bogs as to
afford a security which his years and broad experience
had taught him to value. Into one of these lakes, a
pale blur amid the thick shadows of the shores, the
flock dropped with heavy splashings. A scream or two
of full-throated content, a few flappings of wings and
rufflings of plumage in the cool, and the voyagers
settled into quiet.

All night there was a silence around the flock, save
for the whispering seepage of the snow patches that
still lingered among the thickets. With the first creeping pallor of dawn the geese began to feed, plunging
their long black necks deep into the water and feeling

with the sensitive inner edges of their bills for the swelling root-buds of weed and sedge. When the sun was about the edge of the horizon, and the first rays came sparkling, of a chilly pink most luminous and pure, through the lean traceries of the brush-wood, the leader raised his head high and screamed a signal. With answering cries and a tempestuous splashing the flock flapped for a few yards along the surface of the water. Then they rose clear, formed quickly into rank, and in their spacious V went honking northward over the half-lighted, mysterious landscapes. But, as it chanced, not all the flock set out with that morning departure. There was one pair, last year's birds, upon whom had fallen a weariness of travel. Perhaps in the coils of their brains lurked some inherited memory of these safe resting-places and secluded feeding grounds of the Midgic lakes. However that may have been, they chose to stay where they were, feeling in their blood no call from the cold north solitudes. Dipping and bowing, black neck by neck, they gave no heed to the leader's signal, nor to the noisy going of the flock. Pushing briskly with the black webs of their feet against the discolored water they swam to the shore and cast about for a place to build their nest.

There was no urgent hurry, so they chose not on that day nor the next. When they chose, it was a little bushy islet off a point of land, well tangled with alder and osier and a light flotsam of driftwood. The nest, in the heart of the tangle, was an apparently haphazard collection of sticks and twigs, well raised above the damp, well lined with moss and feathers. Here, in course of days, there accumulated a shining cluster of six

large white eggs.   But by this time the spring freshet
had gone down.   The islet was an islet no longer, but a
mere adjunct of the point, which any inquisitive foot
might reach dry shod.   Now just at this time it happened that a young farmer, who had a curious taste for
all the wild kindred of the wood, and flood, and air,
came up from the lower Tantramar with a wagon-load
of grist for the Midgic mill.   While his buckwheat and
barley were a-grinding he thought of a current opinion
to the effect that the wild geese were given to nesting·
in the Midgic lakes.   "If so," said he to himself, "this
is the time they would be about it."   Full of interest,
a half hour's tramp through difficult woods brought
him to the nearest of the waters.   An instinct, an
intuition born of his sympathy with the furtive folk,
led him to the point, and out along the point to that
once islet, with its secret in the heart of the tangle.
Vain were the furious hissings, the opposing wings, the
wide black bills that threatened and oppugned him.
With the eager delight of a boy he pounced upon those
six great eggs, and carried them all away.   "They will
soon turn out another clutch," said he to himself, as he
left the bereaved pair, and tramped elatedly back to the
mill.   As for the bereaved pair, being of a philosophic
spirit, they set themselves to fulfil as soon as possible his
prophecy.

On the farm by the lower Tantramar, in a hogshead
half filled with straw and laid on its side in a dark
corner of the tool-shed, those six eggs were diligently
brooded for four weeks and two days by a comfortable
gray-and-white goose of the common stock.   When
they hatched, the good gray-and-white mother may

have been surprised to find her goslings of an olive-
green hue, instead of the bright golden yellow which
her past experience and that of her fellows had taught
her to expect. She may have marvelled, too, at their unwonted slenderness and activity. These trivial details,
however, in no way dampened the zeal with which she
led them to the goose pond, or the fidelity with which
she pastured and protected them. But rats, skunks,
sundry obscure ailments, and the heavy wheels of the
farm wagon, are among the perils, which, the summer
through, lie in wait for all the children of the feathered
kin upon the farm; and so it came about that of the six
young ones so successfully hatched from the wild goose
eggs, only two lived till the coming of autumn brought
them full plumage and the power of flight. Before the
time of the southward migration came near, the young
farmer took these two and clipped from each the strong
primaries of their right wings. "They seem contented
enough and tame as any," he said to himself, "but
you never can tell what'll happen when the instinct
strikes 'em." Both the young wild geese were fine
males. Their heads, and long, slim necks were black,
as were also their tails, great wing feathers, bills and
feet. Under the tail their feathers were of snowiest
white, and all the other portions of their bodies a rich
grayish brown. Each bore on the side of its face a
sharply defined triangular patch of white, mottled with
faint brown markings that would disappear after the
first moult. In one the white cheek patches met under
the throat. This was a large, strongly built bird, of a
placid and domestic temper. He was satisfied with the
undistinguished gray companions of the flock. He was

content, like them, to gutter noisily with his discrimi-
nating bill along the shallow edges of the pond, to float
and dive and flap in the deeper centre, to pasture at
random over the wet meadow, biting off the short
grasses with quick, sharp, yet graceful curving dabs.
Goose-pond and wet meadow and cattle-trodden barnyard
bounded his aspirations. When his adult voice came to
him, all he could say was honk, honk, contemplatively,
and sometimes honk-a-honk when he flapped his wings
in the exhilarating coolness of the sunrise. The other
captive was of a more restless temperament, slenderer in
build, more eager and alert of eye, less companionable of
mood. He was, somehow, never seen in the centre of
the flock — he never seemed a part of it. He fed,
swam, rested, preened himself, always a little apart.
Often, when the others were happily occupied with their
familiar needs and satisfactions, he would stand motionless, his compact, glossy head high in the air, looking to
the north as if in expectation, listening as if he awaited
longed-for tidings. The triangular white patch on each
side of his head was very narrow, and gave him an expression of wildness; yet in reality he was no more
wild, or rather no more shy, than any others of the
flock. None, indeed, had so confident a fearlessness as
he. He would take oats out of the farmer's hand,
which none of the rest quite dared to do.

Until late in the autumn, the lonely, uncomraded
bird was always silent. But when the migrating flocks
began to pass overhead, on the long, southward trail,
and their hollow clamor was heard over the farmstead
night and morning, he grew more restless. He would
take a short run with outspread wings, and then, feel-

ing their crippled inefficiency, would stretch himself
to his full height and call, a sonorous, far-reaching
cry — ke-honk-a, ke-honk-a. From this call, so often
repeated throughout October and November, the farmer
named him Kehonka. The farmer's wife favored the
more domesticated and manageable brother, who could
be trusted never to stray. But the farmer, who mused
deeply over his furrows, and half-wistfully loved the
wild kindred, loved Kehonka, and used to say he would
not lose the bird for the price of a steer. " That there
bird," he would say, " has got dreams away down in
his heart. Like as not, he remembers things his father
and mother have seen, up amongst the ice cakes and
the northern lights, or down amongst the bayous and
the big southern lilies." But all his sympathy failed to
make him repent of having clipped Kehonka's wing.

During the long winter, when the winds swept
fiercely the open marshes of the Tantramar, and the
snow piled in high drifts around the barns and wood-
piles, and the sheds were darkened, and in the sun at
noonday the strawy dungheaps steamed, the rest of the
geese remained listlessly content. But not so Kehonka.
Somewhere back of his brain he cherished pre-natal
memories of warm pools in the South, where leafy
screens grew rank, and the sweet-rooted water-plants
pulled easily from the deep black mud, and his true
kindred were screaming to each other at the oncoming
of the tropic dark. When the flock was out in the
barnyard, pulling lazily at the trampled litter, and
snatching scraps of the cattle's chopped turnips,
Kehonka would stand aloof by the water trough, his
head erect, listening, longing. As the winter sun sank

early over the fir woods back of the farm, his wings
would open, and his desirous cry would go echoing
three or four times across the still countryside — ke-
honk-a — ke-honk-a — ke-honk-a ! Whereat the farmer's wife, turning her buckwheat pancakes over the hot
kitchen stove, would mutter impatiently ; but the
farmer, slipping to the door of the cow-stable with the
bucket of feed in his hand, would look with deep eyes
of sympathy at the unsatisfied bird. " He wants something that we don't grow round here," he would say to
himself ; and little by little the bird's restlessness came
to seem to him the concrete embodiment of certain dim
outreachings of his own. He, too, caught himself
straining his gaze beyond the marsh horizons of Tantramar.

When the winter broke, and the seeping drifts
shrank together, and the brown of the ploughed fields
came through the snow in patches, and the slopes leading down to the marshland were suddenly loud with
running water, Kehonka's restlessness grew so eager
that he almost forgot to feed. It was time, he thought,
for the northward flight to begin. He would stand for
hours, turning first one dark eye, then the other, toward
the soft sky overhead, expectant of the V-shaped, journeying flock, and the far-off clamor of voices from the
South crying to him in his own tongue. At last, when
the snow was about gone from the open fields, one
evening at the shutting-in of dark, the voices came.
He was lingering at the edge of the goose-pond, the
rest having settled themselves for the night, when he
heard the expected sounds. Honk-a-honk, honk-a-honk,
honk-a-honk-a, honk, honk, they came up against the

light April wind, nearer, nearer, nearer. Even his keen eye could not detect them against the blackness; but up went his wings, and again and again he screamed to them sonorously. In response to his call, their flight swung lower, and the confusion of their honking seemed as if it were going to descend about him. But the wary old gander, their leader, discerned the roofs, man's handiwork, and suspected treachery. At his sharp signal the flock, rising again, streamed off swiftly toward safer feeding grounds, and left Kehonka to call and call unanswered. Up to this moment all his restlessness had not led him to think of actually deserting the farmstead and the alien flock. Though not of them he had felt it necessary to be with them. His instinct for other scenes and another fellowship had been too little tangible to move him to the snapping of established ties. But now, all his desires at once took concrete form. It was his, it belonged to himself — that strong, free flight, that calling through the sky, that voyaging northward to secret nesting places. In that wild flock which had for a moment swerved downward to his summons, or in some other flock, was his mate. It was mating season, and not until now had he known it.

Nature does sometimes, under the pressure of great and concentrated desires, make unexpected effort to meet unforeseen demands. All winter long, though it was not the season for such growth, Kehonka's clipped wing-primaries had been striving to develop. They had now, contrary to all custom, attained to an inch or so of effective flying web. Kehonka's heart was near bursting with his desire as the voices of the unseen flock died away. He spread his wings to their full extent, ran some ten paces along the ground, and then, with all his energies concentrated to the effort, he rose into the air and flew with swift-beating wings out into the dark upon the northward trail. His trouble was not the lack of wing surface, but the lack of balance. One wing being so much less in spread than the other, he felt a fierce force striving to turn him over at every stroke. It was the struggle to counteract this tendency that wore him out. His first desperate effort carried him half a mile. Then he drooped to earth, in a bed of withered salt-grass, all awash with the full tide of Tantramar. Resting amid the salt-grass he tasted such an exultation of freedom that his heart forgot its soreness over the flock which had vanished. Presently, however, he heard again the sound that so thrilled his every vein. Weird, hollow, echoing with memories and tidings, it came throbbing up the wind. His own strong cry went out at once to meet it — ke-honk-a, ke-honk-a, ke-honk-a. The voyagers this time were flying very low. They came near, nearer, and at last, in a sudden silence of voices, but a great flapping of wings, they settled down in the salt grass all about him.

The place was well enough for a night's halt — a shallow, marshy pool which caught the overflow of the highest spring tides, and so was not emptied by the ebb. After its first splashing descent into the water, which glimmered in pale patches among the grass stems, every member of the flock sat for some moments motionless as statues, watchful for unknown menace; and Kehonka, his very soul trembling with desire achieved, sat motionless among them. Then, there being no sign of peril at hand, there was a time of quiet paddling to and fro, a scuttling of practised bills among the grass-roots, and Kehonka found himself easily accepted as a member of the flock. Happiness kept him restless and on the move long after the others had their bills tucked under their wings. In the earliest gray of dawn, when the flock awoke to feed, Kehonka fed among them as if he had been with them all the way on their flight from the Mexican plains. But his feeding was always by the side of a young female who had not yet paired. It was interrupted by many little courtesies of touching bill and bowing head, which were received with plain favor; for Kehonka was a handsome and well-marked bird. By the time the sky was red along the east and strewn with pale, blown feathers of amber pink toward the zenith, his swift wooing was next door to winning. He had forgotten his captivity and clipped wing. He was thinking of a nest in the wide emptiness of the North.

When the signal cry came, and the flock took flight, Kehonka rose with them. But his preliminary rush

along the water was longer than that of the others, and when the flock formed into flying order he fell in at the end of the longer leg of the V, behind the weakest of

the young geese.   This would have been a humiliation
to him, had he taken thought of it at all; but his attention was all absorbed in keeping his balance.   When the
flock found its pace, and the cold sunrise air began to
whistle past the straight, bullet-like rush of their flight,
a terror grew upon him.   He flew much better than he
had flown the night before; but he soon saw that this
speed of theirs was beyond him.   He would not yield,
however.   He would not lag behind.   Every force of his
body and his brain went into that flight, till his eyes
blurred and his heart seemed on the point of bursting.
Then, suddenly, with a faint, despairing note, he lurched
aside, shot downward, and fell with a great splash into
the channel of the Tantramar.   With strong wings,
and level, unpausing flight, the flock went on to its
north without him.

Dazed by the fall, and exhausted by the intensity of
his effort, Kehonka floated, moveless, for many minutes.
The flood tide, however, racing inland, was carrying him
still northward; and presently he began to swim in the
same direction.   In his sick heart glowed still the vision
of the nest in the far-off solitudes, and he felt that he
would find there waiting for him, the strong-winged
mate who had left him behind.   Half an hour later another flock passed honking overhead, and he called to
them; but they were high up, and feeding time was past.
They gave no sign in answer.   He made no attempt to
fly after them.   Hour after hour he swam on with the
current, working ever north.   When the tide turned
he went ashore, still following the river, till its course
changed toward the east; whereupon he ascended the
channel of a small tributary which flowed in on the

north bank.   Here and there he snatched quick mouthfuls of sprouting grasses, but he was too driven by his
desire to pause for food.   Sometimes he tried his wings
again, covering now some miles at each flight, till by
and by, losing the stream because its direction failed
him, he found himself in a broken upland country,
where progress was slow and toilsome.   Soon after sunset, troubled because there was no water near, he again
took wing, and over dark woods which filled him with
apprehension he made his longest flight.   When about
spent he caught a small gleaming of water far below
him, and alighted in a little woodland glade wherein a
brook had overflowed low banks.

The noise of his abrupt descent loudly startled the
wet and dreaming woods.   It was a matter of interest
to all the furry, furtive ears of the forest for a half mile
round.   But it was in no way repeated.   For perhaps
fifteen minutes Kehonka floated, neck erect, head high
and watchful, in the middle of the pool, with no movement except the slight, unseen oaring of his black-
webbed feet, necessary to keep the current from bearing
him into the gloom of the woods.   This gloom, hedging
him on every side, troubled him with a vague fear.
But in the open of the mid-pool, with two or three stars
peering faintly through the misted sky above him, he
felt comparatively safe.   At last, very far above, he
heard again that wild calling of his fellows — honk-a-
honk, honk-a-honk, honka, honka, honk honk — high
and dim and ghostly, for these rough woodlands had no
appeal for the journeying flocks.   Remote as the voices
were, however, Kehonka answered at once.   His keen,
sonorous, passionate cry rang strangely on the night,

three times. The flock paid no heed to it whatever, but sped on northward with unvarying flight and clamor; and as the wizard noise passed beyond, Kehonka, too weary to take wing, followed eagerly to the northerly shore of the pool, ran up the wet bank, and stood straining after it.

His wings were half spread as he stood there quivering with his passion. In his heart was the hunger of the quest. In his eyes was the vision of nest and mate, where the serviceberry thickets grew by the wide subarctic's waters. The night wind blew steadily away

from him to the underbrush close by; or even in his absorption he would have noticed the approach of a menacing, musky smell. But every sense was now numb in the presence of his great desire. There was no warning for him.

The underbrush, rustled, ever so softly. Then a small, delicately moving, fine-furred shape, the discourager of quests, darted stealthily forth, and with a bound that was feathery in its blown lightness, seeming to be uplifted by the wide-plumed tail that balanced it, descended on Kehonka's body. There was a thin honk, cut short by keen teeth meeting with a crunch and a twist in the glossy, slim blackness of Kehonka's neck. The struggle lasted scarcely more than two heart beats.

The wide wings pounded twice or thrice upon the ground, in fierce convulsion.   Then the red fox, with a sidewise jerk of his head, flung the heavy, trailing carcass into a position for its easy carrying, and trotted off with it into the darkness of the woods.

THE STORY OF A HOMER

(FROM RECREATION.)

BY FRANK M. GILBERT.

I CALL him Steeple Dick because he was raised in a church steeple. To all intents and purposes he was a common blue, town pigeon, just like so many that gain a precarious living flying around the streets and picking up what they can. In almost any large city the steeples and belfries are full of these nomads and they all pass as common pigeons, belonging to nobody; but to anyone who closely noticed our Dick, the bold, fearless look about the head, the full damson eyes, the tapering neck, the square shoulders, strong wings and short, compact body set on sturdy red legs, showed that he was something out of the ordinary. The wattle around his eyes and the other V-shaped wattle over his beak, also gave him a different appearance from the stragglers that picked around by day and roosted in the old steeple at night. Again, the others might grow careless while feeding, and narrowly escape the step of a horse or the wheel of a wagon in the street, or the stone of the small boy; but not so

Dick. He was ever on guard and at the slightest motion was up in the air and out of danger. Though he did not know it, Dick was of royal blood, and thereby hangs a tale.

Across the water, in the kingdom of Belgium, the homer is almost a household god. There it is bred to perfection. No other pigeon is so bold and fearless, so full of bulldog tenacity, so full of royal courage. No other has that unfailing instinct that makes him stop at nothing, whether mountain or sea, ice or torrid heat; but will cause him, when released, to fly in a direct line to his home loft, where his mate and little ones are.

So high in esteem are these birds held that they are used as royal gifts. In 1894 the King of Belgium sent some of these homers to the heir apparent of England, who in turn gave some to a friend who was coming to America. By some means, a grand pair were released on a Western railroad. At the first dash they went high in the air, on their strong wings, with ever widening circles, their keen eyes looking for some familiar point. But all in vain. They had never been trained in America, and were strangers in a strange land. Day after day they flew, trying all points of the compass, but were baffled everywhere. One evening, after the ice of a sleet storm had clogged their wings, they settled on one of the highest buildings they could find in a city they had reached, and, closing up together, sat and shivered through the long night. Next morning brought a snow, and then, knowing that their last hope of any landmark was gone, they began to look for shelter.

It happened they had lit on a church.   On one side of its steeple a slat, long battered by the elements, had given down and through this the royal pair saw many a street straggler come and go.   They flew over and for a few days roosted with the other birds as best they could, caring for little save a place to sleep.   But in a short time the first warm spring breezes began to blow through the steeple, and the breeding instinct became strong.   The pair cast covetous glances at a corner of the steeple which seemed to have been left by the builders especially for a pigeon's nest.   It was not long till, *vi et armis*, it was theirs.

There Dick's career began, and it began alone, for the egg that was to have produced his mate was broken in a struggle for the nest.

Dick's first remembrance was of being imprisoned in something round, smooth, and warm.   He could feel at times a turning over of his prison, and hear a soft little coo.   Something told him he must get out, so, with his diminutive beak, he began a tap-tap that soon made cracks in his prison walls.   Then he would feel his prison turn again, and a gentle picking from the outside would crack the walls still more.   Again he heard that soft coo, and feeling that he must answer in some way, he almost frightened out what little life he had by uttering his first squeak.   Finally there was a break in the wall and a small wing slipped from where it had lain around his neck, and somehow got outside.   Next, a weak little leg wriggled out, and it was only a short time till he felt he was free and lying under a soft, downy breast, listening to the most delightful coos of affection.   Of course he was blind and there was nothing but down on his body, and of course he did not know where his head, legs or wings belonged; but the familiar beak would straighten them out and gradually place them as they should be. Then the beak would move around his head and lift it up, and his own little beak would somehow slip into that large one, from whose depths would come the most delicious food.

One day his eyes opened, and he saw a most beautiful mother looking at him with her loving eyes. Soon she stepped daintily off, and his great, strong father, one of whose feet could easily crush Dick, stepped into the nest, but oh so carefully, that Dick felt nothing till the warm breast was over him.

As Dick waxed in strength he began to "take notice." He would sleep contentedly in the nest, or look over the side, watching the other birds. But they were different from his parents. Their feathers were not so hard or shiny. Not a bird in the steeple had even a wire on its legs, while his mother and father had beautiful silver bands on each leg. If he could have read, he would have found that one band was the band of the Royal Homing Club, and the others were special bands won by wonderful flights. The father had homed from 1,000 miles away, while the mother had a velocity record of 1,500 yards a minute. Dick was very proud of those bands, and often wondered if they would grow on his legs.

Thus passed the days of his babyhood, till he was able to chase his parents out on the church roof and beg for food, or to take short flights with them; when one day they pecked at him and refused to feed him. Then his troubles began. Henceforth he must forage

for himself.   He flew around after the common pigeons
and soon learned how to pick up a precarious living in
the streets.

One sad day his parents disappeared.   No doubt in
the long days of nesting they had thought the matter
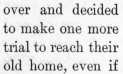
over and decided
to make one more
trial to reach their
old home, even if
they had
to cross
the ocean
to do so.
Whether
they dropped exhausted on some ship and were
helped across, or whether some storm at sea swept
them away forever, no one ever knew.   If they
died, it was while they were struggling on undaunted
and striving to reach the old home loft in far-off
Belgium.

Dick grew strong and full of vigor.   Soon all the
little pin feathers became matured and perfect, and a
beautiful green sheen came on his neck.   No bird could
hope to fly as he did.   He would dart into the air and
soar in wide circles, with a great flapping of wings that
made him the envy of all the others.   He was the king
of the steeple.   He had long ago whipped the miserable
speckled cock that used to perch at the broken slat
every evening and meanly fight and keep out all the
young and timid birds till they were nearly frozen.
He had long ago beaten out the pair of common looking
scrubs that had tried to steal the old home nest as soon

as his parents left, and it was now his, where he perched supreme every night.

Early one morning he noticed a crowd of men, with watches in hand, open some large hampers out of which flew a great lot of pigeons. All started off North save one little hen, which seemed utterly bewildered. She would make short flights, but soon come back to her starting-point, to sit there friendless and alone. Then again she would try, going high into the air, eagerly looking for some familiar landmark, but only to come back to the building where she first stopped.

To one who knows the homer and its ways the explanation is simple. She was a young bird who had never been away from the home loft, even for a short trial flight, and, of course, had no bearings to aid her.

Dick had noticed her several times during the day. He had even flown a little with her, just for exercise; had noticed that she looked a great deal like his mother, and had two bands on her legs; but he had not been really interested in her until he saw her give up, utterly disheartened and worn out, and draw up close to a chimney, where she sat homeless and alone. Then all the chivalry in Dick's heart came in play. He flew over where the stranger timidly sat, and waltzed around in ever decreasing circles, uttering his tenderest love notes. The sun shone on his burnished neck; he spread his tail and walked forward, stopping just far enough away to show how gentle he could be, and how, though not desiring in the least to be pressing, still he wished to lay his heart at the feet of beauty. Never did bird tell such an ardent tale of love. He stopped and drew near the little stranger, and pre-

tended to smooth his feathers, though the rascal knew
that each was in exactly the proper position. Finally
the object of his adoration walked up, stuck out her
little beak, and Dick got his first kiss.

How easy, then, to fly over to the steeple and show
her his home. How he coaxed and cooed while she
preened the feathers on his head and neck, gently closed
his eyes, ever and anon giving him a kiss, and cuddling
close to him in the old nest.

Soon Dick became the busiest pigeon in the city. No
common straw was good enough for little Dorothy's
nest. Each twig, each straw, each bit of hay must be
carefully shaken and investigated before the young
husband would fly to the steeple with it; for the new
nest must be the best one ever built there.

One day little Dorothy showed him an egg, and two
days later another. Oh! how precious those eggs were,
and how carefully the pair slipped on and off the nest.
How they patiently waited till incubation should be
over and the two little squeakers be ready to be fed.

One evening, just the day the eggs were both hatched,
Dick watched and waited, but no little Dorothy came.
Often he thought he must leave the treasured young
ones and look for her, but he could not bear to go.
Finally, with a glad coo, Dorothy appeared at the old
slat. Hardly daring to rest on it, dragging one useless
leg behind her, she fluttered as best she could to the
nest. While she had been hunting carefully for just
the kind of scraps to make the proper food for the
nestlings, a boy had shot her, mangling one thigh.

How tenderly poor Dick tried to help her, but it was
of no avail. With one leg under her and the other

lying a useless thing by the side of the nest, the little
mother took up the night's vigil.

What matter the fever? What matter the agony
that shot up and down her whole side, making her eyes
look sunken and her feathers ruffled with pain; all save
those plastered to her side with blood. Her little nestlings were under her, and that was enough. Of course
Dick took up most of the burden. Early in the morning and late as he could see in the evening, he was out
hunting food for the young; so that Dorothy might
have little to do; but
he could not feed her,
and it was piti-
ful to see her
limping along,
driven away by
the stronger
birds, and gain-
ing a more pre-
carious living
than ever.

The young grew
fat, however, for
Dick cared for
them. Dorothy's leg soon healed, though it had to be
held at an angle from her body, and she still covered
her little ones at night.

One night there was a sudden noise, a door was
pushed open and a blinding light filled the belfry. The
frightened pigeons knew not which way to go. Two
boys began to catch them, stunning some with blows
of a stick or ruthlessly clutching others off the nests.

"Here's a cripple," said one as he swept poor Dorothy off her little ones.

"Never mind," said the other, "slap it in the sack. They won't notice it." Dick was jerked from a corner back of the nest, where he had hidden to escape detection, and in a few moments no pigeons were left in the old steeple save those too young to fly.

The sacks of pigeons were put in a wagon and jolted to a place where in turn the birds were put into long boxes, and left the remainder of the night. Till the next afternoon, they stayed there without a drop of water or a grain of food, when they were taken to a long, low meadow, where a lot of men with guns were gathered.

Then Dick knew what it meant. The birds had been caught for a shooting match. In his great flights over the surrounding country, he had seen the same thing before; pigeons put into little traps, a word given, the birds thrown into the air, only to be cut down by the deadly shot of the marksman who stood at a certain distance back at a line.

But Dick, being a bird of more than ordinary intelligence, had noticed another thing: that good strong birds which started directly away from the crowd and on the other side of the traps, and flew low, confused the shooters, and thus got safely away. In fact, many a crippled bird that had stopped at the steeple had told how it was done. So Dick's heart throbbed with hope, and the old courage of his race surged through his blood and shone in his eyes. If only he could get near little Dorothy, to tell her what to do! By good fortune, in the shifting of the boxes to get fresh birds, he heard her soft coo and hurried to her side. He saw that she was suffering, and that the torture of the close sack and the crowded box had greatly injured the mutilated leg.

Her turn soon came. The boy who took her out cramped the poor stiff leg close to her body, so she might pass muster, and therefore when she was put in the trap she was half crazed with pain. When the trap was pulled she sprang up with every vestige of strength she had; but with only one leg fit to use she toppled over and before she could right herself she fell, a bleeding mass of feathers : killed almost before she left the trap.

Then poor Dick knew that all rested with him, and like a stoic he waited. The boy who pulled him out saw no fear in the brave eyes. He found no resistance in that compact body. Dick was ready.

When the trap flew open, he ran rapidly along the ground a few paces, and sprang into the air with a burst of speed such as gave his mother a record.

"Bang!" went one barrel of the shooter's gun, but not a scratch. "Bang!" went the other, and the shot didn't even reach Dick. He was already thinking of his starving nestlings in the old steeple, when up, seemingly right out of the ground in front of him, rose one of those miserable scouts who hang around a shooting match. Too stingy to take part in the match and pay for their shots, they hang around the outskirts to kill the lucky birds that have escaped, and the poor cripples that, with desperate flutters, have gotten out of bounds.

When Dick saw this fellow, he darted up like a flash, his strong wings beating the air in a perfect agony of fury as he strove to rise out of shooting distance. Too

late! A moment and he fell to the ground, his life
blood staining the copper sheen of his breast, a film
coming fast over the bright and fearless eyes, the feet
clutched tightly together, as with a gasp the bold spirit
departed.

. . . .

That night the moonbeams stole softly through the
windows of the old steeple, and lingered a moment
tenderly on two little dead forms in the lonely nest.
They, too, had had their long hours of suffering. The
first night when their mother's warmth was taken from
them was bad enough, but their crops were full, and
that was a help to keep them warm. All through the
next day no parents came to keep off the chill with
their warm, downy breasts. Not a drop of water, not
a bit of food. The little sister first began to shiver and
gasp and cuddle more closely to the sturdy brother.
He wondered why she grew so drowsy, and why, when
he tried to fondle her with his beak, there was no response, till finally she grew so cold and so still. Then
he in turn began to shiver and gasp, his eyes became
sunken and blue: one last shudder, and all was over.

Thus Steeple Dick, little lame Dorothy, and the two
little ones, orphaned in a day, four of God's feathered
creatures, went to their death to satisfy the craving of
a few men for what they termed sport.

HOW RED WULL HELD THE BRIDGE

(From Bob, Son of Battle.)

By ALFRED OLLIVANT.

———

THE mob with Tammas and Long Kirby at their head had now well-nigh reached the plank-bridge. They still looked dangerous, and there were isolated cries of:

"Duck him!"

"Chuck him in!"

"An' the dog!"

"Wi' one o' they bricks about their necks!"

"There are my reasons!" said M'Adam, pointing to the forest of menacing faces. "Ye see I'm no beloved amang yonder gentlemen, and" — in a stage whisper in the other's ear — "I thocht maybe I'd be 'tacked on the road."

Tammas, foremost of the crowd, had now his foot upon the first plank.

"Ye robber! ye thief! Wait till we set hands on ye, you and yer gorilla!" he called.

M'Adam half turned.

345

"Wullie," he said quietly, "keep the bridge."

At the order the Tailless Tyke shot gladly forward, and the leaders on the bridge as hastily back. The dog galloped on to the rattling plank, took his post fair and square in the centre of the narrow way, and stood facing the hostile crew like Cerberus guarding the gates of hell: his bull-head was thrust forward, hackles up, teeth glinting, and a distant rumbling in his throat, as though daring them to come on.

"Yo' first, ole lad!" said Tammas, hopping agilely behind Long Kirby.

"Nay; the old uns lead!" cried the big smith, his face gray-white. He wrenched round, pinned the old man by the arms, and held him forcibly before him as a covering shield. There ensued an unseemly struggle betwixt the two valiants, Tammas bellowing and kicking in the throes of mortal fear.

"Jim Mason 'll show us," he suggested at last.

"Nay," said honest Jim; "I'm fear'd." He could say it with impunity; for the pluck of Postie Jim was a matter long past dispute.

Then Jem Burton 'd go first?

Nay; Jem had a lovin' wife and dear little kids at 'ome.

Then Big Bell?

Big Bell 'd see 'isself further first.

A tall figure came forcing through the crowd, his face a little paler than its wont, and a formidable knob-kerry in his hand.

"I'm goin'!" said David.

"But yo're not," answered burly Sam'l, gripping the boy from behind with arms like the roots of an oak.

"Your time 'll coom soon enough by the look on yo' wi' niver no hurry." And the sense of the Dalesmen was with the big man; for, as old Rob Saunderson said:

"I reck'n he'd liefer claw on to your throat, lad, nor ony o' oors."

As there was no one forthcoming to claim the honor of the lead, Tammas came forward with cunning counsel.

"Tell yo' what, lads, we'd best let 'em as don't know nowt at all aboot him go first. And onst they're on, mind, we winna let 'em off; but keep a-shovin' and a-bovin' on 'em forra'd. *Then* us 'll foller."

By this time there was a little naked space of green round the bridge-head, like a fairy circle, into which the uninitiated might not penetrate. Round this the mob hedged; the Dalesmen in front, striving knavishly back and brawling to those behind to 'leggo that shovin'; and these latter urging valorously forward, yelling jeers and contumely at the front rank. "Come on!" 'O's afraid? Lerrus through to 'em, then, ye Royal Stan'-backs!" — for well they knew the impossibility of their demand.

And as they wedged and jostled thus, there stole out from their midst as gallant a champion as ever trod the grass. He trotted out into the ring, the observed of all, and paused to gaze at the gaunt figure on the bridge. The sun lit the sprinkling of snow on the dome of his head; one forepaw was off the ground; and he stood there, royally alert, scanning his antagonist.

"Th' Owd Un!" went up in a roar fit to split the air as the hero of the day was recognized. And

the Dalesmen gave a pace forward spontaneously as
the gray knight-errant stole across the green.

"Oor Bob'll fetch him!" they roared, their blood
leaping to fever heat, and gripped their sticks, determined in stern reality to follow now.

The gray champion trotted up on to the bridge, and
paused again, the long hair about his neck rising like a
ruff, and a strange glint in his eyes; and the holder
of the bridge never
moved.   Red and
Gray stood thus, face
to face : the one gay

yet resolute, the other motionless, his great head slowly
sinking between his forelegs, seemingly petrified.

There was no shouting now : it was time for deeds,
not words.   Only, above the stillness, came a sound
from the bridge like the snore of a giant in his sleep,
and, blending with it, a low, deep, purring thunder like
some monster cat well pleased.

"Wullie," came a solitary voice from the far side,
"keep the bridge!"

One ear went back, one ear was still forward; the great head was low and lower between his forelegs and the glowing eyes rolled upward so that the watchers could see the murderous white.

Forward the gray dog stepped.

Then, for the second time that afternoon, a voice, stern and hard, came ringing down from the slope above over the heads of the many,

"Bob, lad, coom back!"

"He! he! I thocht that was comin'," sneered the small voice over the stream.

The gray dog heard, and checked.

"Bob, lad, coom in, I say!"

At that he swung round and marched slowly back, gallant as he had come, dignified still in his mortification.

And Red Wull threw back his head and bellowed a pæan of victory — challenge, triumph, scorn, all blended in that bull-like, blood-chilling blare.

.   .   .   .

In the meantime, M'Adam and the secretary had concluded their business. It had been settled that the Cup was to be delivered over to James Moore not later than the following Saturday.

"Saturday, see! at the latest!" the secretary cried as he turned and trotted off.

"Mr. Trotter," M'Adam called after him. " I'm sorry, but ye maun bide this side the Lea till I've reached the foot o' the Pass. Gin they gentlemen" — nodding toward the crowd — "should set hands on me, why — " and he shrugged his shoulders significantly. " Forbye, Wullie's keepin' the bridge."

With that the little man strolled off leisurely; now dallying to pick a flower, now to wave a mocking hand at the furious mob, and so slowly on to the foot of the Murk Muir Pass.

There he turned and whistled that shrill, peculiar note. " Wullie, Wullie, to me ! " he called.

At that, with one last threat thrown at the thousand souls he had held at bay for thirty minutes, the Tailless Tyke swung about and galloped after his lord.

MALDONADA AND THE PUMA

(FROM THE NATURALIST IN LA PLATA.)

BY W. H. HUDSON.

THE case of Maldonada is circumstantially narrated by Rui Diaz de Guzman, in his history of the colonization of the Plata: he was a person high in authority in the young colonies, and is regarded by students of South American history as an accurate and sober-minded chronicler of the events of his own times. He relates that in the year 1536 the settlers at Buenos Ayres, having exhausted their provisions, and being compelled by hostile Indians to keep within their palisades, were reduced to the verge of starvation. The Governor, Mendoza, went off to seek help from the other colonies up the river, deputing his authority to one Captain Ruiz, who, according to all accounts, displayed an excessively tyrannous and truculent disposition while

in power. The people were finally reduced to a ration
of six ounces of flour per day for each person; but
as the flour was putrid and only made them ill, they
were forced to live on any small animals they could
capture, including snakes, frogs, and toads. Some horrible details are given by Rui Diaz, and other writers;
one, Del Barco Centenera, affirms that of two thousand
persons in the town eighteen hundred perished of
hunger. During this unhappy time, beasts of prey in
large numbers were attracted to the settlement by the
effluvium of the corpses, buried just outside the palisades; and this made the condition of the survivors
more miserable still, since they could venture into the
neighboring woods only at the risk of a violent death.
Nevertheless, many did so venture, and among these
was the young woman Maldonada, who, losing herself
in the forest, strayed to a distance, and was eventually
found by a party of Indians, and carried by them to
their village.

Some months later, Captain Ruiz discovered her
whereabouts, and persuaded the savages to bring her
to the settlement; then, accusing her of having gone
to the Indian village in order to betray the colony, he
condemned her to be devoured by wild beasts. She
was taken to a wood at a distance of a league from
the town and left there, tied to a tree, for the space of
two nights and a day. A party of soldiers then went
to the spot, expecting to find her bones picked clean
by the beasts, but were greatly astonished to find
Moldonada still alive, without hurt or scratch. She
told them that a puma had come to her aid, and had
kept at her side, defending her life against all the

other beasts that approached her. She was instantly released, and taken back to the town, her deliverance through the action of the puma probably being looked on as a direct interposition of Providence to save her.

Rui Diaz concludes with the following paragraph, in which he affirms that he knew the woman Maldonada, which may be taken as proof that she was among the few that survived the first disastrous settlement and lived on to more fortunate times : his pious pun on her name would be lost in a translation : — " De esta manera quedó libre lá que ofrecieron á las fieras : la cual mujer yo la conocí, y la llamaban la Maldonada, que más bien se le podía llamar la Biendonada ; pues por esto suceso se ha de ver no haber merecido el castigo á que la ofrecieron."

If such a thing were to happen now, in any portion of southern South America, where the puma's disposition is best known, it would not be looked on as a miracle, as it was, and that unavoidably, in the case of Maldonada.

NOTE.

In spite of the difficulty of the translation, the sense of the paragraph is, "that one can scarcely believe so good a woman deserved to suffer the fate to which she was condemned. Instead of Maldonada — the bad gifted woman — she should be called Biendonada — the good gifted woman."

THE CAPTAIN'S DOG

By LOUIS A. ENAULT.

Translated by Marie J. Welsh.

THE captain's new wife was fond of cats, but could not bear dogs. If only the captain's dog were a handsome one, he might have won her favor, even if he did not deserve it; but in her eyes the unhappy Zero was without form or color that she should desire him. His good qualities, which could not be seen at first, were his warm and loyal heart, and his subtle and acute intelligence. These were not enough to win his new mistress, and the poor dog was wise enough to understand his position exactly.

Zero was not a setter, but a cross between a French poodle and a spaniel. When he was quite sure that the new Mrs. Pigault did not appreciate him at his true value, he made it a point of duty not to get in her way. He was, however, naturally courteous, and he would have liked nothing better than to place himself entirely at the disposal of his mistress. He was always looking forward to the time when this beautiful and disdainful lady would come to entertain more just feelings towards him. It is quite true that such irreproachable conduct on the part of the dog was difficult to maintain, and I verily believe that many people who had had a better education than Zero would not have acquitted themselves so well in so delicate a position.

This astonishing dog gave still more surprising proofs of tact. While he loved his master with an affection that death only could terminate, he began to show much more reserve and discretion in showing this affection. Hitherto he had been lavish in expressing his affection for his master, as is natural when alone with the person one loves, with nothing to fear from any one else. He had always seized upon every pretext to testify his true sentiments towards him; but now, as though he understood that there was someone who had the right to be jealous, he knew how to restrain himself and to put a mute upon the music of his joy. But when he was happy enough to find himself alone with his master he took his revenge for the long restraint which he had imposed upon himself, and put no limits to the expres-

sion of his passionate love and happiness. This delicacy
of feeling did not escape his master's eye. He knew
how meritorious it was, and was profoundly touched by
it, and would caress the poor animal with an enhanced
tenderness which would fill it with joy for the rest of
the day. Then he would say to himself, "If my wife
loved my dog, every retired captain would be envying
my lot, and I would ask nothing more of heaven than
to spend my life in the company of these two creatures
without caring any more for the rest of the world than
does the figurehead of an old boat."

But Lise did not like Zero. It was a fact about
which it was impossible to have any illusions whatever,
and the master was quite as well aware of it as the dog
was. And to be impartial we must admit that Zero
now did nothing to bring round his enemy to his side.
In the early days when Madame Pigault came to the
house, he showed a disposition to make all kinds of con-
cessions in order to live amicably with her, but when he
saw all his advances repulsed, he made up his mind to
treat her as a stranger, and would not appear even to
be aware of her presence.

At that critical moment in his career he was a little
bit of a glutton. Everybody has his defects, and this
was perhaps the cardinal defect in the dog, who found
himself in a house where there was a good table, after
having lived so long a life of fasting. Unfortunately,
Zero was exposed to temptation and fell, and this defect
was the source of many sad misfortunes.

Madame Pigault loved the good things of this life,
too, and every morning she took for breakfast two fresh
eggs which her two hens laid for her every morning,

with that regularity which is the politeness of poultry. Now it happened one day that the servant, in a distracted or clumsy moment, let fall one of these wonderful eggs as she came across the yard, and it is needless to say that the egg was smashed on the pavement. But this egg was not lost to the world, for Zero, who was strolling about the yard, scented a piece of good fortune, and promptly devoured the white and the yellow of the egg with two laps of his tongue. Madame Pigault's feast that morning was reduced by fifty per cent !

Jeanneton confessed her fault. A fault confessed is a fault forgiven, and no more was said about it. Lise behaved like a princess in this matter, but our hero had found that the taste of the egg exactly suited him. The next morning he hoped for nothing better than to meet with the same luck. Fresh eggs were better for him than a glass of absinthe or vermouth for a man with poor digestion.

At the exact hour when, on the day before, Jeanneton had let fall the half of her mistress's breakfast he came on watch. No doubt he hoped that the same accident would bring him the same happiness as yesterday, but all days are not holidays. Jeanneton that morning made no omelets on the courtyard floor, and Zero had his labor for his pains. He dared not protest, for Jeanneton would have ridiculed him to death; but he was a keen observer, as of course every dog ought to be who has to make his way in the world, and he watched very carefully the comings in and the goings out of the maid servant. It was not long before he found out that every time she carried eggs to the house she came out of a certain cellar where the hens were always allowed their liberty, and were in the habit of laying in little boxes full of hay placed between the barrels and tubs.

Profiting by a moment when Jeanneton was not looking, our embryo thief followed her quietly into the cellar, but it was too late. The field had already been gleaned, and the nests were warm but empty. He was disappointed, no doubt, but not in the least discouraged. Although he had not studied philosophy, he had nevertheless a faculty for arguing, and he knew well how to draw from the premises the conclusions which they contained. He said to himself that since he found no eggs in the cellar when Jeanneton had been there before him, it would be she, on the contrary, who would not find any if he went before she did. When a dog has so much logic you can see that he is on the verge of crime, and the smallest temptation will cause him to fall.

Although he had been an old sailor, Zero could not tell the time by the sun, and as he could not get a chronometer at the marine clock-makers, he despised an ordinary watch. But he had ways of his own of taking note of the time, — ways which were certain, and which enabled him always to be on time. Thus, next morning he got to the cellar five minutes ahead of Jeanneton ; He had no trouble in finding the two nests. . . . .

Zero had now almost achieved his purpose, but at the very moment, as often happens, they say, to those about to commit their first crime, he was touched with remorse for what he was about to do. His conscience, like that of Cæsar, at the moment when the future master of Rome was about to cross the Rubicon, cried out to him, " One step further will be a crime."

The idea of being chastised with a heavy whip at the end of a strong arm presented itself forcibly to his mind, and a slight noise from the outside came to him as a second warning which he could not altogether disregard. He went as far as the door of the cellar and carefully looked all around. Alas! He had lost that frank and loyal look of an honest dog, which is the sure index of a good conscience. On the contrary, there was something sly and restless in his troubled eye, an expression which a physiognomist would have considered a bad augury for his future virtue. One fact was too certain. From the moment when Zero turned his magnificent intelligence to evil deeds he became an incorrigible rascal. A dog of his character, if he took the first step on the road to crime must necessarily travel the whole journey.

Our thief, for he was a thief already in intention, saw nothing suspicious round about him. The kitchen door was shut, and so was the garden gate. The courtyard, too, was deserted. Never was there a more propitious moment, nor an occasion more favorable for helping himself with impunity to the goods which belong to others.

There are moments in our lives when everything seems to conspire to stifle what remains of the moral sense. Dogs know that almost as well as men do.

Zero ran into the cellar. . . . The two eggs were there; each one in its little box shining and white amid the hay, and so fresh that they were still warm. He smelt them an instant as though he could detect their taste through the delicate dazzling shells. For a moment he seemed to reflect, and then all at once a mist seemed to pass before his eyes, and the last little bit of conscience that he might have had was extinguished altogether. He seized one of the eggs which disappeared easily in his capacious mouth, and breaking the shell with his teeth swallowed it with the avidity of a gourmet who has already learned what good things are.

We must not forget, however, that remorse always follows closely on the steps of crime. There still remained some fragments of the shell between Zero's teeth. Like our first father Adam after he had eaten of the fatal apple, Zero sought to hide himself.

But even in the midst of his iniquities he had one good tendency for which we should not omit to give him credit. He no doubt said to himself that crime, like virtue, has its degrees, and that there is no reason why, because one has committed a first fault, one should spend the rest of one's days as a criminal. Or he may have thought that it was enough to have taken half his mistress's breakfast, and that it was but just that he should leave her the other half. His first egg disposed of, Zero looked at the second with feelings of covetousness mixed with regret, but remembering in time the wise man's maxim "He who loves perils will perish," he turned his back upon the tempting nest, and went for a trip along the water front to take the air and digest the proceeds of his crime.

Jeanneton had now just come back from the market with her day's provisions. She consulted the cuckoo clock in the dining-room and saw that it was just a quarter to eight. There was therefore not more than fifteen minutes to lay the table and prepare her mistress's breakfast. Madame was as exact as the captain's old chronometer, and always breakfasted precisely at eight o'clock. If the eggs were not on the table just at that moment, she was out of humor for the whole day. She had an uncompromising appetite, and would not brook a delay of ten seconds. In fact, she regulated her meals by her cuckoo clock. She was furthermore extremely frugal. A cup of milk with these two eggs, and any fruit that might be in season lasted her until dinner time, which as in so many good families among the middle class Normans who remain faithful to the customs of their forefathers, was always at one o'clock.

Jeanneton ran down to the cellar to get the eggs for breakfast. Needless to say, there was only one. She was the more surprised because it was in the full laying season, and the hens had never before failed to do their duty. An earthquake would not have surprised Jeanneton more. She could hardly believe her eyes. She felt in the nest and found it really empty. She turned over the hay, but only one egg could be found.

"That's extraordinary," she thought; "I cannot

understand it. For three months such a thing has not
happened. The hen looks well, and this morning when
I went out to get the coals I saw her sitting upon her
nest. If we cannot rely upon the hens at this season,
what can we rely upon? But that is not all. What
will Madame say? She was somewhat out of humor
all day yesterday."

Naturally, Madame was still less good humored that
day. She was very fixed in her habits, and dearly
loved fresh eggs.

This time, Jeanneton did not come off with any sort
of excuse. In fact, she had to go through a formal
cross-examination. It was a useless cross-examination,
however, for knowing nothing, the poor girl could tell
nothing. She went to the cellar at the accustomed
hour, and instead of finding two eggs as usual, she only
found one. Not a word more could she say.

"Just imagine," said Lise, "anything so strange as
this, and anything so unlikely to happen. See how
well fed these hens are, and this is the full laying
season, too! The whole thing is enough to destroy
one's faith in everything, and as for you, M. Pigault,"
she said, addressing her husband, "instead of sitting
there with your mouth shut while I am fatiguing myself to death with talking, it seems to me you might
say something on the subject."

"I am afraid that is scarcely possible," answered the
captain, in his most peacefully good-humored manner,
"for you hardly leave me time to say a word, my
dear."

"Anyhow you see I have only got one egg to-day.
What do you think of that?" she continued.

"I think that the hens are misbehaving themselves," he said, in his placid and serene manner.

Lise looked at her husband twice to see if he spoke sincerely, or if he was laughing at her, but in certain moments the captain's face was as impenetrable as that of the sphinx, and Madame Pigault could only conjecture his meaning, while she remained in a state of ill humor the whole day long.

ROYAL'S FATE

(From Castle Blair.)

By FLORA L. SHAW.

S UDDENLY in the midst of the fun a splendid Newfoundland dog bounded through the hedge and over the little stream, fairly upsetting Winnie, and splashing the water over them all.

"In the name of all that's wonderful where do you come from?" exclaimed Murtagh, as Winnie, picking herself up, rushed after the dog, crying: "Oh, you beauty! come here."

A low rippling laugh made both Nessa and Murtagh look round, and in a dog-cart on the other side of the hedge they saw a delicate-looking little boy sitting watching Winnie with delight.

"Frankie!" exclaimed Murtagh springing forward.

"Yes," said Frankie. "How do you do? What are you doing? Was it you making that jolly noise? Have you heard why we've come here? There is such a splendid plan. The doctors say I am to go to the seaside somewhere in the south, and some of you are to come."

Murtagh was busy climbing through the hedge and into the dog-cart, so he scarcely heard what Frankie was saying, but now took his place beside him exclaim-

ing : " How are you, old fellow ? Are you any better?
Where did you get him ? He is such a beauty ! "
The last words referred, of course, to the dog, whom
Winnie had caught, and was now leading back to the
stream.

The flush of excitement faded from Frankie's cheek,
and he seemed to have some difficulty in getting his
breath after the volley of questions he had poured out.
In reply to the first part of Murtagh's inquiries he only
seemed to shrink into himself, and shook his head. The
servant who accompanied him began to assure Murtagh
that Mr. Frank was much better, and would soon be
quite well now ; but Frankie seemed to wish to change
the subject, and said hurriedly : " Yes, isn't he splendid !
He was given to me, but I've been training him for
Winnie. He's no good to me, you know ; if he knocks
me over I don't get my breath back for a week. But I
thought she'd like him. He's as quiet as a lamb unless
you set him at anybody, and then he goes at them
like — "

" Like an Irishman," suggested Murtagh ; but though
his words were meant for a joke he looked wistfully at
his cousin, wishing to ask more questions about his
health. He was very fond of Frankie, and it made him
sorry to see the sunken cheeks and wasted hands that
told even to childish eyes how ill the boy was.

Frankie nodded and sat silently looking at Winnie
and the dog with a pleased smile playing round his
mouth.

Winnie had not yet perceived him, and her attention
was entirely absorbed by the dog. Both her arms were
round its neck, and as she walked along by its side,

bending down, she showered upon it every endearing epithet she could think of.

"Perhaps you're lost, and perhaps we won't be able to find your master, however hard we look, and then you'll stay with us; won't you, my beauty?" she was saying when she glanced up and saw Frankie.

Instantly the dog was forgotten, and she flew towards the road, exclaiming: "Frankie! How jolly!"

Frankie laughed again his low, pleased laugh; but having suffered for the rapid questions with which he had saluted Murtagh, he did not attempt to say more than, "Yes; here I am," as Winnie climbed up on the wheel of the dog-cart and pulled down his face to be kissed.

"We're having such fun!" she continued; "get down, and come up to the tower with us." She jumped down herself as she spoke, and threw her arms round the dog, who stood wagging his tail.

"No, I mustn't do that," replied Frankie, looking wistfully at the tower, and then smiling again as his eyes fell to the dog standing by Winnie's side. "I only stopped to see what you'd think of Royal."

"You don't mean to say that this beautiful dog is yours!" exclaimed Winnie. "Oh, Frankie, you are a lucky boy!"

"Yes it is," said Murtagh.

"Your very, very own; not your mother's or anybody's?" inquired Winnie, doubtful whether it were possible for any child to possess such a treasure.

"No," said Frankie; "he isn't mine, he is yours."

"Wha — what do you mean?" asked Winnie astonished, the color deepening a little in her cheeks as the dream-like possibility flashed across her mind.

"I mean what I say," repeated Frankie, his face beaming. "He is your very own dog; I have been training him for you, and I've brought him here for you!"

Winnie did not seem able to take it in. The color spread over her cheeks and mounted to her forehead. Her big eyes grew round and bigger, but she did not dare to believe such a thing could be till Murtagh exclaimed:

"Frankie's given him to you. He's your very own, as own as own can be!"

Then a light broke over her face, and tightening the grasp of her arms round Royal's neck she half-strangled him in an embrace, while all she could say was, "Oh, Frankie!"

Frankie seemed well satisfied with her thanks.

Murtagh laughed and said: "She doesn't believe it now."

"Yes, I do," said Winnie, "only it's too good! I can't seem to know it. Oh, Frankie, I think I shall go cracky with gladness!" Suddenly finding the power of expressing her delight she tore up the hill, calling to Royal to follow, and burst upon the assembled children, exclaiming: "He's mine! He's my very own! Frankie's just given him to me!" Then she raced down again like some mad thing, and ran away at full speed over the heather with Royal at her heels. She came back in about five minutes panting and rosy, with her hand upon the dog's collar, declaring that now she could stay quiet; and her brilliant face would have been reward enough for a more selfish person than Frankie.

Frankie stayed only to display some of Royal's accomplishments, and to show Winnie's name engraved upon the collar. Then he drove away, leaving their new treasure with the children.

But it was getting to be quite afternoon by this time, and nobody had had any dinner yet, so Murtagh careered up the hill, crying: "Come along now, and let's have scene number two in the entertainment. I feel as if I was quite ready for scene number two. How are you, Winnie?"

Winnie's answer was more expressive than elegant, and then they set to work to unpack the hampers. In a very few moments the white cloth was spread upon the ground and covered with Mrs. Donegan's dainties. The children were in no way disappointed in the pleasure of watching the queer expressions of the followers' faces as dish after dish came out of the hampers. Poor hungry followers! they had had nothing to eat since an early hour that morning, and few of them had ever seen such things as Mrs. Donegan had prepared. So it is not to be wondered at, that when they found themselves sitting on the grass round that wonderful feast, with free leave to eat whatever they pleased, the event seemed to them really too good to be true.

Winnie was in ecstasy over their pleasure. At first they were too shy to help themselves to anything, but she jumped up and had soon piled some of their plates. Rosie and the boys did the same, and the followers quickly recovered themselves sufficiently to talk, and eat, and laugh.

" Now, whatever more you want you must really help yourselves," cried Murtagh, returning to his place after having gone once round. " I'm so starving that if I don't get something soon I shall eat one of you."

Royal had waited like a perfect gentleman, as he was, till all were helped; but now he gravely poked his black muzzle into Winnie's hand in a manner that said as plainly as any words, " Give me a little cold pie, if you please." He had not to ask twice. Winnie gave him a great plateful of miscellaneous food, and as on the fast emptying plates there began to appear all manner of suitable scraps, a constant cry of " Here, Royal! Royal!" kept him racing round the tablecloth. One little girl wished to be very polite, and as he was Winnie's dog thought it better to call him Master Royal. That made the others ashamed of their bad manners, but they soon corrected themselves, and from that day forth he was Master Royal to the followers.

At first there was not very much talking, for all were so hungry that they were glad to eat. But when once the edge was taken off their appetites the Irish tongues got loose; and then they chattered, they laughed, they sang snatches of songs, they drank healths in water, and made mock speeches each more ludicrous than the last, till everybody was half incapacitated with laughter. Murtagh was the soul of the party. Nessa wondered where his words and ideas came from, they flowed out so fast. Seated in state at the head of the table she was very gay and happy. She was unusually amused by this wild merry crew, and such spirits as theirs were infectious.

The feast over, Royal was with much mock solemnity

received into the tribe, a ceremony which he disrespect-
fully brought to an abrupt ending by knocking over
four or five of his sponsors. They then divided into
parties, and played robber games among the hills, till
the fading light warned them that even the pleasantest
of days *will* come to an end. The remains of the feast
were divided between the followers. Tommie was
yoked into the cart again, and at last to his satisfaction,
if to nobody else's, his willing head was turned home-
wards.

But even then the children were not tired. It was
wonderful to see how they caracoled round the cart, and
sang and laughed the whole way home; and when,
finally, they drove up in state and deposited Nessa upon
the hall-door steps, the last cheer they gave her was as
hearty as any they had uttered that day.

. . . .

Towards morning Murtagh fell into a disturbed sleep;
but almost before daybreak he was awakened by Bobbo,
who exclaimed as he shook him by the shoulder:
"Get up, Myrrh! We'd better be on the island
early, if we want to save the hut."

In an instant Murtagh was out of bed. Save the
hut! whatever else he might give in about he would
never relinquish that, — their father's hut.

The passionate thoughts of the night before had now
assumed the tangible form of a dogged determination to
resist Mr. Plunkett, and a pleasant sense of anticipated
triumph tingled through his veins as he hurriedly
dressed himself. All the miserable abasement of yesterday's anger was gone. He was going to fight
now!

With his head thrown back and a confident determined look upon his face, he ran down the stairs, saying
to Bobbo: "Call the girls while I fetch Royal. We
shall see who'll be master this time!"

Before it was fully light the four children were on
the island. Rosie, with practical forethought, had possessed herself of such scraps of food as she could find
in the kitchen and servants' hall, and now they lighted
a fire and sat down by it to eat their miscellaneous
breakfast.

"But what are you going to do, Murtagh?" inquired
Rosie, with a note of fretful disappointment in her
voice. It was really an unkind fate which had made
her the sister of such a brother. She had not the least
taste for adventures.

"You'll see when the time comes," replied Murtagh,
whose ideas were in truth very vague. He felt only
sure of one thing, which was that he meant to do
something.

"I don't mind what it is," said Winnie; "I'm ready
for anything!"

"So am I," said Bobbo, "only I vote we don't hurt
the poor beggars if we can help it."

"No; because it's not their fault you know, Myrrh,"
decided Winnie.

"No; but we can't let them land here!" replied
Murtagh determinately. "If they will get hurt we
can't help it. Now look here, we had better collect a
lot of bits of wood, and clods, and things, and pile them
up in front here, where we can get at them easily.
They are sure to come up this front way."

"Oh," cried Winnie in delight, "you're going to pelt

them! Then let us get some of that stiff, yellow mud from the bank. It will do gloriously!"

But their warlike preparations seemed likely to be quite unnecessary. Time passed quietly on. No one came to disturb the peace of the island, and the children were beginning to think they might have spared themselves the trouble of their early watch, when the loose rattle of cart-wheels was heard coming along the road on the left bank of the river.

"Here they come!" cried Murtagh, springing from his seat by the fire and hurrying out to reconnoitre.

The others hastily followed. Through a gap in the bushes they saw two empty carts coming down the road. The driver of each was seated on the shaft smoking a short pipe, and in the corner of one of the carts were visible the handles of picks and mallets.

" Yes," exclaimed Murtagh, " it's them. Now we're in for it! Royal, old boy, are you ready?"

The faces of the other children beamed with excitement. Royal understood well enough that something unusual was the matter, for he answered Murtagh's appeal by a short yap and a pricking up of his ears which meant business. Even Rosie was so carried away by the excitement of the approaching battle as to exclaim in sympathy with Winnie's dancing eyes, "Isn't it jolly?"

The carts stopped on the road, and the men taking their tools began leisurely to descend through the little wood into the bed of the river.

"Now then, steady!" said Murtagh. "I'll talk to them first." He advanced as he spoke along the little path, and standing at the edge of the river he

called out in a loud, firm voice to know what they
wanted.

The men were evidently somewhat discomfited at
finding the island already occupied, and Hickey replied evasively : " Sure, Mr. Murtagh, we didn't expect
to find you up here."

" What do you want here ? " repeated Murtagh.

" Well, Mr. Plunkett's sent us for a load o' them
stones ; and you know orders is orders, so you'll let us
have them quiet, like a good young gentleman, won't
you now ?   Ye've hed ye're bit o' play yesterday
evenin', and there's no gettin' on with work when ye're
hindered that way ! "

" I told you yesterday that you shouldn't touch our
hut," replied Murtagh, " and you sha'n't !   Mr. Plunkett may get his stones from the quarry."

" It's no good standin' blathering here ! " exclaimed
Phelim roughly.   " We've got to have the stones, and
there's an end of it !   Come on, Hickey ; we got the
measure of Mr. Plunkett's tongue last night, and I
don't want no more of it ! "

" Take that for your impudence ! " cried Bobbo, who
without waiting for more snatched a stick from the
heap of missiles and flung it at Phelim's head.

The stick flew harmlessly past, but a shout from the
other children echoed Bobbo's words, and a rapid volley
of mud-balls, sticks, and clods of earth saluted the
onward advance of the men.   So true was the aim, and
so hard and fast did the children pelt, that Hickey and
Phelim ran for shelter round the point of the island,
and tried to effect a landing on the other side.

But on the other side the water was deeper, and the

only standing-room was on a belt of shingle close to
the shore of the island.   The children knew this well,
and when the men emerged upon it from behind the
protecting screen of bushes they were greeted with such
a shower of missiles, that Phelim, whose courage had
been considerably undermined by the sound of Royal's
excited barking, turned and fled blindly into the water.
As he lost his footing and rolled over in the water
deep enough to souse him completely, the children
raised a prolonged shout of triumph, and redoubled
their efforts to dislodge Hickey, who, while returning
their attack with whatever he could lay his hands on,
was good-humoredly swearing at them and imploring
them to stop their fun.

Suddenly in the mist of all the hubbub, over the
noise of the children's shouting, Royal's barking,
Hickey's swearing, Phelim's lamenting, a stern —
" What's the meaning of all this uproar? " made itself
heard, and Mr. Plunkett in shooting costume burst
through the bushes on the right bank of the river.

Missiles were flying in every direction, and the only
immediate answer to Mr. Plunkett's question was a
mud ball, which hit him on the forehead, and a stick
that carried away his hat.

He put his hand angrily to his head, and losing all
his habitual command of language, exclaimed : " What
do you mean by this? "

" We mean," cried Murtagh, who was perfectly wild
with excitement, " that we won't have our rights inter-
fered with, and you may just as well know, once for
all, that we won't have this hut touched if all the walls
in Ireland go unmended."

"Don't be impertinent to me, sir; you'll have whatever you are told to have," returned Mr. Plunkett hotly.

"Where are you going?" he inquired of the men, who, taking advantage of the cessation of active hostilities, were slinking off towards the carts.

"Please, sir, them stones is no good at all at all," Hickey ventured in answer; "they're all rubbish, every one of them, not worth the carting."

"I didn't ask your opinion of the stones. I told you to fetch them. A set of lazy scoundrels! I believe you're every one of you in league to prevent anything being decently done," exclaimed Mr. Plunkett.

"League or no league, the hut shall not be touched!" reiterated Murtagh.

"We shall very soon see that," returned Mr. Plunkett. "Go on to the island, and pull it down at once," he added, turning to the men. "I stand here till the work is begun."

"I'll set the dog on the first one of you who attempts to land," said Murtagh resolutely.

"Do you hear what I say to you?" demanded Mr. Plunkett, as the men stood doubtfully, eying Royal, who, apparently enraged by Phelim's appearance, was furiously barking.

"Please, sir, the dog's very savage; he nearly killed Phelim last night," said Hickey apologetically.

"You pair of cowards! do you mean to tell me you are afraid of the dog?" exclaimed Mr. Plunkett contemptuously.

The men did not answer, but neither did they show the slightest inclination to move, and Winnie called out derisively: "How much for standing there till the work is begun?"

"Do you wish me to begin it myself?" demanded Mr. Plunkett angrily of the two men. "I tell you that hut has to he pulled down before I leave this spot."

He moved along the bank as he spoke, and prepared to jump on to a little island of shingle that lay in the bed of the stream.

"If you come one step nearer I'll set Royal upon you," cried Murtagh, roused to the last pitch of defiance by Mr. Plunkett's determination.

He and Winnie were both of them holding on to Royal's collar, and it was only with difficulty that they could restrain the dog, who seemed ready to attack anything and everything in his excitement.

"If you set your wild dog upon me I give you fair warning that I will shoot him," retorted Mr. Plunkett.

"As if you dare!" cried Winnie incredulously.

Mr. Plunkett's only answer was to spring on to the shingle.

"At him, Royal!" cried Winnie and Murtagh in a breath, loosing their hold as they spoke. With a furious growl Royal bounded into the river. Almost instantaneously Mr. Plunkett raised his gun. There was a loud report, then a piteous whine; the little cloud of smoke cleared away; there was a broad red streak in the water; and Royal turned his dying eyes reproachfully to Winnie.

"Oh, Murtagh! He's done it, he's done it!" she cried, with a beseeching disbelief in her voice that went even to Mr. Plunkett's heart, and though the water was over her ankles she dashed across to the shingle bank.

"Help me to take him out, Murtagh. Don't you see the water's carrying him down? He can't help himself. Royal, darling, I didn't mean it; I didn't think he would. Where are you hurt? oh, why can't you speak?"

The current swept the dog towards her, she managed to throw her arms round his neck and to get his head rested upon her shoulder, while Bobbo and Murtagh going in to her assistance tried to lift his body. But he groaned so piteously at their somewhat clumsy attempt that they stopped, and all three stood still, and in speechless dismay watched the wounded dog. Royal seemed more content, and from his resting-place on Winnie's shoulder licked away the tears that were rolling down her face. But after a time the children's wet feet began to grow numb, and Winnie looked up and signed to Murtagh to try and move him now.

He groaned again. For a moment he seemed to struggle convulsively, his head fell off Winnie's shoulder, his eyes looked up appealingly to hers, his limbs suddenly straightened, and then he was quite quiet as the children supported him through the water, and tried tenderly to lift him on to the bank. He was too heavy for them, and Mr. Plunkett, his hot anger past, came forward saying almost humbly, "Let me help you;" but though the children none of them answered, they turned their faces from him in such an unmistakable manner that he fell back and signed to one of the men to go and help them in his place.

Thus Royal was lifted on to the right bank of the river; and Winnie, sitting on the ground, took his head into her lap, while Murtagh, Bobbo, and Rosie stood round and watched.   But he never moved nor groaned; he was so unnaturally still that a dim terror entered into the children's minds.   Winnie stooped down to kiss him; as she did so her fear became a certainty.

"Murtagh," she said, raising a white frightened face, "He — he's killed him."

Murtagh made no answer, but falling on his knees beside Royal he laid his cheek against the dog's muzzle to feel if there were any breath.   Then his mournful eyes and sad shake of the head confirmed Winnie's words.   Mr. Plunkett and the two men had known it for some minutes, but as Mr. Plunkett stood watching the group of children he felt a strange, unusual moisture rising to his eyes, and he turned and walked away.

As they realized that the dog was dead, really dead, Rosie and Bobbo began to cry; the other two sat dry-eyed gazing at Royal.

The men stood one side respecting their grief for a few moments, but then they came forward and began to make remarks and offer consolation.

"He was a beautiful creathure," said Hickey, "and indeed it would serve old Plunkett right if he got shot with the very same gun.   But there, don't take on so, bless yer hearts; the master'll get yez another dog as fine as ever this was."

While Pat was speaking Phelim stooped down and idly taking one of Royal's paws shook it slowly backwards and forwards.   Winnie put out her hand to prevent the sacrilege, and looking up at Murtagh said, "Take them away, Murtagh, all of them."

"We'd better take the dog with us and bury him," said Phelim; "a big dog like that'll want buryin'."

"No, no," cried Murtagh, with a quick glance towards Winnie which seemed to say he would have protected her from the words if he could. "Come away, all of you, and leave her alone."

And so Winnie was left sitting on the ground with her dead dog's head resting on her lap. Bobbo and Rosie returned to the house to tell the sad news to Nessa. The two men went to find Mr. Plunkett, but Murtagh wandered away by himself into the woods higher up the river.

The men having found Mr. Plunkett at home inquired what they were to do about the hut. Was it to be taken down?

"Yes, of course," returned Mr. Plunkett testily, feeling strongly inclined to say on the contrary that it might be left standing, but ashamed of what he considered a bit of inconsequent weakness.

THE CIVILIZED FOX

(FROM BEING A BOY.)

By CHARLES DUDLEY WARNER.

A BOY on a farm is nothing without his pets; at least a dog, and probably rabbits, chickens, ducks, and guinea-hens. A guinea-hen suits a boy. It is entirely useless, and makes a more disagreeable noise than a Chinese gong. I once domesticated a young fox which a neighbor had caught. It is a mistake to suppose the fox cannot be tamed. Jacko was a very clever little animal, and behaved, in all respects, with propriety. He kept Sunday as well as any day, and all the ten commandments that he could understand. He was a very graceful playfellow, and seemed to have an affection for me. He lived in a wood-pile, in the door-yard, and when I lay down at the entrance to his house and called him, he would come out and sit on his tail and lick my face just like a grown person. I taught him a great many tricks and all the virtues. That year I had a large number of hens, and Jacko went about among them with the most perfect indifference, never looking on them to lust after them, as I could see, and never touching an egg or a feather. So excellent was his reputation that I would have trusted him in the hen-roost in the dark without counting the hens. In short, he was domesticated, and I was fond of him and very proud of him, exhibiting him to all our visitors as an example of what affectionate treatment would do in subduing the brute instincts. I preferred him to my dog, whom I had, with much patience, taught to go up a long hill alone and surround the cows, and drive them home from the remote pasture. He liked the fun of it at first, but by and by he seemed to get the notion that it was a "chore," and when I whistled for him to go for the cows, he would turn tail and run the other way, and the more I whistled and threw stones at him the faster he would run. His name was Turk, and I should have sold him if he had not been the kind of dog that nobody will buy. I suppose he was not a cow-dog, but what they call a sheep-dog. At least, when he got big enough, he used to get into the pasture and chase the sheep to death. That was the way he got into trouble, and lost his valuable life. A dog is of great use on a farm, and that is the reason a boy likes him. He is good to bite pedlers and small children, and run out and yelp at wagons that pass by, and to howl all night when the moon shines. And yet, if I were a boy again, the first thing I would have should be a dog; for dogs are great companions, and as active and spry as a boy at doing nothing. They are also good to bark at woodchuck-holes.

A good dog will bark at a woodchuck-hole long after the animal has retired to a remote part of his residence, and escaped by another hole. This deceives the wood-chuck. Some of the most delightful hours of my life have been spent in hiding and watching the hole where the dog was not. What an exquisite thrill ran through my frame when the timid nose appeared, was withdrawn, poked out again, and finally followed by the entire animal, who looked cautiously about, and then hopped away to feed on the clover. At that moment I rushed in, occupied the " home base," yelled to Turk and then danced with delight at the combat between the spunky woodchuck and the dog. They were about the same size, but science and civilization won the day. I did not reflect then that it would have been more in the interest of civilization if the woodchuck had killed the dog. I do not know why it is that boys so like to hunt and kill animals; but the excuse that I gave in this case for the murder was, that the woodchuck ate the clover and trod it down; and, in fact, was a woodchuck. It was not till long after that I learned with surprise that he is a rodent mammal, of the species *Arctomys monax*, is called at the West a ground-hog, and is eaten by people of color with great relish.

But I have forgotten my beautiful fox. Jacko continued to deport himself well until the young chickens came; he was actually cured of the fox vice of chicken-stealing. He used to go with me about the coops, pricking up his ears in an intelligent manner, and with a demure eye and the most virtuous droop of the tail. Charming fox! If he had held out a little while longer, I should have put him into a Sunday-school book. But I began to miss chickens. They disappeared mysteriously in the night. I would not suspect Jacko at first, for he looked so honest, and in the daytime seemed to be as much interested in the chickens as I was. But one morning, when I went to call him, I found feathers at the entrance of his hole, — chicken feathers. He couldn't deny it. He was a thief. His fox nature had come out under severe temptation. And he died an unnatural death. He had a thousand virtues and one crime. But that crime struck at the foundation of society. He deceived and stole; he was a liar and a thief, and no pretty ways could hide the fact. His intelligent, bright face couldn't save him. If he had been honest, he might have grown up to be a large, ornamental fox.